SILVER·BURDETT

Making Music

Program Authors

Jane Beethoven
Susan Brumfield
Patricia Shehan Campbell
David N. Connors
Robert A. Duke
Judith A. Jellison

Rita Klinger
Rochelle Mann
Hunter C. March
Nan L. McDonald
Marvelene C. Moore
Mary Palmer
Konnie Saliba

Will Schmid
Carol Scott-Kassner
Mary E. Shamrock
Sandra L. Stauffer
Judith Thomas
Jill Trinka

PEARSON

Scott
Foresman

Editorial Offices: Glenview, Illinois • Parsippany, New Jersey • New York, New York
Sales Offices: Needham, Massachusetts • Duluth, Georgia • Glenview, Illinois
Coppell, Texas • Sacramento, California • Mesa, Arizona

ISBN: 0-382-36574-7

SILVER·BURDETT

Making Music

Contributing Authors

Audrey A. Berger	Mary Ellen Junda
Roslyn Burrough	Donald Kalbach
J. Bryan Burton	Shirley Lacroix
Jeffrey E. Bush	Henry Leck
John M. Cooksey	Sanna Longden
Shelly C. Cooper	Glenn A. Richter
Alice-Ann Darrow	Carlos Xavier Rodriguez
Scott Emmons	Kathleen Donahue Sanz
Debra Erck	Julie K. Scott
Anne M. Fennell	Gwen Spell
Doug Fisher	Barb Stevanson
Carroll Gonzo	Kimberly C. Walls
Larry Harms	Jackie Wiggins
Martha F. Hilley	Maribeth Yoder-White
Debbie Burgoon Hines	

Listening Map Contributing Authors

Patricia Shehan Campbell	David Hebert
Jackie Chooi-Theng Lew	Hunter C. March
Ann Clements	Carol Scott-Kassner
Kay Edwards	Mary E. Shamrock
Sheila Feay-Shaw	Sandra L. Stauffer
Kay Greenhaw	

Movement Contributing Authors

Judy Lasko	Wendy Taucher
Marvelene C. Moore	Susan Thomasson
Dixie Piver	Judith Thompson-Barthwell

Recording Producers

Buryl Red, Executive Producer

Rick Baitz	Michael Rafter
Rick Bassett	Mick Rossi
Bill and Charlene James	Buddy Skipper
Joseph Joubert	Robert Spivak
Bryan Louiselle	Jeanine Tesori
Tom Moore	Linda Twine
J. Douglas Pummill	

Contents
Steps to Making Music

 = **Core Lesson**

 = **Music Reading Lesson**

Unit 2 Exploring Music 34

Unit Introduction

Core Lesson =
Music Reading Lesson =

☆ = **Core Lesson**

🖐 = **Music Reading Lesson**

Unit 4 Building Our Musical Skills 110

Unit Introduction
M*U*S*I*C M*A*K*E*R*S Ann Hampton Callaway, Michael Rafter

Core Lesson =

Music Reading Lesson =

vi

✦ = **Core Lesson**

✋ = **Music Reading Lesson**

Unit 6   Making Music Our Own   186

Unit Introduction
M★U★S★I★C   M★A★K★E★R★S   Valerie Dee Naranjo

Core Lesson = ★
Music Reading Lesson = ⬭

Paths to Making Music

STEPS TO Making Music

Enjoy Life

Congratulations, you're in the sixth grade!
You're on your way to bigger and better things.

Being in the sixth grade is not always easy. After all, you still have homework and tests. Part of learning to succeed is knowing how to balance your responsibilities (school) and your personal life (having fun, we hope).

In his song "Your Life Is Now," John Mellencamp reminds us to make the most of each day. Be responsible, and remember to enjoy yourself, your family, your friends, and life.

MUSIC MAKERS

John Mellencamp

John Mellencamp (born 1951) joined his first band when he was in the fifth grade. Since then, he has had an extensive and successful musical career, selling over 25 million albums in the U.S. alone. He has over 36 gold, platinum, and multi-platinum awards and has been nominated for 11 Grammy awards. Mellencamp has given several concerts for Farm Aid and has devoted much of his time to helping autistic children.

Let the Music Begin!

Enjoy Music

Sing "Your Life Is Now."
Enjoy the song. Enjoy life now!

Your Life Is Now

CD 1–1

Words and Music by
John Mellencamp and George M. Green

VERSE

1. See the moon ___ roll ___ a - cross ___ the stars, ___
2. Would you teach your chil - dren to tell the truth? ___

___ See the sea-sons turn ___ like a heart. _
___ Would you take the high ___ road if you could choose? _

Your fa-ther's days are lost ___ to ___
Do you be - lieve you're a vic - tim ___ of a great com - pro -

you, _____ This is _____ your time _
mise? 'Cause I be - lieve _

___ here _ to do ___ what you will _ do. ___
___ you _ could change your _ mind ___ and change our _ lives. ___

4

Express Yourself

If two people read the same sentence, one may say the sentence loud, the other soft. You may say the sentence fast, others may say it slowly. This is known as "expression."

Music also has expressive qualities. Music can be fast or slow, loud or soft. These elements and others make up **musical expression.**

Listen to and **sing** the song "A Brand New Day" from *The Wiz.* How do the singers perform the refrain and verses?

Musical expression comes from the qualities of music that affect how the music sounds. Some of these qualities are loud, soft, slow, and fast.

Youth

by Langston Hughes

We have tomorrow
Bright before us
Like a flame.

Yesterday
A night-gone thing,
A sun-down name.

And dawn-today
Broad arch above
the road we came.

We march!

Arts Connection

Pictured from left to right are cast members from the film musical *The Wiz:* Michael Jackson (Scarecrow), Nipsey Russell (Tinman), Diana Ross (Dorothy), and Ted Ross (Lion).

A Brand New Day

Words and Music by Luther Vandross

REFRAIN

Can't you _ feel a ___ brand new _ day? _

(Last time, repeat ad lib)

Can't you _ feel a ___ brand new _ day? _

VERSE

1. Ev - 'ry - bod - y look a - round 'cause there's a
2. Ev - 'ry - bod - y be glad ___ be - cause the

rea - son to _____ re - joice, ___ you see. _____
sun is shin - ing just _____ for us. _____

Ev - 'ry - bod - y come out _____ and let's com -
Ev - 'ry - bod - y wake up _____ in - to the

mence to sing - ing joy - ful - ly. _____
morn - ing in - to hap - pi - ness. _____

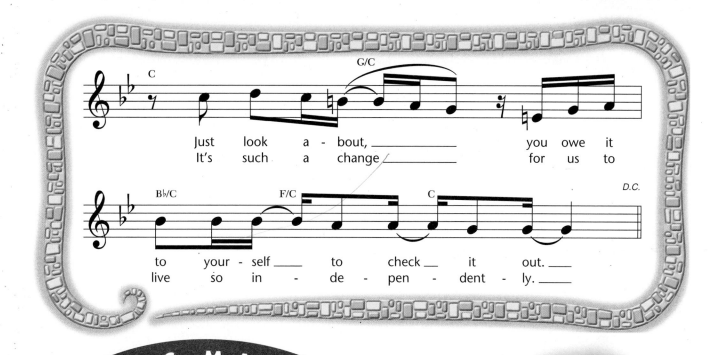

Just look a - bout, _____ you owe it
It's such a change _____ for us to

to your - self ___ to check __ it out. ___
live so in - de - pen - dent - ly. ___

Luther Vandross

Luther Vandross (born 1951) is a performer and a composer. Vandross began playing piano at age three and started his professional career singing jingles and backup for other performing artists. His songwriting breakthrough came in 1972 when "A Brand New Day" was included in the hit musical *The Wiz*. Vandross has written songs for Whitney Houston, Ringo Starr, and Aretha Franklin. His albums typically go platinum.

A Musical Story

Expressive elements are found in all styles of music.
Listen to *Wedding Day at Troldhaugen*. What expressive elements do you hear?

CD 1–5

Wedding Day at Troldhaugen

**from *Lyric Suite*, Op. 65, No. 6
by Edvard Grieg**

Wedding Day at Troldhaugen uses Norwegian melodies. Troldhaugen, Grieg's home, means Troll's Hill. Do you know what trolls are?

Lonesome Cowboy RHYTHMS

Like many cowboy songs, "Red River Valley" got its start far from the Western plains. It eventually ended up in Texas as a cowboy love song.

Using rhythm syllables, **read** and **perform** the rhythms in "Red River Valley."

Rhythms and Ties

Read these patterns using rhythm syllables. How does the **tie** change the rhythm in the second pattern?

1.

2.

tie

A **tie** is a musical symbol that connects two notes of the same pitch to make the sound longer.

CD 1–6

RED RIVER VALLEY

Cowboy Song from the United States

REFRAIN

Come and sit by my side if you love me, — Do not has-ten to bid me a-dieu; But re-mem-ber the Red Riv-er Val-ley — And the girl that has loved you so true.

VERSE

1. From this val-ley they say you are go-ing, —. We will miss your bright eyes and sweet smile; For they say you are tak-ing the sun-shine, — That bright-ens our path-way a-while.

2. Won't you think of the val-ley you're leav-ing? — Oh, how lone-ly, how sad it will be. Oh, — think of the fond heart you're break-ing, — And the grief you are causing me to see.

Fine

D.C. al Fine

Tune In

The Red River marks the border between Texas and Oklahoma. Another Red River flows through Manitoba in Canada and becomes the border between North Dakota and Minnesota.

Listen to the LeLe Bird

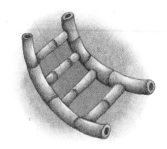

"*Bắt kim thang*" is a Vietnamese song that tells a funny story. **Listen** to the recording while you follow the words of the song.

Sing "*Bắt kim thang*" and listen to the Le Le bird sing *tò tí te*. **Read** and **perform** the rhythm pattern below with its sixteenth-note rhythms. Feel the strong beat of each measure.

The rhythm above shows a strong beat on the **downbeat** of each measure. A conductor moves his or her arm in a downward motion on the downbeat.

> A **downbeat** is the strong beat in music. The first beat in a measure is a downbeat.

▼ Vietnamese folk art is colorful and often full of humor. This illustration of the imaginary Le Le bird follows in that tradition.

CD 1–13

Bắt kim thang

(Setting Up the Golden Ladder)

English Words by Alice Firgau

Traditional Song from Vietnam

Bắt   kim   thang   cà   lang   bí ___   rọ.   Cột   qua   kèo   kèo   qua
Set   the   gold - en   lad - der ___   up;   Now   jump   left,   then   jump

cột.   Chú   bán   dầu   qua   cầu   mà   té.   Chú   bán
right.   What   a   sight!   A   ven - dor   falls   from   the

ếch ___   ở   lại   làm   chi.   Con   le   le   đánh   trống   thổi
bridge;   an - oth - er   calls.   The   Le   Le   bird   plays   trum - pet   and

kèn.   Con   bìm   bịp   thổi   tò   tí   te   tò   te. ___
drum,   And   the   bim   bip   bird   sings   twiddle   dee   dum. ___

Show What You Know!

Show what you know about rhythm. **Perform** this counter-rhythm as you **sing** the song on the syllable *loo*.

Building a Song

Unity in music often comes from repetition. Variety is provided by contrast. In the song "Lean on Me," you will find sections that provide both repetition and contrast. How many different sections of the song can you **identify**?

A Musical Roadmap

As you **sing** "Lean on Me," look for the signs in the music that tell you which way to go.

| 1st, 2nd, and 3rd Endings | *Fine* | *D.C. al Fine* |

CD 1–20

Lean on Me

Words and Music by Bill Withers

VERSE

1. Some - times in our lives ___ we all have pain, ___ we all have
2. Please swal-low your pride _ if I have things _ you need to
3. If there is a load ___ you have to bear ___ that you can't

sor - row. _ But if we are wise ___ we know that there's _
bor - row, _ For no one can fill ____ those of your needs ___
car - ry, ___ I'm right up the road. _ I'll share your load ___

___ al - ways to - mor - row.
___ that you won't let ___ show.   Lean on me ___ when you're not strong _
___ if you just call ___ me.

14

"Magnolia" is a song about childhood memories and a favorite magnolia tree.

Sing "Magnolia." **Identify** the form by choosing a section letter (A or B) when you see a question mark.

CD 1–22

Magnolia

Words and Music by Tish Hinojosa

A

D

1. Tem - pra - no en la ma - ña - na un
2. Ve - ra - no se a - ca - ba tam -
1. ⁊ Ear - ly in the morn - ing,
2. ⁊ Sum - mer - time is end - ing,

Bm   G   A

pa - ja - ri - to can - ta, des - pier - ta la mag - no - li - a.
bién el jue - go pa - ra, ___ ba - jo la mag - no - li - a.
I can hear the birds sing, __ un - der the mag - no - lia tree.
ain't no more pre - tend - ing, __ un - der the mag - no - lia tree.

G   Em

Su can - ción me ha - bla, dul - ce y tan cla - ra,
Ho - jas caen de o - to - ño, a - nun - cian - do in - vier - no,
When I hear it sweet - ly, I am there com - plete - ly,
Au - tumn leaves are fall - ing, win - ter - time is call - ing,

A₇   D   **?**

ba - jo la mag - no - li - a.   Flor blan - ca y bo - ni - ta
ba - jo la mag - no - li - a.   Mi her - ma - ni - ta y yo con
un - der the mag - no - lia tree.   Blos - soms big and white, and
un - der the mag - no - lia tree.   My sis - ter and me, we

A New Structure

Marche militaire

Listen to *Marche militaire* by the Austrian composer Franz Schubert. It has two **A** sections and a **B** section. What is the order of these sections?

by Franz Schubert

The **A** **B** **A** form of this piece reflects a repeating **A** section and a contrasting middle section.

Melodic Roundup

Melodies are often made up of melodic patterns. Using pitch syllables, **read** and **perform** each one. How are the patterns similar?

1. so͵ do mi so

2. la so mi do mi

3. so͵ so͵ do mi re

4. mi re do la͵ do

Tie 'em Up!

Read the melody below using rhythm and pitch syllables. How does the tie change the melody?

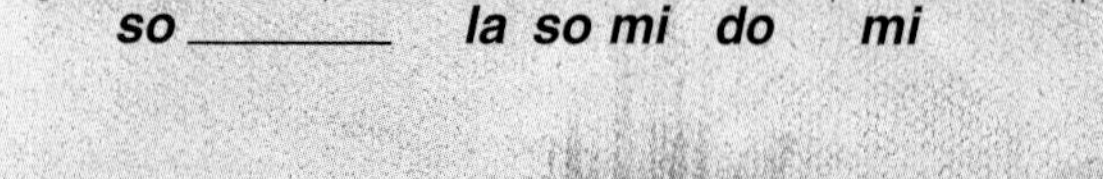

$\frac{4}{4}$ so _____ la so mi do mi

A Prairie Ballad

Sing "Bury Me Not on the Lone Prairie." Which melodic patterns from page 18 appear in the song?

Tune In

This sad ballad was originally written in 1839 about a young sailor's burial at sea. As the song traveled west, cowboys created new words.

CD 2–1
MIDI 1

Bury Me Not on the Lone Prairie

Cowboy Song from the United States

1. "Oh, bur - y me not _____ on the lone prai -
2. "Oh, bur - y me not _____ on the lone prai -
3. "It mat - ters not, _____ I've __ oft been

rie, Where the coy - otes wail, _____
rie," These __ words came slow _____
told, where the bod - y lies _____

____ and the wind blows free; Oh when I
____ and __ mourn - ful - ly from the pal - lid
____ when the heart grows cold. Yet grant, oh

die, _____ don't __ bur - y me
lips _____ of a boy who lay
grant _____ this ____ wish to me,

'neath the west - ern sky, _____ on the lone prai - rie."
on his dy - ing bed _____ at the break of day.
Oh, __ bur - y me not _____ on the lone prai - rie."

REACH FOR THE SKY!

Look at the pictures of the mountains. The mountain on the left is smooth and flowing while the mountain on the right is jagged. Melodies also have contours (shapes). Trace the **melodic contour** of "Gonna Build a Mountain" as you **listen** to the song.

Melodic contour is the shape of a musical phrase.

As you **sing** the song, **read** the notation and notice how the notes in most phrases begin low and then move higher, as though the melody is trying to build a mountain. It's a mountain of melody!

▲ Appalachian Mountains
Blue Ridge Parkway, North Carolina

▲ Mount Reagan
Sawtooth Lake, Idaho

Show What You Know!

Create movements that follow the melodic contour to "Gonna Build a Mountain." Then have the class **perform** your movements with the song.

Gonna Build a Mountain

Words and Music by
Leslie Bricusse and Anthony Newley

1. Gon-na build a moun-tain _____ from a lit-tle hill.
2. Gon-na build a day-dream _ from a lit-tle hope.

Gon-na build a moun-tain, _____ least I hope I will.
Gon-na push that day-dream _ up the moun-tain slope.

Gon-na build a moun-tain, _____ gon-na build it high.
Gon-na build a day-dream, _ gon-na see it through.

I don't know how I'm gon-na do it,
Gonna build a moun-tain and a day-dream,

on-ly know I'm gon-na try.
gon-na make 'em both come true.

From the Musical Production *"Stop the World - I Want to Get Off"* © Copyright 1961 (Renewed) TRO Essex Music Ltd., London, England. TRO - Ludlow Music, Inc., New York, New York, controls all publication rights for the U.S.A. and Canada. Used by Permission.

 MIDI Use the song file for "Gonna Build a Mountain" to explore melodic contour.

Musical Shapes

In Appalachia, craftsmen mold clay into beautiful pottery with different shapes and contours. In music, composers create melodies with different shapes and contours.

Listen to "My Dear Companion." What is the mood and meaning of the words, by Appalachian composer Jean Ritchie?

Now, look at each four-measure phrase on page 23.

- First **describe** the shape, or contour, of each phrase.

- **Compare** the contour of the phrases. How are they similar? How are they different?

- **Create** movements to show the melodic contour of each phrase.

Sing "My Dear Companion." As you sing, pay attention to the shape of each melodic phrase.

Appalachia folk arts include pottery making. Here is an Appalachian craftsman at work. ▼

My Dear Companion

Words and Music by Jean Ritchie

Oh, have you __ seen my dear com - pan - ion,

for he was all this world to me.
(she)

I hear he's gone to some far coun - try,
(she's)

and that he cares no more for ___ me.
(she)

I wish I were some swal - low fly - in',

I'd fly to a high and lone - some place.

There, join the __ wild birds in their cry - in',

Re - mem - ber - ing __ you and your sweet __ face. _____

Vocal Timbres

You recognize the voices of your friends even without seeing them because their voices have different qualities. The unique quality of the sound produced by an instrument or voice is called its **timbre**.

Timbre is the tone color, or unique sound, of an instrument or voice.

The timbre of an individual or group of voices is easy to identify, once you are familiar with it, but describing timbre is not easy. **Listen** to these recordings. Use the words on these pages to describe the vocal timbre in each selection. What factors contribute to the differences in vocal timbre?

CD 2–13
O Christmas Tree

**Traditional German carol
as performed by The Vienna Boys' Choir**

A traditional boys' choir consists of boys with unchanged and changed voices. Note the timbre of the changed voices in the lower register.

mellow

smooth

quivery

CD 2–14
Tamaiti hunahia

**Tahitian choral song
as performed by the Rapa Iti Tahitian Choir**

This ensemble of male and female voices sings a song about a father who rescued his son from death.

pinched   *breathy*

buzzy   *nasal*

CD 2–15
Northfield

as performed by participants at the Alabama Sacred Harp Singing Convention in Birmingham, Alabama

Sacred Harp choral groups of men and women developed in the mid-1800s within the mountain regions of the southern and eastern United States. The tradition continues today in some areas.

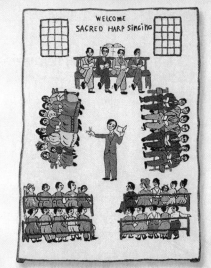

open

relaxed light rough

CD 2–16
Anvil Chorus

**from *Il trovatore*
by Guiseppi Verdi
as performed by the Chicago Symphony Orchestra and Chorus**

The choruses in an opera are sung by male and female singers trained in the operatic vocal style.

pure airy

CD 2–17
Kui.Kyon.pan

as performed by the Monks of the Sera Jé Monastery

In *Kui.Kyon.pan*, Tibetan monks sing in deep, low-bass tones that produce overtones, or harmonics, above the bass tones.

heavy straight

CD 2–18
Strike Up the Band Medley

**by George Gershwin
as performed by the Seven Hills Chorus of Cincinnati, Ohio**

"Sweet Adelines" is a name for *a cappella* women's quartets and choruses. They sing popular American songs of the early and mid-1900s in four-part harmony. The comparable men's singing groups are called "barbershop" quartets and choruses.

tight silvery

SOUNDS OF HARMONY

Have you ever been to a ceremony? "*Wai bamba*" is a ceremonial song performed by the Shona at weddings. The Shona are Bantu-speaking people who live in southeastern Africa, mostly in Zimbabwe.

"*Wai bamba*" has three layers of sound and each layer has its own melody. **Sing** "*Wai bamba,*" adding one layer at a time. As each new layer is added, the **texture** of the music will become thicker and **harmony** will be created.

Harmony is created when two or more different tones sound at the same time.

Texture is the layering of sounds to create a thick or thin quality in music.

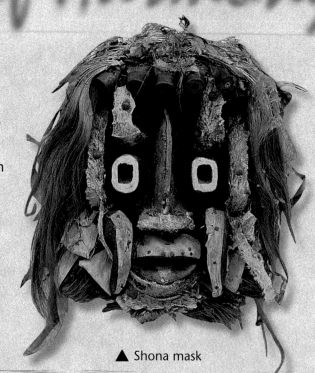

▲ Shona mask

CD 2–19

WAI BAMBA

Shona Wedding Song

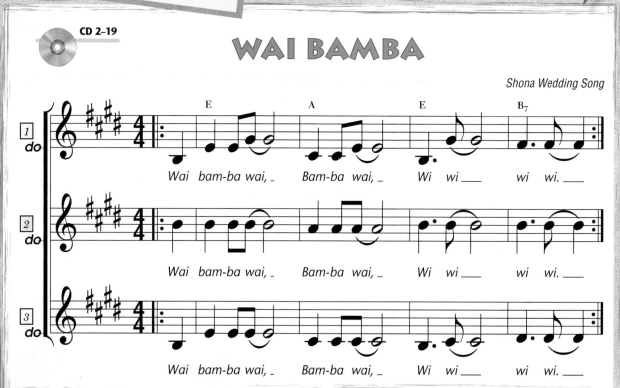

1. Wai bam-ba wai, _ Bam-ba wai, _ Wi wi ___ wi wi. ___

2. Wai bam-ba wai, _ Bam-ba wai, _ Wi wi ___ wi wi. ___

3. Wai bam-ba wai, _ Bam-ba wai, _ Wi wi ___ wi wi. ___

26

Wai bam-ba wai, _ Bam-ba wai, _ Wi _ wi ____ wi wi. ____

Wai bam-ba wai, _ Bam-ba wai, _ Wi wi ____ wi wi. ____

Wai bam-ba wai, _ Bam-ba wai, _ Wi wi wi ____ wi wi wi wi. ____

Talented Thumbs

The *mbira* [mm-BEE-rah] is one of the instruments used to accompany "*Wai bamba.*" The *mbira*, played with the thumb and forefingers, is one of the Shona's most important instruments. The Shona have used the *mbira* in ceremonies for more than 1,000 years. It is frequently praised for its power to soothe the nerves during severe thunderstorms and to calm wild animals of the African jungle.

Listen to this *mbira* performance. **Describe** how the two players use repeated patterns to create a layered texture.

CD 2–21
Chigamba

Traditional song from Zimbabwe as performed by Stella Rambisai Chiweshe Nekati

The *mbira* was traditionally played by men. Stella Rambisai Chiweshe Nekati was one of the first Zimbabwe women to break tradition and learn to play the *mbira*. She is known as the "Queen of Mbira."

▲ *Mbira*

MIDI/Sequencing Software Improvise and record an accompaniment to "*Wai bamba*" using African drum and *mbira* sounds.

Pleasing Polyphony

Listen to "Hey, Ho! Nobody Home." **Describe** what happens to the texture and harmony as you listen to the song. How is it similar to *"Wai bamba"* on page 26? How is the harmony created?

Notice the rhythm notation above measure 1. This notation tells the performer to swing the eighth notes. **Listen** to the recording again, paying attention to the eighth notes sung with swing style. **Sing** "Hey, Ho! Nobody Home."

CD 2–22
MIDI 4

Hey, Ho! Nobody Home

Old English Round

Hey, ho, no - bod - y home,

Meat nor drink nor mon - ey have I none.

Yet I will be mer - ry, ver - y mer - ry.

Hey, ho, no - bod - y home.

Add an Ostinato by Singing or Playing

We can create harmony in layers with one or more **ostinatos.**

Sing these ostinatos with a swing feeling. When you are ready, **perform** them as you accompany "Hey, Ho! Nobody Home."

> An **ostinato** is a musical idea that is continually repeated. Ostinatos can be melodic, rhythmic, or harmonic.

Ostinato 1

do

Hey, ho, Hey, ho, __ I said,

Ostinato 2

do

Hey, ho, Hey, ho.

Ostinato 3

do

Hey, ho, Hey, ho.

Build an Ensemble

For an even richer texture, add these instrumental ostinatos to your "Hey, Ho! Nobody Home" ensemble. Then **improvise** your own parts to use as an introduction and an interlude.

Alto metallophone

Tambourine

Bass metallophone

Obstinate Ostinatos

Musical texture is created through the use of melody and harmony. Ostinatos can be used to build textures. Composer Philip Glass is known for his use of ostinatos. The bass-line ostinatos below are used in Glass's *Open the Kingdom*.

Play these ostinatos on a keyboard or a mallet instrument. How are the ostinatos the same? How are they different?

Days of Fishes (bass)

D   C   Bb   A

Open the Kingdom (bass)

F   E   D   C

In My Way (bass)

D   E   F   E C

Arts Connection

Portrait of Philip Glass by artist Chuck Close (born 1940) ▼

MUSIC MAKERS
Philip Glass

Philip Glass (born 1937) is an American composer who is best known for a style called minimalism. In this style, Glass uses ostinatos to create pleasing harmonies and layered textures. Sometimes his musical pieces are very long, lasting up to twelve hours. Some of Glass's most important works are his operas *Einstein on the Beach* (about Albert Einstein) and *Akhnaten* (about the Egyptian pharaoh Akhnaten). Glass's music is influenced by pop and classical music as well as West African and Indian music.

Hear It Again...And Again!

Follow this map as you **listen** to *Open the Kingdom*. **Identify** the bass and other ostinatos in the piece.

CD 2–24

Open the Kingdom

by Philip Glass and David Byrne

David Byrne was one of the founding members of the rock group Talking Heads.

OPEN THE KINGDOM LISTENING MAP

Review, Assess,

What Do You Know?

1. For each term on the left, identify the type of musical expression.

Performance	Musical Expression
a. fast	• dynamics
b. loud	• tempo
c. soft	
d. slow	

2. Point to the downbeats in this rhythm. How many downbeats are there? Point to the pickups (anacrusis) in this rhythm. How many pickups are there?

What Do You Hear? 1A

 CD 2–25

Vocal Timbre

Listen to these recordings of vocal timbres. Identify the correct vocal performance for each selection.

Excerpt	Vocal Performance
1. _____	**a.** opera chorus
2. _____	**b.** women's "barbershop" chorus
3. _____	**c.** Tibetan monks of Central Asia
4. _____	**d.** boys' choir
5. _____	**e.** men's and women's chorus of Tahiti
6. _____	**f.** sacred harp singing

Perform, Create

CD 2–31

Form

Listen to the recording of "Lean on Me." Using the form symbols on the right, identify the correct form for the selection.

Form

a. ABBA

b. BABA

c. ABAB

Form Symbols

- **A** Verse
- **B** Refrain

What You Can Do

Sing Melodic Patterns

Using pitch syllables, read and perform these melodic patterns.

1. so̦ do mi so

2. la so mi do mi

3. so̦ so̦ do mi re

4. mi re do la̦ do

Play and Create Textures with Ostinatos

Select and perform one of the ostinatos for "Hey, Ho! Nobody Home" on page 29. Then, create a new ostinato to accompany the song. When ready, perform your ostinato as a new texture to the song.

Here to Stay

The 1950s was the decade that popular music and rock 'n' roll took off. It was also a decade that saw spectacular advances in science and technology.

Follow and discuss the 1950s time line below. The number next to a song indicates its highest ranking on the pop music charts that year.

Dwight D. Eisenhower

Lucille Ball

- Patti Page: "The Tennessee Waltz" (#1)
- Color TV transmission
- Korean War erupts

- Jo Stafford: "You Belong to Me" (#1)
- Sony invents the transistor radio
- First commercial jet airliner

1950 1951 1952 1953

- *I Love Lucy* premieres on TV
- First computers sold

- Dwight D. Eisenhower, President
- Perry Como: "No Other Love" (#1)

- Elvis Presley: "Don't Be Cruel" (#1)
- First transatlantic telephone call

1955 1956 1957 1958

- Pat Boone: "Ain't That a Shame" (#1)
- Marian Anderson makes a belated debut at New York's Metropolitan Opera House

- USSR launches Sputnik satellite
- *American Bandstand* premieres on TV

- Stereo recording introduced
- Leonard Bernstein appointed director of the N.Y. Philharmonic
- Danny & the Juniors: "At the Hop" (#1)

Dick Clark: Host of *American Bandstand*

Elvis Presley

34

Exploring Music

SHAKE RATTLE and ROLL

BILL HALEY and his Comets

DECCA RECORDS
EXTENDED PLAY '45'
ED 2168

Shake, Rattle and Roll

1954

- Bill Haley & His Comets: "Shake, Rattle and Roll" (#7)
- Civil rights: *Brown v. Board of Education*
- Radios outnumber daily newspapers

1959

- Frankie Avalon: "Venus" (#1)
- Computer microchip invented
- Xerox invents plain paper copier

Frankie Avalon

Everybody Rock

Sing "Rock and Roll Is Here to Stay," a Top Twenty hit in 1958 for Danny and the Juniors.

CD 2–32

Rock and Roll
Is Here to Stay

Words and Music by David White

VERSE

1. Rock and roll is here to stay, ___ and
2. Rock and roll will al - ways be, ___ I
3. If you don't like rock and roll, ___ just

it will nev - er die. _____ It was meant to
dig it to the end. _____ It'll go down in
think what you've been miss - in'. If you like to

be that way, _ al - though I don't know why. _____
his - to - ry, ___ just you watch, my friend. _____
bop and stroll, _ walk a - round and lis - ten.

I don't care what peo - ple say, ___ Rock and roll is
Rock and roll will al - ways be, ___ It'll go down in
Let's all start to rock and roll, ___ Ev - 'ry - bod - y

36

Danny and the Juniors'
other famous hit, "At the
Hop," is on Billboard's all-
time List of #1 Hits.

here to   stay. __ We don't care what peo-ple say, __
his-to - ry. __   Rock and roll will   al-ways be, __
rock and   roll. __ We don't care what peo-ple say, __

Rock   and   roll   is   here   to   stay. ___
It'll   go   down   in   his - to - ry. _____
Rock   and   roll   is   here   to   stay. ___

REFRAIN

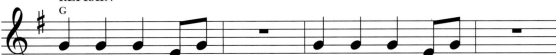

Ev - 'ry - bod - y rock,   Ev - 'ry - bod - y rock,

Ev - 'ry - bod - y rock,   Ev - 'ry - bod - y rock.

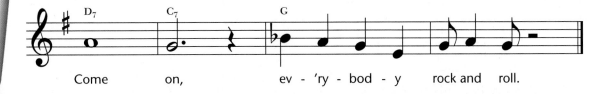

Come   on,   ev - 'ry - bod - y   rock and   roll.

Soft to Loud!

Some sounds can be loud, while other sounds may be soft. What is the loudest sound you heard today? What is the quietest sound?

In music, the intensity of the sound is its dynamic level. There are six main dynamic levels in music. Italian words are used to identify the six different levels.

pp	*p*	*mp*	*mf*	*f*	*ff*
pianissimo	*piano*	*mezzo piano*	*mezzo forte*	*forte*	*fortissimo*
very soft	soft	moderately soft	moderately loud	loud	very loud

On Broadway!

Listen to "Give My Regards to Broadway." Which two dynamic levels are used in the song? Did the dynamics change gradually or suddenly?

The recording of "Give My Regards to Broadway" uses articulation, another expressive element. Articulation is how the notes are performed. The first time, the melody is sung **legato.** The second time, the melody is **staccato.**

Now **sing** "Give My Regards to Broadway." Make sure you change dynamics, as shown in the music.

Legato notes are connected to each other and played or sung smoothly. **Staccato** notes are performed short and separated from each other.

38

Give My Regards to Broadway

Words and Music by George M. Cohan

Give my re - gards to Broad - way, Re -
mem - ber me to Her - ald Square, _____
Tell all the gang at For - ty - sec - ond Street that
I will soon be there; _____
Whis - per of how I'm yearn - ing to
min - gle with the old - time throng, _____
Give my re - gards to old Broad - way and say that
I'll be there ere long. _____

A Written Form of Expression

Poetry is an important form of written expression. Poetry may tell a story. Poetry sometimes uses the same expressions that music uses: slow, fast, loud, soft, accented, or smooth-sounding words.

Listen to a dramatic reading of the poem *Stopping by Woods on a Snowy Evening* by Robert Frost.

CD 2–36

Stopping by Woods on a Snowy Evening

by Robert Frost

In this dramatic reading, the speaker uses vocal inflection, tempo, pauses, dynamics, and other qualities to express the poetry. These are the same kinds of expression used in music.

Robert Frost ▶

A Musical Form of Expression

Listen to a short segment of a choir singing the poem *Stopping by Woods on a Snowy Evening.* How does the musical setting affect the mood of the poem? **Describe** the feeling of the poem when set to music.

CD 2–37

Stopping by Woods on a Snowy Evening

by Randall Thompson

American composer Randall Thompson (1899–1984) set several poems of Robert Frost to music in a piece called *Frostiana* (1959). "The Road Not Taken" is another famous Frost poem in this work.

Stopping by Woods on a Snowy Evening

by Robert Frost

Whose woods these are I think I know.
His house is in the village though;
He will not see me stopping here
To watch his woods fill up with snow.

My little horse must think it queer
To stop without a farmhouse near
Between the woods and frozen lake
The darkest evening of the year.

He gives his harness bells a shake
To ask if there is some mistake.
The only other sound's the sweep
Of easy wind and downy flake.

The woods are lovely, dark, and deep.
But I have promises to keep,
And miles to go before I sleep,
And miles to go before I sleep.

Arts Connection

▲ *Snow Palace* (1986) is a painting by Karl J. Kuerner III. The Kuerner family, from Pennsylvania's Brandywine Valley, lived near another famous American artist, Andrew Wyeth.

Signs of Time

In the nineteenth century, whale hunting was one of Scotland's most important industries. A whaler's life was full of danger and adventure. Many folk songs were inspired by the colorful stories and tales of his struggles at sea.

"Farewell to Tarwathie" is one of the best-known Scottish whaling songs.

The Time Is Three

Find the **time signature** of "Farewell to Tarwathie." Is the first measure complete? On which beat does the melody begin?

Listen to the recording of "Farewell to Tarwathie" and conduct a pattern in $\frac{3}{4}$ meter.

Sing "Farewell to Tarwathie" and conduct in meter in 3.

A **time signature** is the musical symbol that shows how many beats are in a measure and which note gets the beat.

Farewell to Tarwathie

Folk Song from Scotland

1. Fare - well to Tar - wa - thie, A - dieu Mor-mond Hill, And the
2. Fare - well to my com-rades for a while I must part, And __

dear land of Crim-mond, I bid thee fare - well. I'm
like - wise the dear lass who first won my heart, The

bound out for Green - land and read - y to sail, In ____
cold coast of Green - land my heart will not chill, The __

hopes to find rich - es in hunt - ing the whale.
long - er the ab - sence the more lov - ing she'll feel.

3. Our ship is well rigged, and she's ready to sail,
   The crew, they are anxious to follow the whale.
   Where the icebergs do float and the stormy winds blow,
   Where the land and the ocean is covered with snow.

4. The cold coast of Greenland is barren and bare,
   No seedling nor harvest is ever known there,
   And the birds here sing sweetly in mountain and vale,
   But there's no bird in Greenland to sing to the whale.

Listen to these two recordings of Irish and Scottish origin as you
conduct in meter in 3. Which recording is easier to conduct? Why?

Allegretto

**from *Four Scottish Dances*, Op. 59
by Sir Malcolm Arnold**

This British composer also wrote sets
of English, Irish, and Welsh dances.

Highway to Kilkenny

**Traditional Irish tune
as performed by Cherish the Ladies and
the Boston Pops Orchestra**

This performance combines traditional
orchestral instruments with an Irish
folk ensemble.

BALLAD Rhythms

The ballad "Barb'ry Allen" is much older than "Farewell to Tarwathie." It dates back to the seventeenth century. There are hundreds of variations of this ballad on either side of the Atlantic.

Sing "Barb'ry Allen."

Read and clap the rhythm of the words using rhythm syllables.

CD 3–8

BARB'RY ALLEN

Folk Song from the British Isles

1. In Scar - let town, where I was born, There

was a young maid dwell - in', Made

ev' - ry youth cry, _____ "Well - a - day," For

love of Bar - b'ry Al - len.

Show What You Know!

Read and clap these patterns using rhythm syllables. Then find one pattern used in "Farewell to Tarwathie," on page 43, and one pattern used in "Barb'ry Allen," on page 44.

1.

2.

3.

4.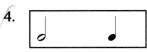

5.

6.

7.

8.

2. 'Twas in the merry month of May,
   When green buds they were swellin',
   Sweet William on his deathbed lay,
   For love of Barb'ry Allen.

3. He sent his servant to the town,
   To the place where she was dwellin',
   Cried, "Master bids you come to him,
   If your name be Barb'ry Allen."

4. Then slowly, slowly she got up,
   And slowly went she nigh him,
   And when she pulled the curtains back
   Said, "Young man, I think you're dyin'."

5. "Oh, yes, I'm sick, I'm very sick,
   And I never will be better,
   Until I have the love of one,
   The love of Barb'ry Allen."

6. Then lightly tripped she down the stairs,
   She trembled like an aspen.
   "'Tis vain, 'tis vain, my dear young man,
   To long for Barb'ry Allen."

7. She walked out in the green, green fields,
   She heard his death bells knellin'.
   And every stroke they seemed to say,
   "Hard-hearted Barb'ry Allen."

8. "Oh, father, father, dig my grave,
   Go dig it deep and narrow.
   Sweet William died for me today;
   I'll die for him tomorrow."

9. They buried her in the old churchyard,
   Sweet William's grave was nigh her,
   And from his heart grew a red, red rose,
   And from her heart a brier.

10. They grew and grew o'er the old church wall,
    'Till they could grow no higher,
    Until they tied a lover's knot,
    The red rose and the brier.

A Favorite Form

The musical form **a a b b** has both built-in repetition and contrast. It is used in all types of music, from early folk songs to today's bluegrass fiddle tunes.

Sing "*El cóndor pasa,*" a song from the Andes region of South America. **Identify** the four sections that make up the song. How does the **b** section differ from the **a** sections?

CD 3–16

El cóndor pasa

English Words by Aura Kontra

Music by Daniel Almonica Robles

a Am

El a - mor ___ co - mo un cón - dor ba - ja - rá, mi co - ra -
Love is like a con - dor glid - ing towards the earth, It comes to

C   Am   E₇   Am   E₇

zón, ʼl gol-pea - rá, _____ des-pués se i - rá. _____ Mmm _____
me, fill-ing me with hap-pi-ness. _ And then it's gone. _____ Mmm _____

Am   **a**

_____ La _ lu - na en el de - sier - to bri - lla - rá Tú ven -
_____ As the moon-light leaves its glow on de - sert sands, You ap -

C   Am   E₇   Am   E₇

drás. So - la - men-te un be - so, _ me de - ja - rás. _____ Mmm _____
pear, bring-ing back the love I lost. _ And then you, too, are gone. _ Mmm _____

Instruments of the Andes

Listen to the following Andean instruments in *"El cóndor pasa"*—*quena* (flute), *zampoña* (panpipes; pictured on page 46), *charango* (small fret lute), and *ch'ajch'as* (rattles).

Andean *ch'ajch'as* ▶

◀ *Quena*

Tune In

Did you know that the Andean *ch'ajch'as* (rattles) are made from the toenails of llamas?

¿Quién sa - be si ma - ña - na vol - ve - rás, _____ qué ha -
Who knows __ when my love will draw you back a - gain. _ What to

rás, _____ no pen - sa - rás? Yo sé que nun - ca vol - ve -
do, _____ will you re - turn? Who knows if love is meant to

rás, más pien - so que _____ no vi - vi - ré co - mo po -
be when it has flown _____ back whence it came. I do not

dré. _____ Mmm _____
know. _____ Mmm _____

Move with "*El cóndor pasa*"

You can **move** to show the form of "*El cóndor pasa*." You will use smooth, gliding movements. Practice and then **perform** the movements.

▲ **Section ⓐ** In a circle formation, move to the left, using a cross-step pattern, for the first six measures of the song.

▲ Move to the right, using a cross-step pattern, for the next six measures.

▲ **Section ⓑ** In place, create smooth, flowing patterns, using your whole body.

Greatest Hits of the 1500s

Sing "Greensleeves," a sixteenth-century melody also known as the English carol "What Child Is This?" "Greensleeves" also uses **a** **a** **b** **b** form. Notice that the second **a** and **b** phrases are slightly different. One way of showing this is **a** **a'** **b** **b'**.

CD 3–20

Greensleeves

Folk Song from England

a

VERSE

1. A - las, my love, __ you do me wrong __ to cast me off __ dis-
2. My men were cloth - ed all in green __ And they did ev - er

a'

cour - teous - ly; And I have lov - ed you so long __ De-
wait on thee; All this was gal - lant to be seen __ And

light - ing in _____ your com - pa - ny.
yet _____ thou wouldst __ not love _____ me.

REFRAIN **b**

Green - sleeves __ was all my joy, _____ Green - sleeves __ was

b'

my de - light, Green - sleeves was my heart of gold, __ And

who but my La - dy Green - sleeves?

Element: FORM | SKILL: PLAYING | Connection: CULTURE

Playing with Form

Repetition and contrast help define phrases and sections in musical form. **Listen** to the recording of *"La paloma se fué,"* a folk song from Puerto Rico. Follow the notation and **identify** the **a** and **b** melodic phrases. How many times does each phrase repeat?

Notice that the phrases can be combined to create an **A** **B** section form. Music can have both phrase and section form.

Sing *"La paloma se fué."* As you sing, notice how the **A** **B** sections contrast with each other in melody, rhythm, and texture.

Arts Connection

▲ *Trío Musical* (2003) by Puerto Rican painter, Obed Gómez

Forming Rhythms

Rhythms and instrumental accompaniments can define contrasting sections in music.

Clap, or say, these rhythm patterns. Then, **perform** them as an accompaniment to *"La paloma se fué."* Perform the rhythms in different sections of the song to create contrast.

CD 3–22

La paloma se fué
(The Dove that Flew Away)

English Words and Arrangement by Alejandro Jiménez
Folk Song from Puerto Rico

¿Se - ño - res no han vis - to la pa -
Oh say, sirs, have you seen la pa -

lo - ma que vo - ló del pa - lo - mar? ¿Se - ño - res no han
lo - ma that has flown a - way from home? Oh say, sirs, have

vis - to la pa - lo - ma que vo - ló del pa - lo - mar?
you seen la pa - lo - ma that has flown a - way from home?

Se fué la pa - lo - ma, se fué la pa - lo - ma, se fué pa - ra no vol -
It's gone, la pa - lo - ma, it's gone, la pa - lo - ma, it's gone and will not re -

ver. Se fué la pa - lo - ma, se fué la pa - lo - ma, se
turn. It's gone, la pa - lo - ma, it's gone, la pa - lo - ma, it's

fué pa - ra no vol - ver.
gone and will not re - turn.

Glorious Gospel

"Glory, Glory, Hallelujah" is a gospel song. Like most gospel songs, it encourages the singers to let go of their fear, worry, and anger and let only good thoughts come through. The influences of gospel music can be heard in the popular music we listen to every day.

Describe the contour of the melody after you **sing** "Glory, Glory, Hallelujah."

CD 3–27
MIDI 6

Glory, Glory, Hallelujah

Traditional Gospel Song

REFRAIN Glo - ry, glo - ry, hal - le - lu - jah!
    1. I feel bet - ter, so much bet - ter,
    2. Feel like shout - in' "Hal - le - lu - jah!"

Since I laid my bur - den down.

Glo - ry, glo - ry, hal - le - lu - jah!
I feel bet - ter, so much bet - ter,
Feel like shout - in' "Hal - le - lu - jah!"

Repeat Refrain after each verse

Since I laid my bur - den down.

Gospel Choir Moves

With their upbeat sense of celebration, gospel songs make singers and listeners let go—and move! The movements used by gospel choirs influenced the way popular music is performed today. Through movement we experience the rhythm of the music and the feeling of the lyrics.

Using "Glory, Glory, Hallelujah," **move** to express the lyrics of the song.

Perform these movements as you **sing** the phrase *glory, glory, hallelujah.*

▲ *Glory, Glory*–Hands flicker, moving upward.

▲ *Hallelujah*–Draw a rainbow arc overhead.

Gospel B3

One of the most famous sounds in gospel music is that of a Hammond B3 organ. The sound of a "B3" can be found on MIDI keyboards. Locate a gospel organ sound on your MIDI keyboard and **play** this chord accompaniment to "Glory, Glory, Hallelujah." Experiment with playing a variety of rhythm patterns on the accompaniment.

GO with the Melody

Listen to a different performance of *Glory, Glory, Hallelujah*. How would you **describe** the way the singer performs the melody?

CD 3–29

Glory, Glory, Hallelujah

Traditional Gospel Song as performed by Carol Woods and the Linda Twine Singers

This gospel performance also features call and response and improvisation on the Hammond organ.

Here is the song melody:

Glo-ry,   glo - ry,   hal - le - lu - jah!

Here is an ornamented melody:

Glo-ry,   glo - ry, __   hal-le - lu - jah! _

▲ Plain egg

▲ Slightly ornamented eggs

▲ Highly ornamented Fabergé egg

Dress Up the Melody

Singers sometimes add extra notes to the melody. These extra notes are called *ornamentation*. The singer may **improvise** the ornamentation on the spot. Name some performers who improvise ornamentation in this way.

> The term **improvise** means to make up music as it is being performed.

Perform this familiar melody, using bells, keyboard, or your voice. Then **improvise** ornamentation on the melody.

Frè - re   Jac - ques,   Frè - re   Jac - ques,

Here is one possibility for improvising ornamentation for *"Frère Jacques."*

Frè - re ___ Jac - ques,   Frè - re ___ Jac - ques,

Composers use ornamentation to add variety to a composition. They may write the ornamentation into the score or expect the performer to improvise it. The trill is a type of ornamentation used frequently by Baroque composers. **Play** this melody, without the trills, on a mallet or keyboard instrument.

Listen to the melody above performed on a trumpet with the ornamentation. Point to the notes that are trilled.

CD 3–30
Prince of Denmark's March

by Jeremiah Clarke
as performed by the Canadian Brass

This famous piece, sometimes titled *Trumpet Voluntary,* is often used as processional music at weddings and other formal ceremonies.

A SINGING "TONIC"

In this scale, the **tonic** note is *do*.

> The **tonic** is the home note of a scale. In a major scale, the tonic is *do*.

so₁ la₁ ti₁ do re mi fa so la ti do¹

A Major Scale

This scale is the *do*-diatonic scale, or major scale, starting on F. You can always find *do* on the staff by looking at the key signature.

Finding *do*

When there are flats in the key signature, the last one on the right is always *fa*. Find the note *fa*, then go down four notes to find *do*.

When there are sharps in the key signature, the last one on the right is *ti*. Find the note *ti*, then go up one note to find *do*.

Sing each of these scales. Then **play** one on the metallophone.

F-*do* pentatonic scale

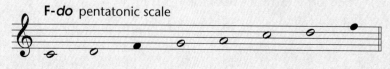

F-*do* diatonic scale

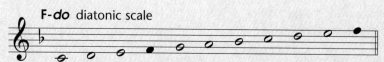

Use the key signature to find *do* in "*Adiós, amigos.*"

Spot the Scale!

Sing "Adiós, amigos." Then identify each F-do in the music.
(One is shown in the color box.)

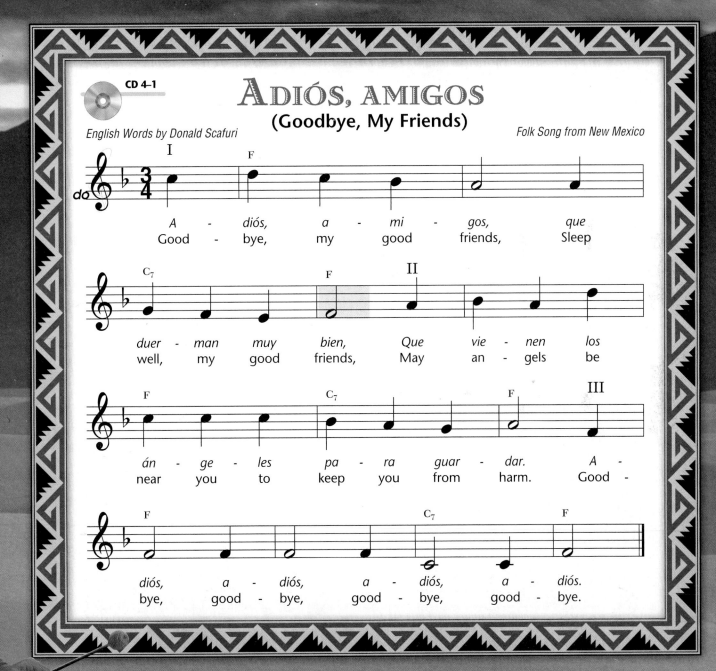

CD 4–1

ADIÓS, AMIGOS
(Goodbye, My Friends)

English Words by Donald Scafuri

Folk Song from New Mexico

A - diós, a - mi - gos, que
Good - bye, my good friends, Sleep

duer - man muy bien, Que vie - nen los
well, my good friends, May an - gels be

án - ge - les pa - ra guar - dar. A -
near you to keep you from harm. Good -

diós, a - diós, a - diós, a - diós.
bye, good - bye, good - bye, good - bye.

Migrate to Minor

Butterflies are found all over the world and live in many varied climates. Their beauty has inspired artists to create art and musicians to create songs. "La mariposa" ("The Butterfly") is one such song.

Listen to "La mariposa" from Bolivia. It is based on a different scale. **Sing** "La mariposa" and listen to the sound.

Scale Review

You already know how to use the key signature to find *do*. When a scale ends on *do*, the scale is called *major*.

When a scale ends on *la*, it is called *minor*. In minor scales, the tonic is *la*.

Every key signature has a major scale and a minor scale that belong to it.

CD 4–8
MIDI 7

La mariposa
(The Butterfly)

English Words by Aura Kontra   *Folk Song from Bolivia*

La la la la lai   la   lai   la lai   la   lai   lai   lai   lai   lai,

La la la la lai   la   lai   la lai   la   lai   la la la la la   lai   lai   lai.

Al   son de   las   ma - tra - cas   to - dos can - tan   y   bai - lan
Hear   the rat - tles'   rhyth-mic beat,   Call - ing   us   to   sing and dance

La mo-re-na-da.
to the live-ly sound.

Con las pal-mas,
Clap your hands now, *(clap)*

con los ta-cos.
kick your heels up, *(stamp)*

¡Vi-va la fies-ta!
turn your part-ner 'round.

¡Vi-va la fies-ta!
Turn your part-ner 'round,

¡Vi-va la fies-ta!
turn your part-ner 'round. *(clap)*

A Minor Mystery

Play the scale in the color box. Use the key signature to find *do*. Can you figure out its tonic?

so, la, ti, do re mi fa so la ti do¹

Show What You Know!

Create rhythm patterns using the notes in these scales. **Play** the patterns on a mallet instrument. Label the scales "major" or "minor."

1.

2.

SHADES of SOUND

Timbre is an important part of musical style. People around the world sing in different ways. **Listen** to the vocal timbre of "*Yü guang guang*," a Cantonese lullaby from Hong Kong. Then **sing** the song. Does your vocal timbre sound the same?

CD 4–15

Yü guang guang

English Words by Aura Kontra

(Moonlight Lullaby)

Folk Song from Hong Kong

月 —— 光 —— 光 —— 照 —— 地 —— 堂
yü —— gwahng — gwahng —————— tsee - oo day - ee tong
1. Moon - light is shin - ing ———— sil - v'ry on the earth.
2. Har - vest —— time —————— now — is —— here.

虾 仔 你 乖 乖 —— 瞓 落 —— 床 ——
hah tzai nay gwai gwai —— fuhn lah - oo tchong —
Come now, my dear child, —— sleep and be still. ——
Work - ing all day, the —— barn we —— fill. ——

World Voices

Listen to some of the ways people from around the world use their voices to create unique vocal styles. How would you **describe** each vocal timbre?

CD 4–19
Vocal Styles Around the World

This montage includes these vocal styles: Navajo tribe of the American Southwest, Tuvan people of central Asia, Celtic style of Scotland and Ireland, popular music of Cuba, and African American gospel music.

天	早___	阿	媽	要	廣	播___	秧	咯___

teeng   dsee - yoo ah   mah   yee oo gong   tsah(p) ___ yong   law ___

Moth - er ___ will soon plant   the   young   rice ___ seed - lings   and

Sleep,   ba - by, __ sleep __   and   grow   big   and _ strong __   For

阿	爺	睇	牛	俱	上___	山 __	崗___

ah   yeh   tai ngow koy   tsü(ng) _   sahn _   gong ___

your grand-fa-ther will   watch ___   the cat - tle __ a - graz-ing on the hill.

your grand-fa-ther needs you   to watch the cat - tle __ a - graz-ing on the hill.

Musical Colors

Musical performers are often known by the timbre of their instrument or voice.

Louis Armstrong, the great jazz trumpeter and singer, is known for his playing and singing style. Sing "What a Wonderful World," a song associated with Armstrong's unique vocal timbre.

CD 4–20

What a Wonderful World

Words and Music by George David Weiss and Bob Thiele

I see trees of green, red ros - es too,
I see them bloom for me and you, ___and I think ___ to my-self,
What a won-der-ful world. I see skies of blue and
clouds of white, the bright,___ bless-ed day, the dark, ___ sa-cred night, ___and I
think ____ to my-self, What a won - der - ful world.

CD 4–22

What a Wonderful World

by George Weiss and Bob Thiele
as performed by Louis Armstrong

What a Wonderful World is considered
Armstrong's signature song.

Wonderful Timbres, Wonderful Styles

Popular hit songs are often rerecorded by artists using different timbres and styles of music.

Listen to singer Eva Cassidy perform the song *What a Wonderful World*. **Describe** the timbre of her voice.

Then **listen** to rock singer Joey Ramone perform his version of *What a Wonderful World*. Notice how Ramone and the band use a distorted guitar timbre along with **power chords**.

Power chords are chords containing only a root and fifth (no third), often used by rock guitarists.

CD 4–23

What a Wonderful World

by George David Weiss and Bob Thiele as performed by Eva Cassidy

This live recording at *Blues Alley* features the smooth vocal timbre of Eva Cassidy, whose voice has been described as "one of the best in her generation."

CD 4–24

What a Wonderful World

by George David Weiss and Bob Thiele as performed by Joey Ramone

Joey Ramone was lead singer for the rock band The Ramones. *What a Wonderful World* is from his solo album.

Cool Cat Scat

Try your hand at scat singing, one of Louis Armstrong's trademarks, by following these simple steps:

- **Sing** a familiar song like "When the Saints Go Marching In," using the original words.

- **Sing** the same song in scat style by substituting syllables such as *bah* and *dah* for the words.

- **Create** your own scat syllables to go with the melody.

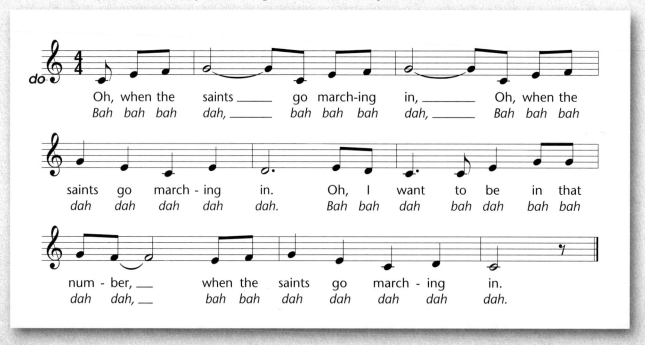

Hot Cat

Listen to Louis Armstrong play *Hotter Than That*. Which instrument has the "buzzy" tone? What techniques do the Dixieland band instruments use to sound "jazzy"?

CD 4–25
Hotter Than That

by Lil Hardin Armstrong
as performed by Louis Armstrong
and the Hot Five

This famous recording from 1927 features Armstrong's spectacular trumpet playing and his trademark "scat singing" solos.

M·U·S·I·C M·A·K·E·R·S

Louis Armstrong

Louis Armstrong (1901–1971) was one of the most important musicians in jazz history. Born in New Orleans, Louisiana, he became the leading Dixieland trumpet player, known for his virtuoso solos. Armstrong also had a unique singing voice, and he popularized scat singing (using nonsense syllables).

In his later years, Armstrong became America's goodwill ambassador, playing and singing concerts all over the world. Some of his biggest song hits were "Hello, Dolly," "Blueberry Hill," "Mack the Knife," and "What a Wonderful World."

Partners for Peace

Sometimes two songs fit together and can be performed at the same time. Their performance creates harmony.

Part 1 of the song below is "Sing a Song of Peace." Part 2 is "This Is My Country." **Sing** each separately. When you know each well, sing them as partner songs.

Arts Connection

Garden of Eden by Jacob Bouttats (17th century, Flemish). Describe your feelings about this painting. What suggestions can you make for people to live peacefully together? ▶

CD 4–26

Sing a Song of Peace

Words by Jill Gallina
"This Is My Country"–Words by Don Raye

Music by Al Jacobs
Arranged by Jill Gallina

Sing a song of peace through the world,   till ev-'ry land is sing-ing. __

This   is   my   coun-try, land   of my birth;

Classical Partners

Classical composers also combine different themes as partners. The French composer Georges Bizet [jorj bee-ZAY] did just that with the two melodies below.

Theme 1

Theme 2

Listen to how the two melodies are used in *Farandole*. As you follow the listening map, locate the themes and the canon.

CD 4–28

Farandole

from *L'Arlésienne Suite No. 2* by Georges Bizet

Bizet uses the melody of a well-known Christmas tune and combines it with a second theme that is in sharp contrast to the first.

Farandole

LISTENING MAP

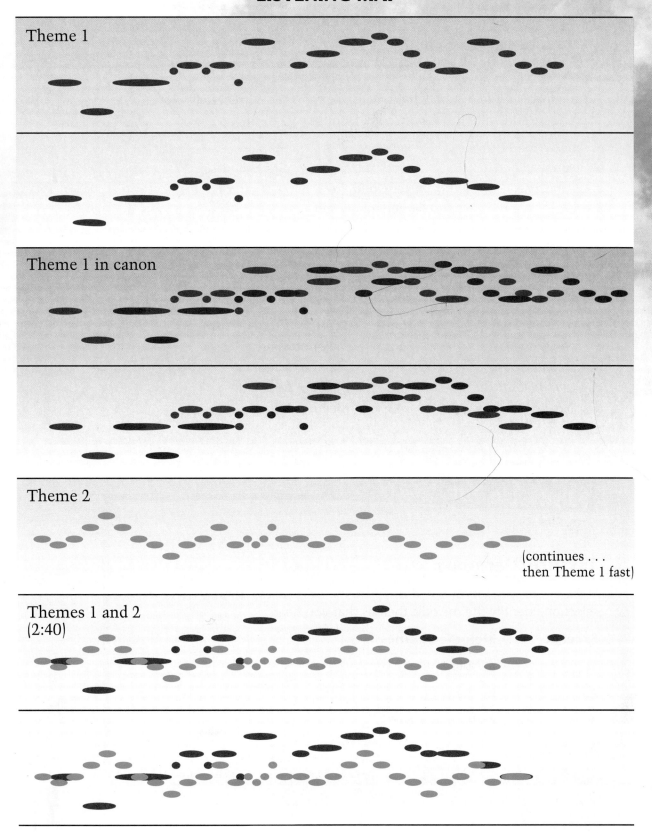

Theme 1

Theme 1 in canon

Theme 2

(continues . . .
then Theme 1 fast)

Themes 1 and 2
(2:40)

Review, Assess,

What Do You Know?

1. For the following terms, match the Italian term to the correct definition. Then name and write the dynamic marking for each term.

   a. *mezzo forte*   • very soft
   b. *piano*   • loud
   c. *pianissimo*   • very loud
   d. *forte*   • moderately soft
   e. *mezzo piano*   • soft
   f. *fortissimo*   • moderately loud

2. Look at the notation for the songs below. Point to the name of the scale on which each melody is based. Identify *do* in each song.

Song	Page	Scale	Do
a. "*Adiós, amigos*"	57	Major or Minor	____
b. "*El cóndor pasa*"	46	Major or Minor	____
c. "*La mariposa*"	58	Major or Minor	____
d. "Farewell to Tarwathie"	43	Major or Minor	____

What Do You Hear? 2A

 CD 4–29

Texture/Harmony

Listen to the two melodic themes of Bizet's *Farandole* on page 68. For each selection, identify the melodic themes that you hear.

Excerpt	Melodic Themes
1. ____	**a.** theme 1
2. ____	**b.** theme 2
3. ____	**c.** themes 1 and 2
4. ____	

Perform, Create

CD 4–35, 36

Timbre

Listen to two recordings of *What a Wonderful World.* As you listen, identify the words that describe the timbres of the voices and instruments on the recordings.

Excerpt	Timbre		
1. _____	**a.** smooth violins	**e.** buzzy voice	
2. _____	**b.** piano	**f.** mellow drums	
	c. trumpet	**g.** clear voice	
	d. soft guitar	**h.** children's voices	

What You Can Do

Move to Show Form

Analyze and describe the form of "*El cóndor pasa*," page 46. Create two movements (**a** and **b**) that go with the song. Perform each movement with the corresponding section of the song.

Read and Play Rhythms in 3

Follow the notation of "Farewell to Tarwathie," page 43, and conduct the beat in 3. Play the rhythms in the song on a nonpitched rhythm instrument. Create new rhythms in 3 that can be performed with the song.

Expressing History through Music

The musical *Evita* (1978), by composer Andrew Lloyd Webber and lyricist Tim Rice, tells the story of Argentina's Eva Perón. Eva ("Evita") rose from poverty to become a successful radio actress. She met and married Juan Perón, who became president of Argentina. Eva Perón was politically active alongside her husband and helped the women's political movement in Argentina.

Tune In

The musical *Evita* was a tremendous success, with over 2,900 performances in London and 1,567 performances in New York. In 1996, *Evita* was made into a movie.

Patti LuPone played Eva Perón in the 1979 stage production of *Evita*.

Learning the Language of Music

EVITA

PRINCE EDWARD THEATRE

Evita and Her People

Sing "Don't Cry for Me, Argentina" from *Evita*.
The opening of the song is in **recitative** style.

A **recitative** is a sung narration with *rubato* tempo and minimal accompaniment used to carry the story forward.

CD 4–37

Don't Cry for Me, Argentina

Words by Tim Rice

Music by Andrew Lloyd Webber

Tempo rubato

It won't be eas - y, you'll think it strange when I try ___ to ex-plain ___ how I feel, That I still need your love af-ter all ___ that I've done, ___ You won't be-lieve me, all you will see is a girl you once knew, Al - though she's dressed up to the nines, at six - es and sev-ens with you.

1. I had to let it
2. And as for

hap-pen, I had to change;
for-tune, and as for fame;

Could-n't stay all my life down at
I nev-er in - vit - ed them

DynamiCS bring Music to LIfe

A change in loudness is a common and effective means of musical expression. These changes can be sudden or gradual.

Crescendo means "gradually louder."
Decrescendo means "gradually softer."

Adjust the Volume

Gradual dynamic changes are indicated by the markings **crescendo** [kreh-SHEN-doh] and **decrescendo** [deh-kreh-SHEN-doh].

Crescendo   Decrescendo

Dynamic Sibelius

Dynamics and musical expression are important in the music of Finnish composer, Jean Sibelius [jahn sih-BAY-lee-uhs]. The use of *crescendos* and *decrescendos* affect the mood, intensity, and expression of his music.

M·U·S·I·C M·A·K·E·R·S

Jean Sibelius

Jean Sibelius (1865–1957) loved his homeland, and much of his music depicts this love for his country and its people. Born in Finland of Swedish parents, Sibelius grew up in a bilingual household. His parents spoke Swedish at home, but he learned to speak Finnish in school. Sibelius learned to play the violin when he was quite young and composed his first work at age ten for violin and cello. His brother played the cello, and his sister played the piano.

Vocal Dynamics in Hymns

Listen to "This Is My Song," and follow the dynamic markings in the score. Are the dynamic changes sudden or gradual? **Sing** "This is My Song." **Perform** the dynamics of the song as you sing.

CD 5–1

This Is My Song

English Words by Lloyd Stone

Music by Jean Sibelius

1. This is my song, O God of all the na-tions,
2. My coun-try's skies are blu-er than the o-cean,

A song of peace for lands a-far and mine.
And sun-light beams on clo-ver-leaf and pine.

This is my home, the coun-try where my heart is;
But oth-er lands have sun-light too, and clo-ver,

Here are my hopes, my dreams, my ho-ly shrine;
And skies are eve-ry-where as blue as mine.

But oth-er hearts in oth-er lands are beat-ing
Oh, hear my song, thou God of all the na-tions,

with hopes and dreams as true and high as mine.
A song of peace for their land and for mine.

Dynamics Used in Symphonic Music

Few composers before Beethoven (1770–1827) placed dynamic markings in their music. Since Beethoven's time, composers have used dynamic markings to create more expressive music.

As you **listen** to *Finlandia*, discover the changes in dynamic levels. Are there any **sforzandos** [sfohrt-SAHN-dohs] in *Finlandia*?

Sforzando is a sudden accent on a note or chord.

CD 5–3
Finlandia

by Jean Sibelius

Finlandia, written in 1899, is a tone poem. A tone poem is music that tells a story or describes an event. This music was later used in the movies *Die Hard 2* and *The Hunt for Red October*.

A Fine Finnish Folk Dance

The *kerenski* [keh-REHN-skee] was a popular folk dance in Finland during the 1920s and is still danced today.

Perform the dance, using movements modeled by your teacher.

CD 5–4
Kerenski

Folk Dance from Finland

The Finnish version of this dance was named for Aleksandr Fyodorovich Kerensky (1881–1970), a premier of Soviet Russia.

◄ Finnish folk dancers

Tune In

The *kerenski* has elements of Russian dancing, which is not surprising, since Finland was a part of Russia from 1809 to 1917.

Dynamic Travels

Listen to "I Walk the Unfrequented Road" and decide if the dynamic changes are sudden or gradual.
Sing the song and show the dynamics as you sing.

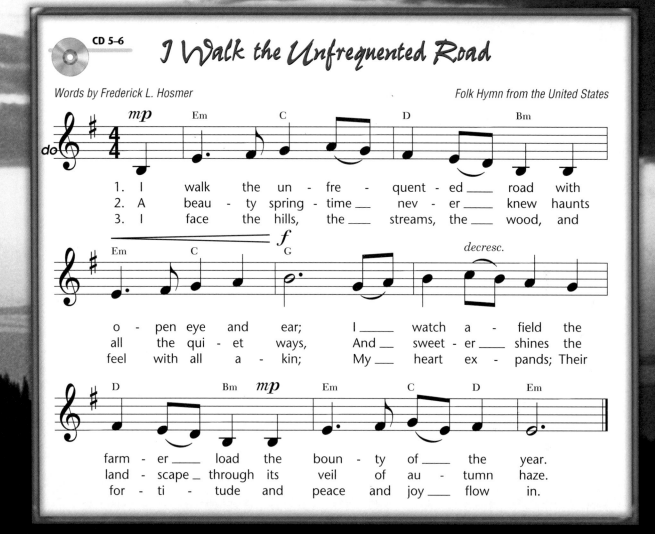

CD 5–6

I Walk the Unfrequented Road

Words by Frederick L. Hosmer

Folk Hymn from the United States

1. I walk the un - fre - quent - ed ____ road with
2. A beau - ty spring - time ____ nev - er ____ knew haunts
3. I face the hills, the ____ streams, the ____ wood, and

o - pen eye and ear; I ____ watch a - field the
all the qui - et ways, And ____ sweet - er ____ shines the
feel with all a - kin; My ____ heart ex - pands; Their

farm - er ____ load the boun - ty of ____ the year.
land - scape ____ through its veil of au - tumn haze.
for - ti - tude and peace and joy ____ flow in.

Playing for Time

To make a composition interesting, composers may use a variety of musical tricks. One technique involves playing with the rhythm by performing it twice as slow or twice as fast as the original. This is called **augmentation** or **diminution.**

Augmentation means that the rhythm is notated to be twice as slow.
Diminution means that the rhythm is notated to be twice as fast.

Stretch It Out

The song "Do, Re, Mi, Fa," from a school songbook published in 1852, uses only half-note and eighth-note rhythm patterns. **Sing** in unison, then in canon. Keep a steady beat by conducting as you sing.

CD 5–8

Do, Re, Mi, Fa

The School Round Book, 1852

Do,　　re,　　mi,　　fa,

I'm quite tired of this sol - fa - ing, I've for - got all you've been say - ing.

▼Augmentation　　　　　▼Normal　　　　　▼Diminution

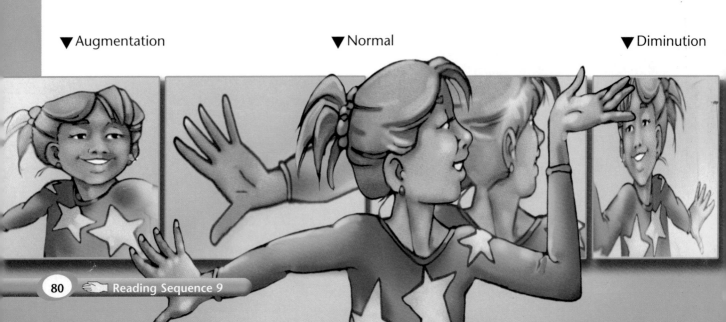

Time to Augment

To augment the rhythm of "*Do, Re, Mi, Fa,*" the half notes are changed to whole notes. How are the eighth notes changed?

Notice that when the time signature stays the same, bar lines must be added. Instead of the original four measures, there are now eight measures—twice as many!

Sing and conduct the new augmented rhythm of "*Do, Re, Mi, Fa.*"

AUGMENTATION

Do,   re,   mi,   fa,

I'm quite tired of   this sol - fa - ing,   I've for - got   all   you've been say - ing.

Tighten It Up

To notate "*Do, Re, Mi, Fa*" in diminution, the half notes are changed to quarter notes. How are the eighth notes changed?

Again, the original song has four measures. **Read** the notation below to **identify** the number of measures the diminution version of the song will have.

Conduct and **sing** the rhythm syllables for this diminution of "*Do, Re, Mi, Fa.*"

Do, re, mi, fa,   I'm quite tired of this sol-fa-ing, I've for-got all you've been say-ing.

Show What You Know!

Follow these directions to show what you know about augmentation and diminution.

1. Conduct and say the rhythm syllables for the pattern notated below.

2. Notate, conduct, and say the syllables for a rhythmic augmentation of this pattern.

3. Notate, conduct, and say the syllables for a rhythmic diminution of this pattern.

Joyful Rhythms

"*Hava nashira*" is an Israeli song. The Hebrew text means *let us sing a song of praise*. Using rhythm syllables, **perform** the rhythm patterns.

Then use pitch syllables to **sing** the melody. When you are ready, **sing** "*Hava nashira*" as a three-part round.

CD 5–16

Hava nashira
(Sing and Be Joyful)

Round from Israel

I

Ha - va na - shir - a,   shir   hal - le - lu - jah.
Sing   and   be   joy - ful,   sing   hal - le - lu - jah.

II

Ha - va na - shir - a,   shir   hal - le - lu - jah.
Sing   and   be   joy - ful,   sing   hal - le - lu - jah.

III

Ha - va na - shir - a,   shir   hal - le - lu - jah.
Sing   and   be   joy - ful,   sing   hal - le - lu - jah.

Expand, Contract, and Create Rhythms

You can use this song to practice rhythmic augmentation and diminution. **Notate** and **perform** the rhythmic augmentation and diminution of the rhythms in "*Hava nashira*."

Notation Software Use notation software to compose an eight measure rhythm in meter in 4. Then, notate a rhythmic augmentation and diminution of your rhythm.

William Schuman

William Schuman (1910–1992) is one of the most honored American musicians of the twentieth century. Beginning with a tango composed at age 16, his works include ten symphonies, three concertos, five ballets, and even a "baseball opera" (*The Mighty Casey*). In 1943, his cantata, *A Free Song*, won the first Pulitzer Prize in Music.

In addition to his talents as a composer, Schuman was an innovative music educator, administrator, and arts advocate. He served as president of the Juilliard School of Music and later as president of Lincoln Center for the Performing Arts, both in New York City.

Listen to this classroom discussion in which William Schuman talks about *Chester* and William Billings.

CD 5-24
Interview with William Schuman

This historic recording was made in the mid-1960s while Schuman was president of Lincoln Center.

A New England Overture

The hymn tune *Chester* was written in 1770 by William Billings, one of America's earliest native-born composers. During the American Revolution, this melody could be heard around campfires, played by fifers, and sung as a marching song by the Continental army.

Listen to this arrangement of *Chester* by William Schuman. **Identify** the augmentation and diminution of the *Chester* melody when you hear it.

CD 5-25
Chester

**from *New England Triptych*
by William Schuman**

Chester was named for a town in colonial Massachusetts.

Backbeat Rhythm

In $\frac{4}{4}$ time, the main beats occur on beats 1 and 3, while the **backbeats** occur on beats 2 and 4. In most African American styles of music—such as jazz, blues, and gospel—the backbeats are emphasized more than beats 1 and 3.

A **backbeat** is the strong offbeat in a measure, such as the snare drum playing on beats 2 and 4 in rock rhythms.

- To move to the backbeat, **move** your feet in a left–together–right–together motion on each four-beat pattern.
- Start by counting all the beats as you move.
- When everyone is moving together, add the claps on backbeats 2 and 4.

▲ **1.** Left

▲ **2.** Together

▲ **3.** Right

▲ **4.** Together

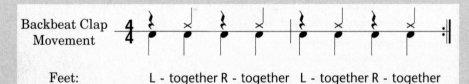
Backbeat Clap Movement

Feet: L - together R - together   L - together R - together

Spirituals with a Backbeat

Many spirituals have a strong sense of backbeat. The song "Ain't Gonna Let Nobody Turn Me 'Round" is an African American spiritual that was sung during the Civil Rights struggles of the 1960s.

Sing "Ain't Gonna Let Nobody Turn Me 'Round." When you know the song well, add the movement and clapping patterns on the backbeats.

CD 5–26
MIDI 8

Ain't Gonna Let Nobody Turn Me 'Round

African American Civil Rights Song

1. Ain't gon-na let no-bod-y turn me 'round, _ turn me 'round, _ turn me 'round. _ Ain't gon-na let no-bod-y turn me 'round, _ I'm gon-na
2. Ain't gon-na let no jail ____ turn me 'round, _ turn me 'round, _ turn me 'round. _ Ain't gon-na let no jail ____ turn me 'round. _ I'm gon-na
3. Ain't gon-na let no doubt-ers turn me 'round, _ turn me 'round, _ turn me 'round. _ Ain't gon-na let no doubt-ers turn me 'round. _ I'm gon-na

keep on a-walk-in', keep on a-talk-in', March-in' to the free-dom land. ____

MIDI Use the song file for "Ain't Gonna Let Nobody Turn Me 'Round" to explore backbeat rhythms.

Musical Bridges

The musical form **a** **a** **b** **a** is the most common popular song form. In an **a** **a** **b** **a** song, the **a** phrases are basically the same. The **b** phrase is different from the **a** phrase and provides variety and contrast.

Sing "Bridges," an **a** **a** **b** **a** song about building bridges between people.
Describe how the **b** phrase is different.

CD 5–28

Bridges

Words and Music by Bill Staines

1. There are bridg-es, bridg-es in the sky, They are shin-ing in the sun. __
2. There are can-yons, there are can-yons, They are yawn-ing in the night. __
3. Let us build a bridge of mu-sic, Let us cross it with a song. __

They are stone and steel and wood and wire, They can change two things to one. __
They are rank and bit-ter an-ger, They are all de-void of light. __
Let us span an-oth-er can-yon, Let us right an-oth-er wrong. __

They are lan-guag-es and let-ters, They are po-et-ry and all. __
They are fear and blind sus-pi-cion, They are ap-a-thy and pride, __
And if some - one should ask us Where we're off and bound to-day, __

They are love and un-der-stand-ing, __ And they're bet-ter than a wall. __
They are dark and so fore-bod-ing, __ And they're oh, so ver-y wide. __
We will tell them "build-ing bridg-es," __ And be off and on our way. __

The Joy of Bach

Listen to *Jesu, Joy of Man's Desiring,* by Johann Sebastian Bach. The listening map will help you **analyze** the form.

by Johann Sebastian Bach

This chorale is from Bach's *Cantata No.147.* It is one of Bach's best-known pieces.

Jesu, Joy of Man's Desiring

Johann Sebastian Bach

LISTENING MAP

Sing a Standard

When a song becomes well-known and is played for many years, it is often called a "standard." "Blue Skies," by the famous American composer Irving Berlin, is a standard that uses **a a b a** song form.

Sing "Blue Skies." How many measures are in each phrase? Are all of the **a** phrases exactly the same?

CD 5–31

Blue Skies

Words and Music by Irving Berlin

a   Dm   A   F   G   F

Blue   skies _____ smil-ing at   me,   noth-ing but   blue   skies _

C7   F   **a** Dm   A

_____ do   I   see. ____   Blue - birds _____ sing-ing a

F   G   F   C7   F

song,   noth-ing but   blue - birds _____ all   day   long. _

Pump Up the Bass

Once you know "Blue Skies," add this part on all of the **ⓐ** phrases. Some students can **sing** it, while others may wish to **play** it on instruments.

Oo _____

Oo _____

Tune In

Irving Berlin, the composer of "Blue Skies," lived more than 100 years. He wrote many other standard songs such as "White Christmas," "God Bless America," and "Easter Parade." He had a custom-made piano that allowed him to automatically transpose to other keys.

Nev-er saw the sun   shin-ing so bright,   nev-er saw things

go-ing so right.   No-tic-ing the days   hur-ry-ing by;   when you're in love,

my, how they fly.   Blue   days _____   all of them gone,   noth-ing but

blue   skies _____   from now   on. _____

In Rare Form

A B C A is a rare musical form. In this form, there are three different sections before the music returns to the "home" **A** section.

When John Lennon and Paul McCartney of the Beatles took on the task of writing "Birthday," they were competing with the well-established version of "Happy Birthday." **Sing** "Birthday" and notice where each section begins.

CD 6–1

Birthday

Words and Music by John Lennon and Paul McCartney

You say it's your birth-day, _ It's my birth-day, too, _ yeah. _

They say it's your birth-day, _ We're gon-na have a good time;

I'm glad it's your birth-day, _ Hap-py birth-day to __ you. _

These items from the Beatles era are now collectors' items. ▶

Yes, we're go-in' to a par-ty, par - ty, ___ Yes, we're go-in' to a

par - ty, par - ty, ___ Yes, we're go-in' to a par-ty, par - ty, ___

do

I would like you to dance, _ (Birth-day_) Take a cha-cha-cha-chance, _

D. C. al Fine

(Birth-day_) I would like you to dance, _ (Birth-day_) Dance!

Blues Bass

The chord progression and bass line of the **A** section of *Birthday* are based on the 12-bar blues form. This form typically uses just three different chords. Here are the three chords in the key of A. Notice that all three include the 7th.

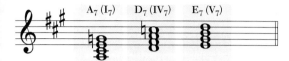

Birthday Blues

As you listen to *Birthday*, play the chords or the bass part below. Follow the color boxes and chord progression to help you **identify** the form as 12-bar blues.

▲ Paul McCartney, playing a Hofner left-handed bass guitar.

Notice the Roman numerals below the chords at the bottom of the page. They tell the step of the scale on which the chord is built. I means the first step of the scale. Rock players often say, "Let's play a I-IV-V progression in A."

CD 6–1

Birthday

by John Lennon and Paul McCartney

McCartney's bass line is probably the most important musical element in *Birthday*.

Can You Boogie?

Another type of bass line that outlines chords is **boogie-woogie.** You can **play** this boogie-woogie on a keyboard instrument.

Boogie-woogie is a special blues chord progression that uses blues chords and swing rhythm. Boogie-woogie is sometimes called "eight-to-the-bar."

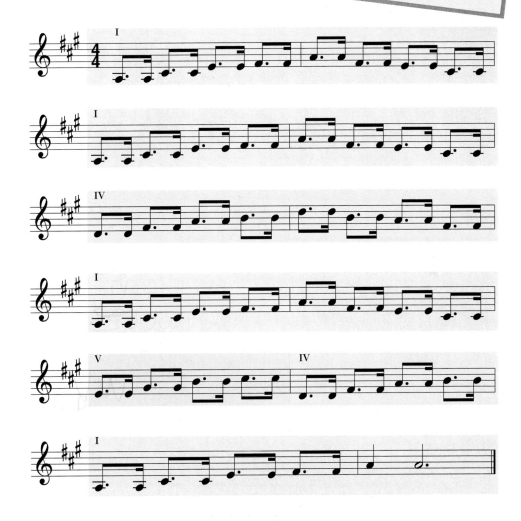

Listen to this classic example of boogie-woogie style.

CD 6–3

Boogie-Woogie

**by Pine Top Smith
as performed by the Tommy Dorsey Orchestra**

Boogie-Woogie, recorded in 1938, was one of Dorsey's most successful arrangements.

◀ Big band leader Tommy Dorsey

SCALES à la mode

You have already discovered the difference between a major scale (*do* to *do*ˈ) and a minor scale (*la* to *la*ˈ). But did you know that each of the other notes has its own scale, too?

These natural scales are called **modes.** Below are two well-known modes—dorian and aeolian.

> A **mode** is a musical scale with a specific set of half-steps and whole-steps that give it its unique sound.

re to *re*ˈ	dorian mode
la to *la*ˈ	aeolian mode

Just like in major and minor scales, the arrangement of whole and half steps gives each scale, or mode, its own **unique** sound.

Sing the dorian and aeolian modes with pitch syllables and hand signs, starting on D. Watch out for the half steps! Did you notice that these modes sound similar?

CD 6–4

Scarborough Fair

Folk Song from England

1. Are you go - ing to Scar - bor-ough Fair?
2. Tell her to make me a cam - bric shirt;
3. Tell her to wash it in yon - der well;

Pars - ley sage, rose - mar - y, and thyme. With - Where

Re -

mem - ber me to one who lives there; _
out a seam or fine nee - dle work; _
nev - er rain or wa - ter fell; ___

She once was a true love of mine.

Tune In

Modes have been used since medieval times. Gregorian chants are modal.

Make It Modal

The notes of the *so* diatonic scale produce the mixolydian mode. There is another way to create the mixolydian mode, using *do* as the tonic. It is easy to make the *do* scale fit the mixolydian pattern by substituting *ta* for *ti* as the seventh scale degree. (Remember that *ta* is one half step lower than *ti*.)

do   re   mi   fa   so   la   ta   do'

This scale shows the lowered seventh degree and is sometimes called the flatted-seventh scale, or "flat-seven scale," for short.

A Ballad from the Ozarks

Listen to the song "Harrison Town" and follow the melody. Which phrase does not include the flatted-seventh degree, *ta*? Next, **sing** the song.

Stay in the Mode

Read this mixolydian melody and **identify** the flatted-seventh. Use C as *do* to **sing** this melody.

Fine

$\frac{2}{4}$ do'   so   do'   so   ta   so   do'   so   :||

D. C. al Fine

re'   ta   do'   so   re'   ta   do'   so

Harrison Town

Folk Song from the Ozarks
Adapted by Jill Trinka

Melodic Motives

Composers use **motives** in many styles of music. Occasionally, a motive becomes very well known and is attributed to a musical composition and its composer. **Sing** or **play** this motive.

> A **motive** is a short musical idea or pattern that repeats in a composition.

Listen to an excerpt of the opening movement from this symphony.

 CD 6–14
Symphony No. 5 in C Minor

Movement 1
by Ludwig van Beethoven

The opening motive of Beethoven's *Fifth Symphony* is one of the most famous in all music.

The Winning Motive

Listen to a humorous play-by-play analysis of this same movement.

 CD 6–15
New Horizons in Music Appreciation

Movement 1
from Beethoven's *Fifth Symphony*
by Professor Peter Schickele

Peter Schickele, alias "P. D. Q. Bach," and Robert Dennis describe this musical event as if they were announcing a sports competition.

 Take It to the Net Visit *www.sfsuccessnet.com* to learn more about Beethoven.

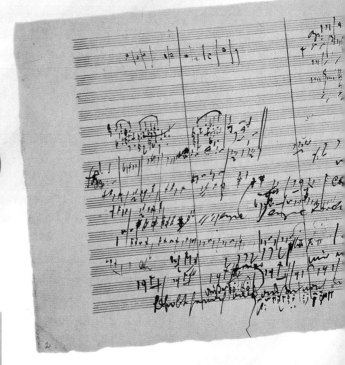

Sketches by Ludwig van Beethoven for *Symphony No. 5* ▼

Ludwig van Beethoven

Ludwig van Beethoven (1770–1827) is one of history's most well-known composers. He wrote many compositions in his lifetime including nine symphonies, five piano concertos, and 16 string quartets. His *Symphony No. 5* is one of the most recognized and famous symphonies of all time.

Beethoven was born in Bonn, Germany, just six years before the United States of America declared independence from England. His father taught him violin and piano at an early age. When Beethoven was 11, he became an assistant organist at the local court and later played viola in the court orchestra.

Beethoven spent most of his career in Vienna, Austria, where he met Wolfgang Amadeus Mozart and Franz Josef Haydn. He associated with Vienna's nobility, who often helped him with his career. Beethoven began to lose his hearing in the late 1790s and spent the last nine years of his life completely deaf.

Tune In

Beethoven carried sketchbooks around with him so that he could write down his musical ideas. These sketchbooks give us a glimpse of how Beethoven composed his music.

Swinging Motives

American composer George Gershwin based many of his songs and compositions on motives.

Listen to and **sing** Gershwin's "I Got Rhythm." Then **identify** the motives that repeat throughout the song.

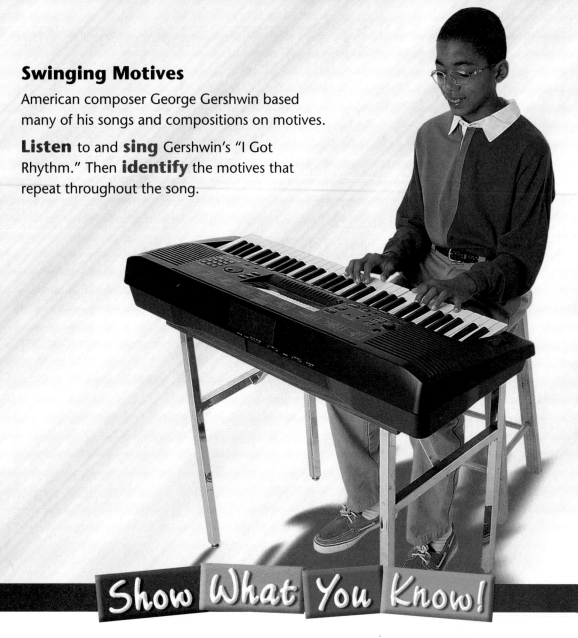

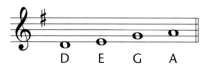
Show What You Know!

Here is the motive used in the song "I Got Rhythm." How many times is it used in the piece? What happens to the melody of the motive in measures 3 and 4?

Using a keyboard or other melody instrument, **play** the four notes shown below—D, E, G, and A. **Create** your own motive by adding a new rhythm to these same notes.

D E G A

I Got Rhythm

Words by Ira Gershwin

Music by George Gershwin

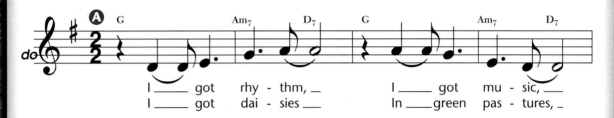

A

I ___ got rhy - thm, ___ I ___ got mu - sic, ___
I ___ got dai - sies ___ In ___ green pas - tures, _

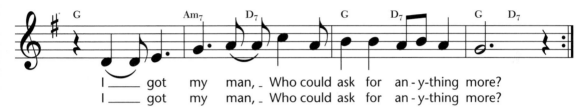

I ___ got my man, _ Who could ask for an - y-thing more?
I ___ got my man, _ Who could ask for an - y-thing more?

B

Old Man Trou - ble, _ I ___ don't mind him, _ You _ won't

A

find him _ 'Round _ my door, I ___ got star - light, _

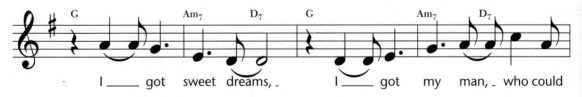

I ___ got sweet dreams, _ I ___ got my man, _ who could

ask for an - y-thing more, Who could ask for an - y-thing more?

Sounds of Strings

Large orchestras, composed of string instruments of all sizes, can be found in different parts of the world. **Listen** to the sound and timbre of three different examples.

Strings from Italy

Listen to a movement from Vivaldi's *The Four Seasons*. The string instruments are primarily bowed, but occasionally they are played *pizzicato* [pit-sih-KAH-toh], or plucked.

CD 6–18
Concerto No. 2, "Summer"

Movement 3 ("*La tempesta*") from *The Four Seasons* by Antonio Vivaldi

The Four Seasons, a set of four concertos, was first published in Amsterdam, Netherlands, in 1725. This movement is a musical depiction of a summer rainstorm.

Arts Connection

The Concert (c. 1690) by A. D. Gabbiani. This painting of a Baroque string ensemble features cello (left), harpsichord (center), and violins of various sizes. ▼

Strings from China

The Chinese string orchestra is composed of instruments that are both plucked and bowed. Some Chinese instruments trace their origins to as early as 200 B.C. The *erhu* [ehr-hoo], perhaps the best-known Chinese string instrument, is over 1,000 years old. It is a two-string alto instrument that has a sound box covered with snakeskin. It is played with a horsehair bow.

Listen to the solo *erhu* and Chinese string orchestra in this selection inspired by a beautiful moonlit pool.

CD 6–19
The Moon Mirrored in the Pool

Erhu ▶

by Hua Yanjun

Hua Yanjun (1890–1950) was poor and blind most of his life. The Chinese people hear "sadness" in this composition.

The Ukrainian Bandura Orchestra

The *bandura*, the national folk instrument of Ukraine, dates back to the fourteenth century. It was played by wandering minstrels *(kobzars)* and warriors *(cossacks)*.

The *bandura* is a large string instrument with a wide oval body. There are no frets, so each string plays only one pitch. There are 55 to 64 strings that are tuned in half steps, which range from bass to treble.

Listen to this traditional Christmas carol performed by one of the leading *bandura* orchestras in the United States. **Identify** the performing techniques of plucking, strumming, and tremolo.

◀ **Bandura**

CD 6–20
Shchedryk

**Traditional Ukrainian Carol
as performed by the Ukrainian Bandurist Chorus**

This Ukrainian carol is known by the familiar title *Carol of the Bells*.

Tune In

The world's finest violin makers—Stradivari, Amati, Guarneri—all lived and worked in Italy during the 1600s and 1700s. Their violins, some worth millions of dollars, have never been surpassed in quality.

Melody/Countermelody

Listen to the song "Going upon the Mountain," a folk song from the Illinois Ozarks. As you listen, follow the notation and determine the form of the song. How many sections are there? How many melody lines do you hear, and where do they occur?

This song has a melody and two **countermelodies.** When you can **sing** the melodies together, you will be singing in harmony.

> A **countermelody** is a melody that often runs counter to, or against, the main melody.

Mountain Traditions

The Ozark Mountains are forest-covered hills in parts of Missouri, Arkansas and Oklahoma. The Ozarks are filled with folk traditions important to the region and to music. One of these traditions is the hoedown.

A hoedown is a dance tune often played in duple meter and performed by string bands which may consist of fiddle, banjo, acoustic bass, guitar, and mandolin.

Arts Connection

Swing Your Partner by Jane Wooster Scott, 1988. ▼

Sing a Mountain Melody

Sing "Going upon the Mountain." Remember to sing your words clearly and with precise rhythm in this lively song.

 CD 6–21

Going upon the Mountain

Folk Song from the Ozarks

VERSE

do

1. Go - ing up - on the moun-tain to raise a crop of cane, To
2. I used to __ ride the old gray horse, but now I ride the roan, You

make a bar - rel of 'las - ses to sweet-en old Li - za Jane.
may court your __ own true love but you'd bet - ter leave mine a - lone.

REFRAIN

It's a bye, bye, my dar - ling girl, bye, bye, I'm gone.

Bye, bye, my dar - ling girl, with the gol - den slip - pers on.

That Mountain Sound

Listen to *The Battle of New Orleans* as performed by Ozark songwriter, Jimmie Driftwood. **Analyze** his vocal timbre and singing style. What musical elements contribute to the mountain folk sound?

 CD 6–23

The Battle of New Orleans

by Jimmie Driftwood
as performed by Johnny Horton

Jimmie Driftwood was a history teacher in Arkansas when he wrote his first hit in 1958, *The Battle of New Orleans*. He has written over 6,000 songs in the Ozark folk tradition.

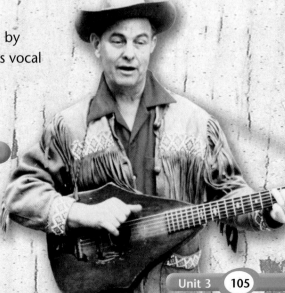

Counter that Melody

Look at these countermelodies. In which section are they performed? How do the melody and countermelodies contrast each other? **Sing** each countermelody. Experiment with ways to contrast the countermelodies with the melody.

When you are ready, **perform** both the melody and countermelodies to "Going upon the Mountain." **Sing** in the spirit of a festive hoedown.

Countermelody 1 (Refrain, 1st time)

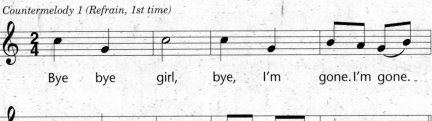

Bye   bye   girl,   bye,   I'm   gone. I'm gone. __

Bye   bye   girl,   gold - en slip - pers on.

Countermelody 2 (Refrain, 2nd time)

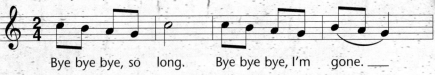

Bye bye bye, so   long.   Bye bye bye, I'm   gone. ___

Bye bye bye, so   long.   Gold - en slip - pers on.

Create a Hoedown Dance

Learn these movements for "Going upon the Mountain." Experiment with creating different body percussion rhythms for each verse. When ready, **perform** the movements with the song.

- **Starting position:** Partners form two large circles facing each other.

- **Verse:** As you sing, the inner circle partner creates a body percussion rhythm for four measures. The outer circle partner matches the body percussion rhythm on the next four measures.

- **Refrain:** Both circles turn to their right and move forward with a shuffle step. At the end of the refrain, new partners face each other and begin the body percussion movements on the verse.

Add an Ensemble

Learn these instrumental parts to accompany "Going upon the Mountain." How do the mallet parts contrast in each section? Add the percussion instruments once you have learned the mallet parts.

When you are ready, **perform** the ensemble as the class sings the song.

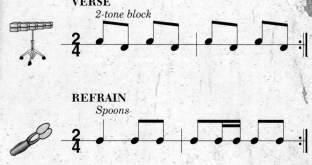

◄ Hootenanny Granny dancing at a hoedown

Review, Assess,

What Do You Know?

1. Match the correct definition to the vocabulary word. On a separate piece of paper, draw the musical symbols for the dynamic terms.

Vocabulary
a. *crescendo*
b. *sforzando*
c. *decrescendo*
d. motive

Definition
• a short musical idea
• gradually getting louder
• suddenly loud
• gradually getting softer

2. Look at the rhythms below. Point to the rhythm on the right that is the augmentation of the rhythm in the left column.

3. Look at the rhythms below. Point to the rhythm on the right that is the diminution of the rhythm in the left column.

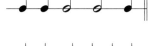

Perform, Create

CD 6–24

Timbre

Listen to these examples of string instruments playing. For each selection, identify which techniques of producing sound are used. Selections may use more than one string technique.

	STRING TECHNIQUES			
EXCERPT	BOWING (ARCO)	STRUMMING	PLUCKING (PIZZICATO)	TREMOLO
1. Symphony No. 5				
2. The Moon Mirrored in the Pool				
3. Shchedryk				
4. Concerto No. 2, "Summer"				

What You Can Do

Show Form with Movement

Listen to the song "Bridges," page 86. Identify the form of the song using the letters **a** and **b** . Create a movement for each letter and then perform the movements with the appropriate phrases of the song.

Sing Modes

Sing "Harrison Town" on page 97 using pitch syllables. Use *ta* to indicate the flatted seventh of the scale. Then, sing the song with lyrics using hand signs each time you sing the motive *ta-la-so.*

Sing Textures

As a class, sing "Going upon the Mountain" on page 105. Form small groups and perform the countermelodies as the class sings the song. As a challenge, sing "Harrison Town" as a countermelody to "Going upon the Mountain."

Jazz—Hot, Swing, and Big Band

American big band jazz of the 1930s is often categorized as both "swing" and "hot." These slang terms describe jazz that is fast, exciting, energetic, and rhythmic. The big band sound and improvised jazz solos added to the excitement.

The excitement of big band jazz is heard in music performed by Glenn Miller (1904–1944), an arranger and bandleader. The Glenn Miller Orchestra was one of the most popular bands of the 1930s and 1940s.

Listen to one of Glenn Miller's most famous big band pieces, *In the Mood.*

CD 6–28

In the Mood

by Joseph Garland
as performed by the Glenn Miller Orchestra

The big band sound is made up of trumpets, trombones, saxophones, and a rhythm section (piano, guitar, bass, and drums).

Building Our Musical Skills

Bouncin' Along

Sing the jazz song "Hit Me with a Hot Note and Watch Me Bounce."
After you know the song, snap your fingers on the offbeats as you sing.
Be cool.

"Hit Me with a Hot Note and Watch Me Bounce" is a jazz classic by
Duke Ellington. This song is featured in the Broadway musical *Swing*.

CD 6–29

Hit Me with a Hot Note and Watch Me Bounce

Words by Don George

Music by Duke Ellington

1. Hit me with a hot note and watch __ me bounce, _
2. Hit me with a hot note and watch __ me burn, _
3. Hit me with a hot note and watch __ me bounce, _

Hit me with a hot note and watch __ me bounce, _ When
Slap me down with rhy-thm from stem ___ to stern, _ When
Knock me out with mu-sic in great ___ a - mounts, _ Oh,

trum - pets heat up, Gim - me a rug to beat up,
sax - es flare up, How can I keep my hair up?
let that beat wave, We're gon-na have a heat wave,

Hit me with a hot note and watch _ me bounce. _ _ me bounce. _
Hit me with a hot note and watch _ me bounce. _
Hit me with a hot note and watch _

112

Ann Hampton Callaway and Michael Rafter

Ann Hampton Callaway is a jazz singer and songwriter. Born in Chicago, she began her career as a singer in Chicago jazz clubs, and later in New York cabarets. Callaway is well-known for her ballads and scat singing. As a songwriter, Callaway wrote "At the Same Time," page 115, which was recorded by Barbra Streisand. She also wrote the opening theme to the TV show *The Nanny*. Callaway has appeared in the Broadway musical *Swing*, and has toured internationally, performing songs from her acclaimed CD, *To Ella with Love*.

Michael Rafter is a conductor, music supervisor, producer, and an arranger. In addition to *Swing*, he has worked on the Broadway musicals *Les Misèrables*, *The King and I*, *Gypsy*, *The Sound of Music*, and *Thoroughly Modern Millie*. Rafter worked with Bette Midler in the TV movie *Gypsy*, which won an Emmy for Musical Direction. Rafter has worked as an arranger and recording producer for *Making Music*.

Listen to Ann Hampton Callaway and Michael Rafter discuss their careers in music.

CD 6–33
Interview with Ann Hampton Callaway and Michael Rafter

Start that trom-bone slid - in', ___ While I gath - er steam, -

Keep that tem - po rid - in' ___ And I'll ___ come in ___ right on ___ the beam. -

Take Your Time

Tempo, the speed of the music, is an important element of musical expression. Tempo can be fast, slow, or anywhere in between. **Listen** to "At the Same Time." Is the tempo fast or slow?

TEMPO TERM	DEFINITION	M.M.
Largo	Very slow	40–66
Adagio	Quite slow	66–76
Andante	Moderate, walking tempo	76–108
Moderato	Moderate	108–120
Allegro	Fast	120–168
Vivace	Lively	168–176
Presto	Very fast	176–184
Prestissimo	As fast as possible	184–208

A Musical Clock

Music has markings to tell performers the tempo. Tempo is indicated by metronome markings (M.M.). Like a clock, a metronome is set to play the desired number of beats per minute. For example, M.M. = 64 means there are 64 beats per minute.

Tempo is also indicated by special Italian words. Select the best tempo for "At the Same Time" from the list.

Listen to *Oye mi canto*. How does the tempo affect the character of the music? What instruments create rhythmic excitement? How does the tempo compare to "At the Same Time"?

CD 6–34
Oye mi canto

by Gloria Estefan, Jorge Casas, and Clay Ostwald
as performed by Gloria Estefan and the Miami Sound Machine

Oye mi canto (Hear My Voice) begins in a brisk tempo in pop-rock style. The song changes to Cuban style with a rhythm section of Latin percussion and brass.

see. Think of all ___ the ways ___ we have ___ of

see - ing. _____ Think of all ___ the ways ___ there are ___ of

be - ing. _____ Think of all ___ the dreams that could come true, ___
All of life ___ is in our trem - bling hands, ___

_____ Yes, ___ if the hands ___ we're reach - ing with ___ could
_____ It's time to o - ver - come ___ our fears and join ___ to

come to - geth - er, join - ing me and you.

When it comes to think - ing of to - mor - row, _____

we must pro - tect our ___ frag - ile des - ti - ny. In ___

___ this pre - cious life, ___ there's no time to bor - row, ___ The

Meter–
THE FOUNDATION OF MUSIC

Meter is defined by the number of beats in a measure and the note value that gets the beat. Now we are going to look at a new meter.

Listen to "Swanee" while you keep a steady beat. Show the meter by patting the strong beats on your knees and clapping the weak beats.

CD 7–3

Swanee

Words by Irving Caesar

Music by George Gershwin

Swa - nee, How I love ya, How I love ya, My dear old Swa - nee; I'd give the world to be A-mong the folks in D - I - X - I - E - ven now there's some - one Wait-ing for me, Pray-ing for me Down by the Swa - nee, The folks up north will see me no more When I get to the Swa-nee shore.

Feel the Beat!

You can learn to recognize meters by feeling how beats are grouped in measures. Try tapping each of these patterns as you **sing** along with the recording of "Swanee." Which pattern feels correct for this song?

Now **read** the rhythm of the first four measures of "Swanee." How many beats are written in each measure? How many beats do you feel?

It doesn't quite add up, does it? The music sounds and feels like meter in 2, but it is written in 4. In this song, a different kind of note equals the beat.

Hear It, Feel It, Read It!

You can determine the meter of a song by looking at the time signature. The top number in a time signature shows how many beats are in each measure. The bottom number represents the beat note.

In $\frac{4}{4}$ meter, there are four beats in each measure, and the quarter note is the beat note.

In $\frac{2}{2}$, how many beats are in a measure? What note is the beat note?

$\frac{4}{4}$ meter is sometimes written like this. C

$\frac{2}{2}$ meter, or **cut time,** can be written like this. ¢

Look again at the music for "Swanee" and **identify** the meter and time signature.

> **Cut time** is a meter of 2 beats per measure; the half note gets the beat. This is also called $\frac{2}{2}$ meter.

What's the Meter?

You have learned that "Swanee" has two beats per measure with the half note getting the beat, and that it is in meter in 2. Another term for *meter in 2* is **duple meter.**

You have also discovered that each half note is subdivided into two quarter notes. When the beat is divided into two equal parts, it is called **simple meter.**

> **Duple meter** has two beats in each measure.
>
> In **simple meter** the beat is divided into two equal parts. Usually, the quarter note gets the beat.

Simple meter in $\frac{2}{4}$

A Springtime Meter

Sing the romantic ballad "One Morning in May." As you sing, feel the strong and weak beats. How many beats are in each measure? What is the meter of the song? Another term for *meter in 3* is **triple meter.**

Perform the rhythm below. How is each beat subdivided? When the beat is divided into three equal parts, it is called **compound meter.**

> **Triple meter** has three beats in each measure.
>
> In **compound meter** the beat is divided into three equal parts. The dotted quarter note gets the beat.

Compound meter

Show What You Know!

Play these rhythm patterns. Tap the beat note and **identify** the type of meter (duple, triple, simple, or compound). Then **sing** the melody using pitch syllables.

a.

mi' re' do'   so mi so   la fa la   so mi ____ so

do' re' do'   ti la so   so do' ti   do'

b.

so   so la   so fa mi fa   fa   re so   mi fa mi re do

CD 7–8

One Morning in May

Folk Song from the Appalachian Mountains

1. One morn-ing, one morn-ing, one morn-ing in May, I
2. "Good morn-ing, good morn-ing, good morn-ing to thee, Oh
3. We had-n't been stand-ing but a min-ute or two, When

met a fair cou-ple a - mak-ing their way, And
where are you go-ing my pret-ty la - dy?" "Oh
out from his knap-sack a fid - dle he drew, And the

one was a maid - en so bright and so fair, And the
I am a - go-ing to the banks of the sea, To ___
tune that he played made the val - leys all ring, Oh ___

oth - er was a sol - dier and a brave vol - un - teer.
see the wa - ters glid - ing, hear the night - in - gale sing."
see the wa - ters glid - ing, hear the night - in - gale sing.

4. "Pretty soldier, pretty soldier,
      will you marry me?"
   "Oh no, pretty lady, that never can be;
   I've a wife in old London
      and children twice three;
   Two wives and the army's
      too many for me."

5. "I'll go back to London
      and stay there one year,
   And often I'll think of you, my little dear,
   If ever I return,
      'twill be in the spring
   To see the waters gliding,
      hear the nightingale sing."

A FAMOUS FORM

Arts Connection

▲ *B126* by Japanese artist Kuwayama Tadasky (born 1935)

Repeating a musical idea, or returning to it, creates unity in music. Introducing new musical ideas provides variety.

A **round** provides unity by repeating the same melody over and over. Variety in a round comes from how the different phrases of the melody combine with each other.

> A **round** is a composition in which two or more parts enter in succession with the same melody.

Sing "Dance for the Nations" in unison. Then sing it as a round.

CD 7–15

DANCE FOR THE NATIONS

Words and Music by John Krumm

'Round and 'round we turn, we hold ___ each oth - ers' hands, And

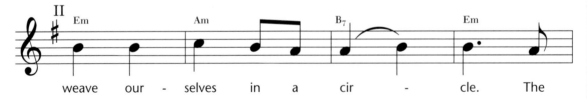

weave our - selves in a cir - cle. The

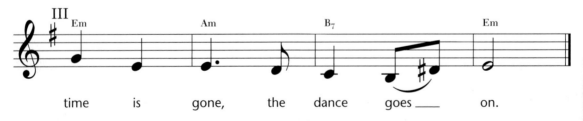

time is gone, the dance goes ___ on.

Move Around

Move to "Dance for the Nations" by following these simple steps: Form three concentric circles with fewer people in the inside circle, more in the middle, and the most on the outside. Hold hands.

◄ On the first phrase of the round, move sideways to the left on each beat: Left, Right, Left, Right

On the second phrase of the round, move sideways to the right on each beat: Right, Left, Right, Left

On the third phrase of the round, swing your hands every two beats: Forward – Backward – Forward – Backward ►

Rap a Round

It's easy to **compose** a spoken rap. First draw eight blank measures, as shown.

Below each line, write words that take up eight beats. Then **notate** the rhythm of the words.

To **perform** your rap as a round, place the number 1 at the beginning. Place the number 2 where the second part starts.

CANON FORM

There are many types of **canons.** One important trait of canons is their imitative entrances. The melody may enter at a different pitch, or the same pitch. When the melody enters at different pitches, the harmony of the canon may change. The melody may be exactly the same, or slightly varied. The canon form has a lot of variation in its use.

> A **canon** is a form in which each part performs the melody, entering at different times on the same or different pitches.

A round is a type of canon. *"Dona nobis pacem"* is a perpetual, or infinite, canon in which each part enters at different times, performs the melody, and then repeats the melody as many times as desired. Not all canons follow this structure.

A Canon for Peace

"Dona nobis pacem" is a canon with a message of peace—*grant us peace.* Look at the song notation and locate where each part begins.

Listen to the canon and follow the melody part all the way through. Then, **sing** the melody of *"Dona nobis pacem"* in unison.

Do - na no - bis pa - cem, pa - cem,

Do - na _____ no - bis pa - cem.

II

Do - na no - bis pa - cem,

Do - na no - bis pa - cem.

III

Do - na no - bis _____ pa - cem,

Do - na no - bis pa - cem.

Tune In

In a "crab" canon, the melody is performed backwards. In some canons, the melody is performed upside down.

Here are some general sight-reading tips.

- Determine the key of the song, then find and **sing** do. In this song, what pitch is do?

- **Sing** the scale of the song using pitch syllables. In this song, which scale do you sing? This puts the sound of the scale (key) in your head and helps you to hear the notes.

- Next, learn to recognize the important pitches of the melody as you sing them. Here is an example using the first phrase of "*Dona nobis pacem*." **Sing** this phrase using pitch syllables. Then, gradually add more notes to your melody until you are finally singing all of the pitches correctly.

When you are ready, **listen** to the Pronunciation Practice track to learn the words in Latin. Then, **sing** the song in unison, and again as a canon.

Listen to a Canon

Listen to *Canon for Violin and Cello*. As you listen, follow the imitative entrances of each instrument.

CD 7–20

Canon for Violin and Cello

by Jean Sibelius
as performed by Annette Barbara Vogel and Fulber Slenczka

Sibelius' *Canon for Violin and Cello* was written in 1889 and is more classical in style than his later Romantic compositions.

Add a Bass Ostinato

One way to add interest to a canon is to add mallet instruments to the accompaniment. Learn this ostinato on a bass mallet instrument. When you are ready, **play** the accompaniment with the class as they sing "*Dona nobis pacem*" as a canon.

Latin Is the Language

The language of "*Dona nobis pacem*" is Latin, a language that is not spoken very much today. Why do schools teach Latin? In what famous place in Italy might you hear Latin? Do you know what professions write in Latin? What common objects have Latin words inscribed on them?

Art for Peace

Pablo Picasso (1881–1973) is recognized as one of the most influential artists of the 20th century. Born in Malaga, Spain, Picasso created over 22,000 works of art in his lifetime. He is known as one of the founders of *cubism*, a new style of art, in the early 1900s. Peace is one of the recurring themes found in his work.

𝒜rts Connection

La Ronde by Pablo Picasso. This work is also titled as *Ronde de l'amitie, Circle of Friendship,* or *Circle of Youth.* ▶

FugueForm

In rounds and canons, melodies enter at different times. The **fugue** is a relative of the round and canon.

> A **fugue** is a musical form in which the main melody is stated in one voice and then imitated by two or more voices, each entering successively.

A Famous Fugue

Johann Sebastian Bach (1685–1750) is one of the most famous composers of fugues. His *"Little" Organ Fugue in G Minor* starts with a subject, the main melody. **Sing** the first two measures of the subject.

The subject enters again at different intervals throughout the fugue. **Sing** the second version of the subject, below.

Subject 2 sounds an interval of a 4th lower than subject 1. Are the rhythms of subjects 1 and 2 the same?

The fugue also has a countersubject, a second melody that plays along with the subject. Other changes to the melodies occur during the episodes, or contrasting sections of the fugue. The subject keeps coming back at various times throughout the piece to provide unity.

The Subject Is Fugue

Listen to the *"Little" Organ Fugue in G Minor.* Count the number of times the subject enters. Then **listen** to the Canadian Brass perform the same piece.

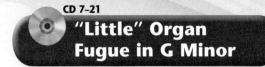

CD 7–21

"Little" Organ Fugue in G Minor

by Johann Sebastian Bach

The pipe organ is called the "king of instruments" because of its powerful sound.

CD 7–22

"Little" Organ Fugue in G Minor

**by Johann Sebastian Bach
as performed by the Canadian Brass**

This performance features two trumpets, French horn, euphonium, and tuba.

▼ Organ pipes. Air flows through the pipes of an organ to create musical sound.

BUILDING INTERVALS

"*Lo yisa*" is a song of peace. What English words convey this message? The Hebrew words to "*Lo yisa*" are from the Book of Isaiah. **Listen** to the Pronunciation Practice track to learn the words in Hebrew. **Sing** "*Lo yisa.*"

CD 7–23

Lo yisa
(Vine and Fig Tree)

Hebrew Words from the Book of Isaiah
English Version by Leah Jaffa and Fran Minkoff

Music by Shalom Altman

Lo yi - sa goy el goy che - rev, Lo yil - m'-
And ev - 'ry man 'neath his vine and fig tree, Shall live in

du od mil - cha - ma. ma. Lo yi - sa goy el
peace and un - a - fraid. fraid. And in - to plow-shares

goy che - rev, Lo yil - m'-du od mil - cha - ma. mil - cha - ma.
turn their swords, Na - tions __ shall learn war no more. war no more.

Intervals = Distance

In music, the distance between notes is given in **intervals.** These intervals are counted in numbers. The interval of a second is one of the most common intervals in music.

> An **interval** in music is the distance between two notes.

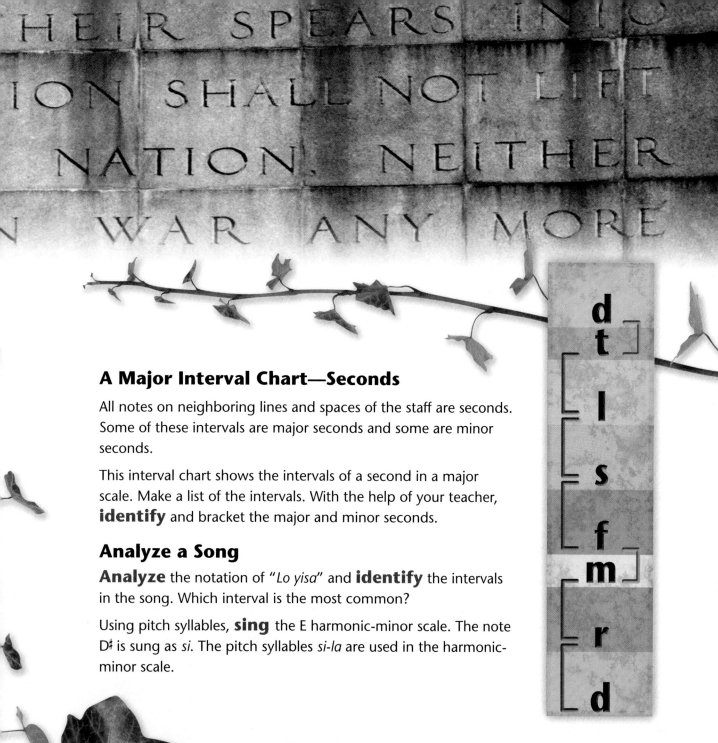

A Major Interval Chart—Seconds

All notes on neighboring lines and spaces of the staff are seconds. Some of these intervals are major seconds and some are minor seconds.

This interval chart shows the intervals of a second in a major scale. Make a list of the intervals. With the help of your teacher, **identify** and bracket the major and minor seconds.

Analyze a Song

Analyze the notation of "*Lo yisa*" and **identify** the intervals in the song. Which interval is the most common?

Using pitch syllables, **sing** the E harmonic-minor scale. The note D♯ is sung as *si*. The pitch syllables *si-la* are used in the harmonic-minor scale.

d
t
l
s
f
m
r
d

Building Scales One Step at a Time

You can use mallet instruments to hear how major and minor seconds sound. Use C as *do*. **Play** up the scale (C-D-E-F-G-A-B-C) and **listen** to the major and minor seconds. Match the sound to your list of intervals.

Now use F as *do*. **Play** up the scale as before. On what pitch does the interval sound incorrect? Fix this by exchanging the B bar for a B-flat bar. **Play** the scale again. Does it sound correct this time?

Which pitches will you need if you use G as *do*?

Moving Motives

A motive can be repeated at different pitches to create a **melodic sequence.** Melodic sequences can move upward (ascending) or downward (descending).

> A **melodic sequence** is the repetition of a melodic pattern usually at different stepwise pitch levels.

Here is a descending melodic sequence. Notice that the first pitch of each motive descends—*so-fa-mi.*

do   so   fa   mi

Here is an ascending melodic sequence. Notice that the first note of each motive ascends—*so, la, ti.*

do   so   la   ti

Spotting Sequences

Analyze the melody of "Alleluia," a three-part canon by Mozart. In which phrases can you **identify** a melodic sequence? What is the starting pitch of each motive in the sequence?

Sometimes composers change the rhythm of the repeated motives. **Identify** the motives in "Alleluia" that have rhythmic changes.

Arts Connection

Engraving of Franz Joseph Haydn conducting and playing in a string quartet ▶

Singing Sequences

Sing "Alleluia." As you sing, conduct in 4/4, then in 2/2.

CD 7–30

Alleluia

Music by Wolfgang Amadeus Mozart

I
Al - le - lu - ia, Al - le - lu - ia.

II
Sing al - le - lu - ia, al - le - lu - ia, sing al - le - lu - ia, al - le - lu - ia.

III
Sing al - le - lu - ia, al - le - lu - ia, sing al - le - lu - ia, al - le - lu - ia.

Listening Sequences

Listen to this canon by Haydn. Can you **identify** a melodic sequence?

CD 7–35
Canon No. 110 in G

by Franz Joseph Haydn

This Haydn canon is a four-part canon.

Tune In

Haydn wrote so many canons that he framed and hung them in his bedroom. He once said, "I was not rich enough to buy myself beautiful paintings, so I made myself a wallpaper that not everybody can have."

SEQUENCE-iT

In music, as you have learned, ideas can repeat at a higher or lower pitch. This repetition is called a "sequence."

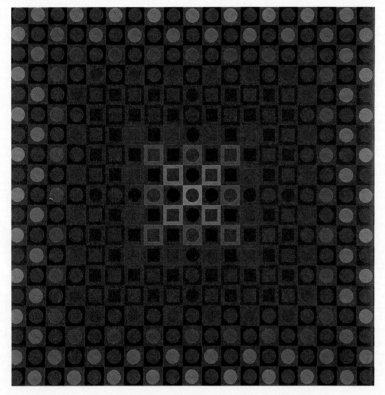

Look at the melodic ideas, or motives, in "Strike Up the Band." The main motive is shaded purple. The secondary motive is shaded orange. **Sing** "Strike Up the Band" to discover how George Gershwin used motives and sequences to build this song.

Arts Connection

◄ The form of this painting, *Alom* by Victor Vasarely (1908–1997), is composed of repeated patterns that are positioned at different levels and angles.

Show What You Know!

Find this motive in "Strike Up the Band" and **identify** the sequences based on this motive. **Create** one additional sequence for this motive.

CD 7–36
MIDI 11

STRIKE UP THE BAND

Words by Ira Gershwin

Music by George Gershwin

Let the drums roll out! ____ Let the trum-pet call! ____ While the

peo - ple shout! ____ Strike up the band! ____ Hear the

cym - bals ring! ____ Call - ing one and all ____ to the

mar - tial swing. ____ Strike up the band! ____ Yan - kee

Doo, Doo-dle-oo, Doo-dle - oo, We'll come through, Doo-dle-oo, Doo-dle - oo, For the

Red, White and Blue, Doo-dle - oo, Lend a hand! ____ With our

flag un - furled, ____ For a brave, new world! ____

Hey, lead - er! Strike up the band! ____

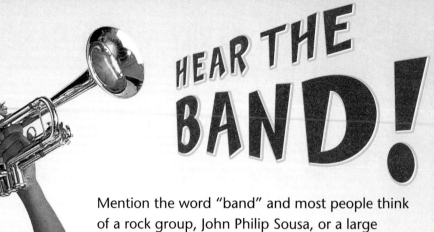

HEAR THE BAND!

Mention the word "band" and most people think of a rock group, John Philip Sousa, or a large parade band. But there are many different types of bands around the world.

Sing "Alexander's Ragtime Band" by Irving Berlin. Berlin was influenced by the ragtime piano style of Scott Joplin and others.

CD 8–1

ALEXANDER'S RAGTIME BAND

Words and Music by Irving Berlin
Arranged by Carmen Culp and Don Kalbach

Countermelody

Come on and hear,   come on and hear Al - ex-

Melody

Come on and hear,   come on and hear   Al - ex-

an - der's Rag-time Band.   Come on and hear,

an - der's Rag-time Band.   Come on and hear,   come on and

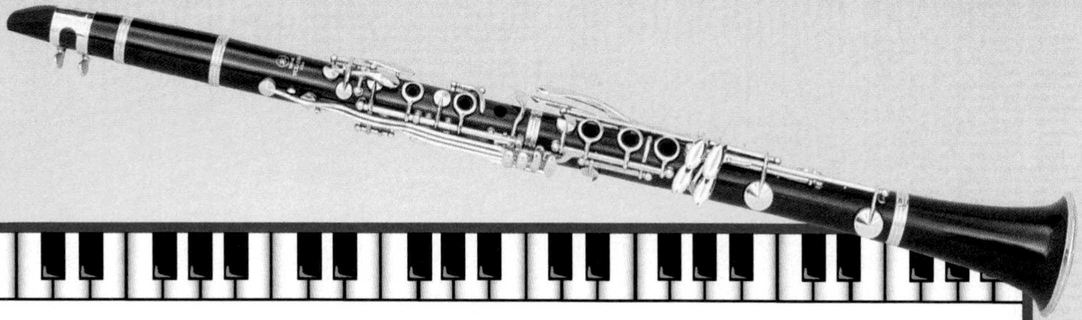

1
A♭
E♭
come on and hear, It's the best band in the land. Play like you
2
hear, It's the best band in the land. They can play a bu-gle call like you
1
E♭
nev - er heard be-fore, So you'll ask for more;
2
nev - er heard be-fore, So nat - u - ral that you'll al-ways ask for more;
1
F7
B♭7
It's the best band in the land, hon-ey lamb.
2
It's the best band in the land, hon-ey lamb. Come on a -
1
E♭
B♭7
Come on a-long, come on a-long, Let me take you by the
2
long, come on a - long, Let me take you by the

The Concert Band

The concert, or symphonic, band is found in just about every school and university in America. This ensemble plays music of many different genres—from classical to pop to patriotic.

The concert band is made up of woodwinds, brass, and percussion. (See the Sound Bank for information on specific band instruments.)

Listen to this piece from the British concert band literature.

CD 8–3

Suite No. 2 in F

Movement 1, "March"
by Gustav Holst

Holst based this suite on English country tunes.

Listen to another selection for concert band and **identify** the families of instruments mentioned above.

CD 8–4
Fanfare for Freedom

by Morton Gould
American composer Morton Gould (1913–1996) wrote this patriotic fanfare in 1971.

MUSIC MAKERS
Gustav Holst

Gustav Holst (1874–1934) was an English composer and well-known teacher and educator. His most famous work is *The Planets*, a suite for orchestra. His two "military" suites are among the best and most important works for concert band. Holst loved English folk songs of the sixteenth and seventeenth centuries. He was also influenced by the music and folklore of India and the Far East.

Reggae Harmonies

CD 8–5

Give A Little Love

Words and Music by Al Hammond and Diane Warren

REFRAIN

D   A₇

We got to give a lit-tle love,   have __ a lit-tle hope,   make __

D   A₇   D   **2**   A₇   D   **3**

_____this world a lit-tle bet - ter. Oh-oh whoah,   Oh - oh whoah.

VERSE
D   A₇   D

1. Liv-ing in   this cra-zy world, __   so caught up in the con-fu - sion.
2. Got the wars __ on our minds, __   got the trou-bles on our shoul - ders.

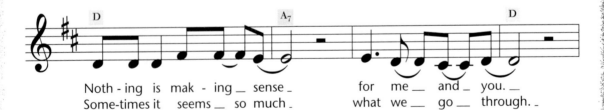

D   A₇   D

Noth - ing is mak - ing __ sense __   for me __ and __ you. __
Some-times it   seems __ so much __   what we __ go __ through. __

D   A₇   D

May-be we can find a way, __   there's __ got to be a so - lu - tion,
May-be if we take the time, __   time __ to un-der-stand each oth - er,

Reggae Is Pop

Reggae is a popular music style that was born in Jamaica. It is a blend of African American music, rock, and traditional African Jamaican music. This modern reggae song uses mostly two chords.

Sing "Give a Little Love."
Listen to the harmonies and the rhythm as you sing.

REFRAIN

How to make a bright-er day, __ What do __ we do?
We can learn to make it right. _ What do __ we do? } We got to

give a lit-tle love, have __ a lit-tle hope, make __ this worlda lit-tle bet - ter.

Try a lit-tle more, hard - er than be-fore, let's do what we can do to-geth - er. Oh _

whoah - oh, _____ We can ev-en make it bet - ter, yeah. _

1.
Oh whoah, _ la, la, la, On-ly if we try. ___ (last time repeat refrain ad lib) ___ We got to

2.
___ If ev-'ry - bod - y took some-bod - y by the hand, _

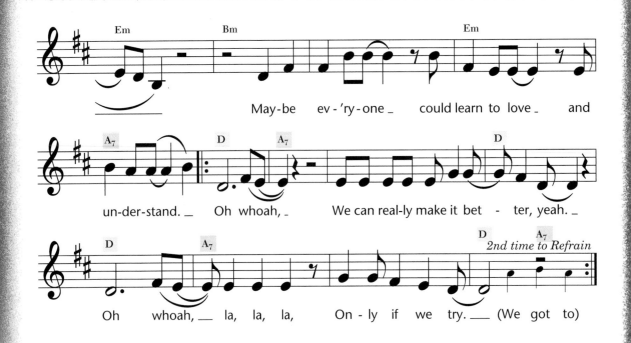

Two Chords—No Problem!

Learn to play the two chords shown below on guitar or keyboard. Then **perform** an **accompaniment** for "Give a Little Love" by following the chord symbols above the music.

An **accompaniment** is the musical background, such as chords and rhythms, that supports the melody.

D chord

A₇ chord

142

Reggae Rhythm Box

Perform this reggae-style rhythm complex when you sing the refrain.

(Beats)	1				2				1				2			
Clap			X				X				X				X	
Guitar Chords			D				D				A_7				A_7	
Shakers	X	X	X	X	X	X	X	X	X	X	X	X	X	X	X	X
Bass		D				D				A				A		

Listen to Ziggy Marley's performance of *Reggae Is Now*.

CD 8–7
Reggae Is Now

by Ziggy Marley
performed by Ziggy Marley and the Melody Makers

Ziggy Marley's performance of *Reggae Is Now* features reggae-style rhythms and call-and-response form.

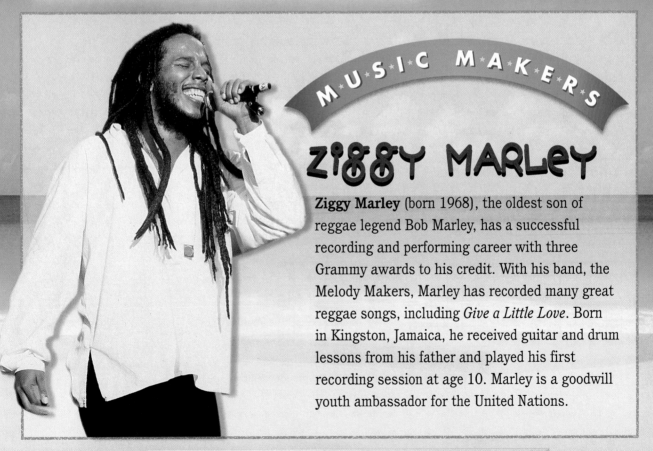

MUSIC MAKERS

ZIGGY MARLEY

Ziggy Marley (born 1968), the oldest son of reggae legend Bob Marley, has a successful recording and performing career with three Grammy awards to his credit. With his band, the Melody Makers, Marley has recorded many great reggae songs, including *Give a Little Love*. Born in Kingston, Jamaica, he received guitar and drum lessons from his father and played his first recording session at age 10. Marley is a goodwill youth ambassador for the United Nations.

Visit **Take It to the Net** at www.sfsuccessnet.com to learn more about the music of Jamaica.

Guitar Textures

Vaqueros and cowboys roamed the western plains from Mexico to Canada from the 1860s to the 1880s, driving cattle from one place to another. They played simple chords on their guitars and sang to entertain themselves.

Sing *"El payo."* **Listen** to the simple harmonies as you sing. How many different chords are used?

Cowboy Chords

"El payo" is harmonized with three chords: I (F), IV (B♭), and V_7 (C_7). These chords are built on the first, fourth, and fifth degrees of the F scale.

I	ii	iii	IV	V_7	vi	vii°	I
C			F	B♭			
A			D	G			
F			B♭	E			
				C			

The I, IV, and V_7 chords appear above in **root position.** To **perform** *"El payo"* on the guitar, place a capo on fret 3 and play the chords D (I), G (IV), and A_7 (V_7).

> **Root position** is a chord in which the pitch called the root is the lowest note of the chord. For example, C is the root of a C chord.

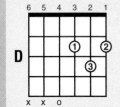

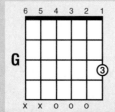

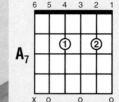

El payo

(The Cowpoke)

English Words by Alice Firgau

Folk Song from Mexico

Guitar: capo 3

1. Es - ta-ba un pa - yo sen - ta - do ___ En tran-cas de un __ co - rral; ___ Y el
1. Oh, Nick, a sad, _ old cow-poke, _ Would sit all day on a fence. ___ The

ma - yor-do-mo le di - jo, ___ "No es-tés tris - te, Ni - co - lás." ___ "Si
fore-man saw him and told him, _ "Your sad-ness does-n't make sense." __ "Just

quie - res que no_es-té tris - te ___ Lo que pi - da me_has de dar." __ Y_el
give me all that I ask for ___ And you'd cheer my low mor - ale." __ The

ma - yor - do - mo le di - jo, ___ "Ve pi - dien - do, Ni - co - lás." ___
fore-man smiled then and told him, __"Well, start ask - ing, Nick, old pal." __

2. "Necesito treinta pesos,
Una cuera y un gabán."
Y_el mayordomo le dijo,
"No_hay dinero, Nicolás."
"Necesito treinta pesos
Para poderme casar."
Y_el mayordomo le dijo,
"Ni_un real tengo, Nicolás."

2. "I need some thirty *pesos*,
A jacket, coat, and a hat."
The foreman smiled then and told him,
"No money have I for that."
"I need those thirty *pesos*
For to marry my sweet gal."
The foreman smiled then and told him,
"I have none, my dear, old pal."

Review, Assess,

What Do You Know?

Match the notation on the left with the correct definition or symbol on the right.

Notation	Definition/Symbol
1. ♩♪ ♩♪	**a.** 𝄴
2. $\frac{4}{4}$	**b.** simple meter
3. $\frac{2}{2}$	**c.** compound meter
4. ♩♪♪ ♩♪♪	**d.** 𝄵

What Do You Hear? 4A

 CD 8–12

Form

Listen to the following selections. Identify the term in the right column that best describes the form of the selection.

Selection	Form
1. "Dance for the Nations"	**a.** verse form (ballad form)
2. *Canon for Violin and Cello*	**b.** fugue
3. "Barb'ry Allen"	**c.** round
4. *"Little" Organ Fugue in G Minor*	**d.** canon

Perform, Create

What Do You Hear? 4B

CD 8–16

Timbre

Listen to the timbre of these selections and match each with the correct musical ensemble.

Selection

1. *Suite No. 2 in F*
2. *The Stars and Stripes Forever*
3. "Alexander's Ragtime Band"
4. *Kerenski*

Musical Ensemble

a. big band

b. concert band

c. polka band

What You Can Do

Sing with Expression

As a class, sing "Swanee," page 118, with the recording. Follow the notation and conduct a two-beat pattern. Then sing the song without the recording at a slow tempo and again at a fast tempo. Point to the correct Italian terms below for "slow" and "fast."

- *moderato*
- *adagio*
- *prestissimo*
- *allegro*

Sing Sequences

Sing the melody of "Alleluia," page 133. Perform small steady-beat movements as you sing. Point to the melodic sequence in the second line of the music. Is this sequence ascending or descending?

Play Chords

Play the D and A chords on guitar or keyboard. Sing "Give a Little Love," page 140, with the recording. Add harmony by playing the accompaniment part on guitar or keyboard with the recording. Play the chords accurately and in time with the song.

Play a Song for Me

The 1960s was a decade of social and political change, and popular music experienced a transformation of its own. As the Beatles and other British groups stormed the U.S., America answered with poet/songwriter Bob Dylan and groups like the Byrds.

Listen to this recording of the Byrds singing Dylan's *Mr. Tambourine Man*.

Then turn the page and **sing** your own rendition of the song.

CD 8–20
Mr. Tambourine Man

by Bob Dylan
as performed by the Byrds

The Byrds' unique folk-rock style features distinctive harmonies and a 12-string Rickenbacker guitar sound.

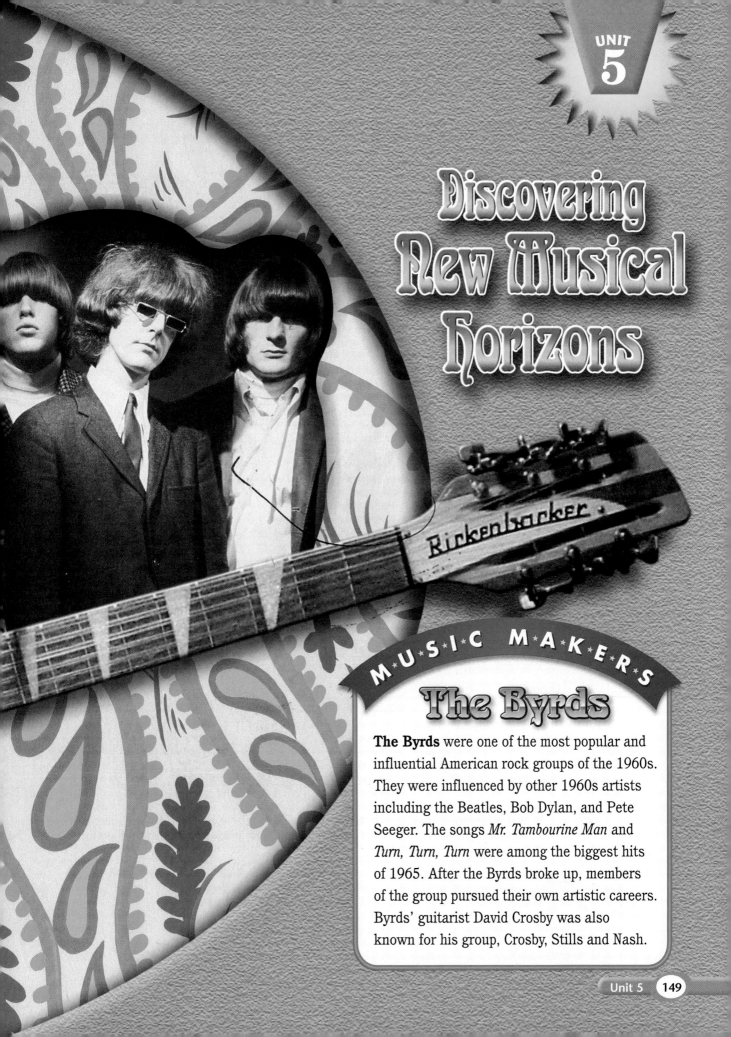

Discovering New Musical Horizons

Rickenbacker

MUSIC MAKERS

The Byrds

The Byrds were one of the most popular and influential American rock groups of the 1960s. They were influenced by other 1960s artists including the Beatles, Bob Dylan, and Pete Seeger. The songs *Mr. Tambourine Man* and *Turn, Turn, Turn* were among the biggest hits of 1965. After the Byrds broke up, members of the group pursued their own artistic careers. Byrds' guitarist David Crosby was also known for his group, Crosby, Stills and Nash.

Mr. Tambourine Man

Words and Music by Bob Dylan

REFRAIN

do

Hey! Mis-ter Tam-bou-rine _ Man, _ play a song _ for me, I'm not

sleep-y and there is no place I'm go-in' _ to. _

Hey! Mis-ter Tam-bou-rine _ Man, _ play a song _ for me, in the

jin-gle jan — gle morn-in' I'll come fol — low-in' you.

VERSE

Though I know that eve — nin's em-pire has re-turned in-to _
wear-i-ness _ a-maz-es me I'm brand-ed on my _

sand, van-ished from my _ hand, left me blind-ly here to stand but still not
feet. I have no one to _ meet and the an-cient emp-ty street's too dead for

1.
sleep-in'! _
dream-in'. _

2. *D. C. al Fine*
My

150

Bob Dylan had mega-hits of his own in the 1960s. His song *Like a Rolling Stone* (1965) is a classic of the folk-rock genre.

▲ Pete Seeger

Bob Dylan ▶

THE BEATLES

▲ The Beatles

sPEED UP/SLOW DOWN

Have you ever watched an ice skater spin? The skater usually begins the spin slowly and gradually speeds up, or accelerates.

Like the skater's spin, some music begins at one speed or tempo and gradually speeds up. We use the Italian term **accelerando** for this type of tempo change. When music gradually slows down, the tempo change is called a **ritardando.**

> **Accelerando** is a gradual increase in tempo.
>
> **Ritardando** is a gradual decrease in tempo.

The song "*Hava nagila*" usually accompanies a dance. It begins at a slow tempo and accelerates to the end. As you **sing** the song, **listen** for the *accelerando*.

▲ View of Jerusalem

HAVA NAGILA

Jewish Folk Song

An Exhibition of Tempo

The job of the conductor is to lead a group of musicians in playing a piece of music. The conductor gives the music expression by telling the musicians how to play. One of the most famous conductors in the world is Zubin Mehta. He conducts the Israel Philharmonic Orchestra and makes guest appearances with many other orchestras around the world.

Listen to Zubin Mehta conduct an excerpt from Russian composer Mussorgsky's *The Great Gate of Kiev*. How does Mehta use tempo changes, such as *ritardandos,* to make the music more expressive?

CD 8–27
The Great Gate of Kiev

from *Pictures at an Exhibition*
by Modest Mussorgsky
as performed by Zubin Mehta and
the New York Philharmonic

This selection features both tempo and meter changes.

M·U·S·I·C M·A·K·E·R·S

Zubin Mehta

Zubin Mehta (born 1936) is known for his grandiose and intense conducting style. He is a world-class conductor. Born in the city of Mumbai (formerly Bombay), India, Mehta initially wanted to become a doctor; however, his father, who co-founded the Bombay Symphony Orchestra, encouraged his son to pursue music. At the age of eighteen, Mehta went to the famous Academy of Music in Vienna, Austria. Mehta has been the musical director in Montreal, Los Angeles, New York City, and Florence, Italy. Presently, he serves as the permanent Music Director for the Israel Philharmonic Orchestra.

Israeli Dance

"Hava nagila" is a favorite song for dancing the *hora*. The movements to *"Hava nagila"* can be performed at different tempos.

Perform the movements below. The traditional *hora* is danced moving to the left. The music begins slowly and gradually becomes faster.

1. Step Left
2. Step Right (in front or in back of Left)
3. Step Left
4. Lift Right
5. Step Right
6. Lift Left

▼ The *hora* is danced in a circle and uses steps and lifts. Dancers feel the energy increase as the music and dancing get faster and faster.

Syncopated Rhythms

"Let Us Sing Together" uses **syncopated** rhythms at the end of each phrase. **Read** and speak the rhythm syllables in the song.

Tap a quarter-note beat as you speak the rhythm syllables of the last two measures of "Let Us Sing Together." The first two beats of the last measure consist of a short-long-short pattern. This short-long-short pattern is syncopated.

> **Syncopation** is a term used to describe accented rhythms that occur off the beat.

Sing "Let Us Sing Together," first in unison and then as a four-part canon.

CD 8–28
MIDI 13

Let Us Sing Together

Traditional Czech Folk Melody

Everybody Play

Play these rhythms using percussion instruments. **Identify** the short-long-short syncopation.

Syncopated Waltz

The American composer Scott Joplin used a similar syncopated pattern in his piano composition *Bethena Waltz*. As you **listen** to this piece, focus on the melody played in the right-hand part.

CD 8–33
Bethena Waltz

by Scott Joplin

Scott Joplin is probably the most famous composer of American ragtime music. He wrote *Bethena Waltz* in 1905.

◄ Scott Joplin

Double the Speed

A common syncopated rhythm pattern is ♪ ♩ ♪ .

At the same tempo, you can write this rhythm to be twice as fast ♫ ♪ ♫ ♪ .

This technique is called *rhythmic diminution*.

"Lost My Gold Ring" is a song from Jamaica that was originally brought to the New World by enslaved Africans. It is a singing game. **Read** the rhythm patterns in the song, using rhythm syllables. **Sing** "Lost My Gold Ring." Choose rhythm patterns from the song and **create** an accompaniment.

CD 9–1 **Lost My Gold Ring**

Singing Game from Jamaica

do-

Bid - dy, Bid - dy, hold on, lost my gold ring;

One go to Kings - ton, come back a - gain.

Notating Syncopation

Ties can also create syncopation. **Play** these syncopated rhythms as you tap an eighth-note beat with your foot.

1.

2.

3.

Time for Ragtime

Listen to how tied rhythms and syncopation are used in Scott Joplin's *Elite Syncopations.*

 CD 9–9
Elite Syncopations

by Scott Joplin

Ragtime got its name from "ragging" (syncopating) the melody against the straight rhythms in the left hand.

In 1899, Scott Joplin published "Maple Leaf Rag." It became the first published sheet music to sell more than a million copies.

Perform these syncopated rhythms. Then, **create** your own eight-beat syncopated rhythm and **perform** it on a percussion instrument of your choice.

1.

2.

Theme and Variations

A familiar melody can be used as a musical **theme.** The first time you hear a theme, it is usually a simple tune. Then the composer varies, or changes, the theme. Some ways to vary a theme are

- Change the tonality.
- Change the meter.
- Use different rhythms.
- Change the style.
- Use different instruments.
- Vary the tempo and dynamics.

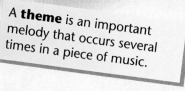

A **theme** is an important melody that occurs several times in a piece of music.

Play the theme of "Scattin' A-Round." **Create** a **variation** by using $\frac{3}{4}$ meter.

Sing the theme of "Scattin' A-Round." Then **create** a variation by changing the tonality from major to minor. Which note will you change?

A **variation** is a significant change in a musical theme.

Now scat **sing** "Scattin' A-Round," using neutral syllables. What variation techniques are used in Variations 1 and 2?

CD 9–10

Scattin' A-Round

Traditional Round
Arranged by Will Schmid

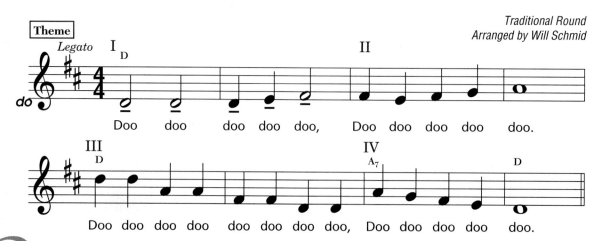

Listen to *Variations on "The Carnival of Venice,"* one of the best-loved trumpet solos of all time. It is an example of theme and variations.

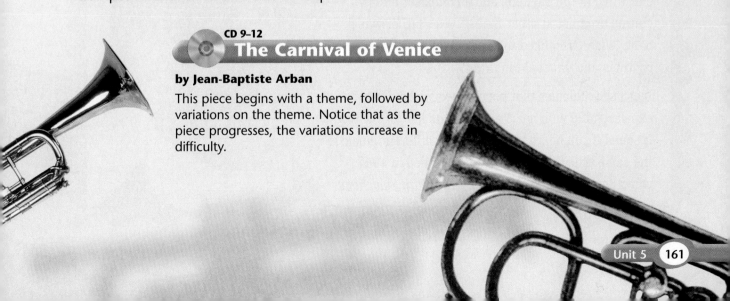

CD 9–12

The Carnival of Venice

by Jean-Baptiste Arban

This piece begins with a theme, followed by variations on the theme. Notice that as the piece progresses, the variations increase in difficulty.

AMERICAN Variations

In *Variations on "America,"* composer Charles Ives wanted to show the patriotic song "America" in the musical styles of different countries. He wrote *Variations on "America"* when he was sixteen years old.

Listen to *Variations on "America."* Follow along with the listening map and **identify** each variation.

CD 9–13

Variations on "America"

by Charles Ives

Listen for the Irish jig in Variation 4 and the Spanish dance in Variation 5.

M·U·S·I·C M·A·K·E·R·S

Charles Ives

Charles Ives (1874–1954) was an interesting character in American music. He was an insurance executive in the daytime, and a composer and church organist at other times. Ives's father was a band leader who liked to experiment with complicated rhythms and unusual tonalities.

Ives used melodies that people recognized. He experimented with musical questions like, "How would it sound if you heard two bands play different music at the same time?" His talent was rewarded in 1947, when he won a Pulitzer prize for his *Third Symphony.*

Variations on "America"
LISTENING MAP

Introduction

(1:02)
Theme: "America," muted brass

(1:48)
Variation 1: Strings and woodwinds, brass

(2:27)
Variation 2: Legato clarinet and strings, brass

(3:11)
Variation 3: Dissonant brass and strings f

(3:39)
Variation 4: Light woodwinds, strings

(4:29)
Variation 5: Brass, strings, trumpets in minor with Spanish rhythms

(5:13)
Variation 6: Brass choir (short)

(5:28)
Variation 7: Solo trumpet with melody in woodwinds, strings, trumpets, and low brass

(6:27)
Coda: Starts with part of Introduction, alternates motives of variations to a grand finale

Melodic Distances

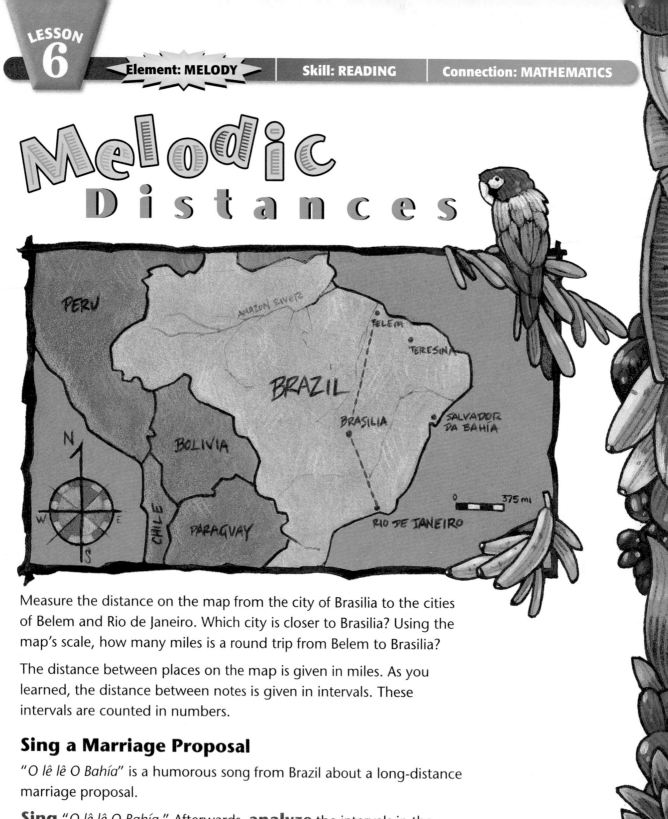

Measure the distance on the map from the city of Brasilia to the cities of Belem and Rio de Janeiro. Which city is closer to Brasilia? Using the map's scale, how many miles is a round trip from Belem to Brasilia?

The distance between places on the map is given in miles. As you learned, the distance between notes is given in intervals. These intervals are counted in numbers.

Sing a Marriage Proposal

"O lê lê O Bahía" is a humorous song from Brazil about a long-distance marriage proposal.

Sing "O lê lê O Bahía." Afterwards, **analyze** the intervals in the song.

Distance = Intervals

The distance between notes is called an interval. Below are some of the intervals in "Like a Bird." Find each interval in the chart below using pitch syllables, staff notation, and keyboard. Then **play** each of these intervals on a melody instrument.

- Octave
- Second
- Third
- Fourth
- Fifth

Then **listen** to "Like a Bird" and **identify** these intervals in the song.

Keyboard

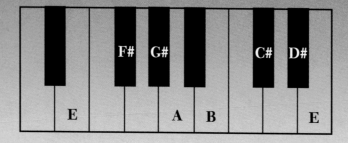

Notation

Pitch Syllables

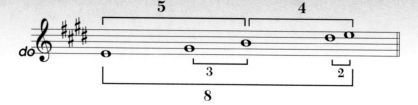

Cherubini's Birds

Luigi Cherubini [keh-roo-BEE-nee] (1760–1842) was an Italian-born composer who lived in Paris. Cherubini's song "Like a Bird" is a three-voice canon.

Listen to "Like a Bird" and conduct it in $\frac{2}{2}$ meter. First **sing** the song in unison and then as a three-part canon.

CD 9–21

Like a Bird

Words by E. Bolkovac

Music by Luigi Cherubini

Like a bird up in the sky, I'd like to

soar with the sky an o-pen door, With-out rea-son with-out

why, Just to fly up in the sky, To feel I'm free with noth-ing stop-ping

me, To fly up in the sky!

Show What You Know!

Notate the E-major scale on a piece of paper. Then **play** it on a keyboard or other instrument. **Identify** each of these intervals: second, third, fourth, fifth, and octave. Draw brackets and label each interval.

Rows of Tones

Music that uses major and minor scales is called "tonal." (You can find a *do* tone in the music.) In the twentieth century, composers began experimenting with all of the notes of the **chromatic scale.** Here are the 12 notes of the chromatic scale, in order.

A **chromatic scale** is a scale with consecutive half-steps.

Some early twentieth-century composers wrote music based on "tone rows"—using the 12 notes of the chromatic scale in a non-tonal order. (You can't find a *do* tone in the music.) This music was called "serial," or "atonal" music.

Here is the 12-tone row that Alban Berg used in his *Lyric Suite.*

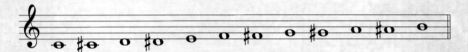

Violin 1

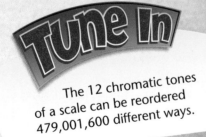

The 12 chromatic tones of a scale can be reordered 479,001,600 different ways.

A music score by Alban Berg ▶

A Row with Tones

Listen to a section of Alban Berg's *Lyric Suite*. How would you **describe** this style of music?

CD 9–26
Allegretto gioviale

**from *Lyric Suite*
by Alban Berg**

This suite, using a 12-tone row, was composed for string quartet in 1926.

Create Your Own Tone Row

Create a tone row. Use all 12 notes of the chromatic scale with resonator bells. Place them in a non-tonal order. Write the notes down. Then **play** the same notes, but play them in different octaves. Splitting notes into different octaves makes the tone row sound different.

M·U·S·I·C M·A·K·E·R·S
Alban Berg

Alban Berg (1885–1935) was born in Vienna of middle class parents. His early compositions were traditional (tonal). In later life, Berg composed in the atonal, or serial style. This style of writing music was developed by his teacher, Arnold Schoenberg. Berg's music used more traditional harmonies and "romantic" themes than other atonal composers.

Berg's most famous work was his opera, *Wozzeck*. Many people were not used to Berg's atonal style of writing in *Wozzeck*. Performances of the opera caused scandal, yelling, and even fighting in the audience.

Arts Connection

Painting of Alban Berg by Arnold Schoenberg ▶

Different Cultures and Timbres

As you travel to different places, or listen to recordings, you may notice how people from different cultures sing with different timbres. Each culture often has its own unique sound, favorite vocal styles, and favorite instruments to play. Enjoy our tour of some of the world's vocal sounds.

Listen to *Vocal Timbres Around the World*. What differences do you hear?

CD 9–27

Vocal Timbres Around the World

This montage features Bobby McFerrin's *Grace*, Keb' Mo's *Every Morning*, Emanual Dufrasne's *Leró pá Cico Mangual*, and Ricky Skaggs' *Crying My Heart Out Over You*.

Bobby McFerrin ▶

Sing the melody of "Four Strong Winds" in unison. Then add the harmony part. How would you **describe** your vocal timbre?

CD 9–28

Four Strong Winds
(from *Song to a Seagull*)

Words and Music by Ian Tyson
Arranged by Robert Evans

VERSE

1. Think I'll go out to Al – ber – ta, Weath-er's good there in the
2. If I get there be-fore the snow flies, And if things are go - ing

fall, Got some friends that I can go to work - in' for, _____
good, You could meet me if I sent you down the fare. _____

Still I wish you'd change your mind, If I asked you one more
But by then it would be winter, Ain't too much for you to

time, But we've been through that a hun-dred times or more. _____
do, And those winds sure can blow cold a - way out there. _____

REFRAIN

Four strong winds that blow lone - ly, Sev - en seas that run

high, All those things that don't change, come what may, _____

_____ But our good times are all gone, And I'm bound for mov - in'

on, I'll look for you if I'm ev - er back this way. _____

Element: TEXTURE/HARMONY | **Skill: SINGING** | **Connection: CULTURE**

Spanish TEXTURES

People who begin a new life in another part of the world take their folk tales, history, and music with them. In Texas, the *musica norteña* style is a blend of Mexican and German heritages. The song "*Así es mi tierra*" is in the *norteña* style.

Sing the melody, then sing the harmony part for "*Así es mi tierra*." Next, sing the song in two-part harmony as a **duet.**

> A **duet** is a piece written to be played or sung by two performers.

CD 9–30
MIDI 14

Así es mi tierra
(This Is My Land)

Words and Music by Ignacio Fernandez Esperón

A-sí es mi tie-rra, mo-re-ni-ta y lu-mi-no-sa; A-sí es mi
This is my coun-try, It's a land that's bright with beau-ty; This is my

tie-rra, tie-ne el al-ma he-cha de a-mor. A-sí es mi
coun-try, It's a land that's made to love. This is my

tie-rra, a-bun-dan-te y ge-ne-ro-sa; ¡Ay, tie-rra
coun-try, It has giv-en so much to me; Oh, my dear

2nd time to next stanza

mí-a co-mo es gra-to tu ca-lor!
coun-try, Wel-come are your gifts of love.

Harmony Produces Texture

Perform the harmony part of "*Así es mi tierra*" again. Notice that the harmony supports the main melody. It is not a separate melody. This texture is known as **homophonic.**

Homophonic texture is a melody supported by harmony.

Arts **Connection**

◀ *Empanadas* by Carmen Lomas Garza

Sus al - bo - ra - das tan lle - ni - tas, de_a - le - grí - a. Sus se - re -
When morn-ing light comes, Peo-ple greet the day with glad-ness. In hap-py

na - tas tan pro - pi - cias al a - mor. A - sí_es mi
sing - ing we hear mel - o - dies of love. This is my

tie - rra, flor de la me - lan - co - lí - a. ¡Ay, tie - rra
coun - try, Leav-ing fills me with such sad - ness; Oh, my dear

mí - a co - mo_es gra - to tu ca - lor!
coun - try, Wel-come are your gifts of love.

Caribbean Harmonies

Homophonic texture, using harmony in thirds, is also a part of the music of Caribbean and other Latin cultures. Singers often create harmony by singing intervals of a third above or below a melody.

Listen to *"Habemos llegado,"* a folk song from Puerto Rico. As you listen, indicate where the homophonic texture and harmony in thirds occur. Use the Pronunciation Practice track to learn the Spanish words, melody, and harmony parts. When you are ready, **sing** *"Habemos llegado."*

From Harmony to Chords

Caribbean singers are often accompanied by guitars or *cuatros*. These chord instruments play chords based on the harmony of a song.

Analyze the three chords in *"Habemos llegado."* **Sing** the root of each chord and then **play** it on keyboard.

A *cuatro* is a small guitar with four- or five-course double strings. You may hear it played in the music of South America, Mexico, and the Caribbean.

CD 10–1

Habemos llegado
(We Have Arrived)

English Words by David Eddleman

Folk Song from Puerto Rico

do

Dm   Gm   Dm

1. Ha - be - mos lle - ga - do a su a - ma - do ho - gar.   Ha -
2. Ói - ga - me, se - ño - ra, le ven - go a can - tar.   Ói -
1. We stand at the door of your dwell - ing so dear,   We
2. So hark, la - dy dear, to the song that I sing,   So

Dm   Gm   Dm

be - mos lle - ga - do a su a - ma - do ho - gar.   Con
ga - me, se - ño - ra, le ven - go a can - tar.   Que es
stand at the door of your dwell - ing so dear;   With
hark, la - dy dear, to the song that I sing;   My

Root position   Playing position

Play the chords for "*Habemos llegado*" on keyboard, or bells. Experiment with creating rhythms that may accompany the song.

Keyboard chords for Habemos llegado

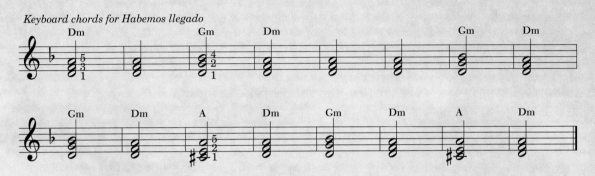

▼ A modern ten-string *cuatro*

con - chas, con	per - las, con	bri - sas del	mar;	con
u - na pro - me - sa	que	quie - ro pa - gar;		que es
shells and with	pearls and with	sea breez - es	near,	With
prom - ise to	keep is the	song that I	bring,	My

con - chas, con	per - las, con	bri - sas del	mar.
u - na pro - me - sa	que	quie - ro pa - gar.
shells and with	pearls and with	sea breez - es	near.
prom - ise to	keep is the	song that I	bring.

STEPS TO Harmony

Sing *"Vive l'amour."* Some of the lyrics are not in English. Do you know what language you will be singing? What part of the song will be in unison and what part will be in harmony?

Revisiting Intervals

The distance between two pitches is an interval. When sounded together, some intervals produce harmonies that are more pleasant to our ears than others. Two such intervals are thirds and sixths.

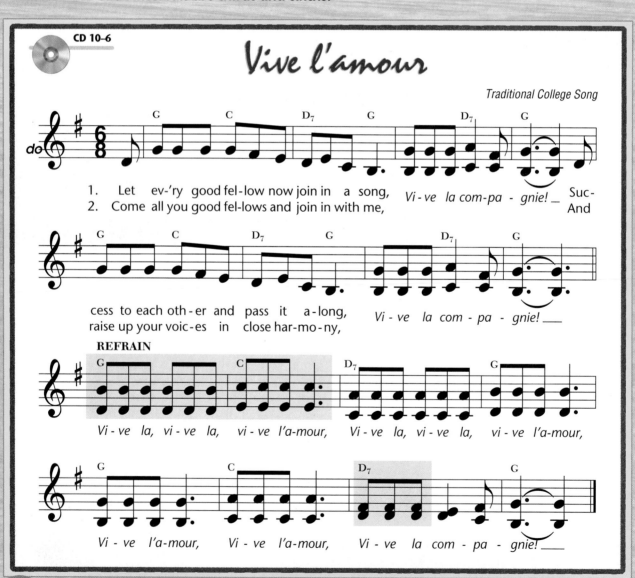

CD 10–6

Vive l'amour

Traditional College Song

1. Let ev'ry good fel-low now join in a song,
2. Come all you good fel-lows and join in with me,

Vi-ve la com-pa-gnie! — Suc-
And

cess to each oth-er and pass it a-long,
raise up your voic-es in close har-mo-ny,

Vi-ve la com-pa-gnie! ___

REFRAIN

Vi-ve la, vi-ve la, vi-ve l'a-mour, *Vi-ve la, vi-ve la, vi-ve l'a-mour,*

Vi-ve l'a-mour, *Vi-ve l'a-mour,* *Vi-ve la com-pa-gnie! ___*

It's a Third

On the staff the interval of a third is from one line to the very next line or from one space to the very next space.
Play these thirds on a keyboard. Which color box in the song contains thirds?

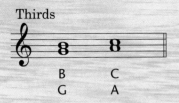

Thirds

B   C
G   A

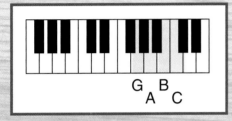

G   B
  A   C

Sounds Like a Sixth

Sixths are related to thirds. If you move the top note of a third an octave lower, you get a sixth.
Play these sixths on a keyboard.
Which color box in the song contains sixths?

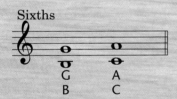

Sixths

G   A
B   C

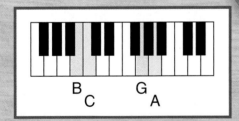

B   G
  C   A

Harmonizing a Melody

You can sometimes harmonize a melody with the intervals of a third or a sixth. First, **play** this melody on a keyboard. Then **create** harmony by playing a third below the melody. Next harmonize the melody again by playing a sixth above the melody.

Harmonies of Angels

Pie Jesu is a duet sung by a woman soprano and a boy soprano. Part of this duet is sung in thirds.

Follow the listening map on page 179. As you **listen** to the music, identify the sections where you hear thirds in the melody.

CD 10–8
Pie Jesu

from *Requiem*
by Andrew Lloyd Webber

Now **listen** to a solo performance.

CD 10–9
Pie Jesu

from *Requiem*
by Andrew Lloyd Webber
as performed by Charlotte Church

MUSIC MAKERS

Charlotte Church

Charlotte Church (born 1986) is one of today's biggest young superstars. Church's international career began at age 11 when she performed *Pie Jesu* on a British television show. Her debut album, *Voice of an Angel*, has sold over two million records.

Church has expanded her singing repertoire from that of opera to a variety of musical styles that include Broadway musicals, Gaelic songs, and popular music. By age 16, her achievements included four albums with international sales of over 10 million records, a platinum record in the United States, and performances to sellout crowds.

Church has performed for many famous people including President Clinton, Prince Charles, and the Queen of England.

Mapping Harmony

Follow the listening map for *Pie Jesu*. Where are the singers singing in thirds?
Where are they singing in sixths?

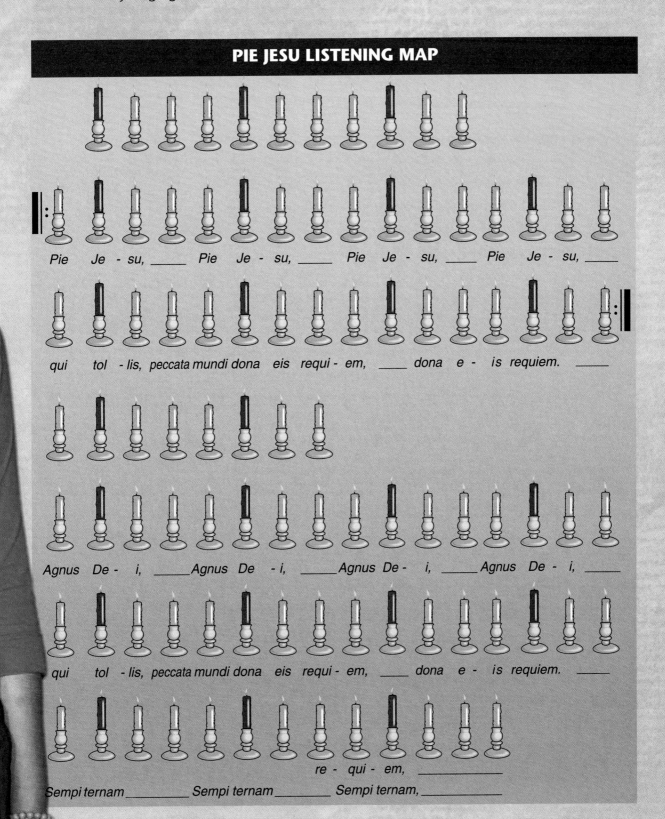

PIE JESU LISTENING MAP

Pie Je - su, _____ Pie Je - su, _____ Pie Je - su, _____ Pie Je - su, _____

qui tol - lis, peccata mundi dona eis requi - em, _____ dona e - is requiem. _____

Agnus De - i, _____ Agnus De - i, _____ Agnus De - i, _____ Agnus De - i, _____

qui tol - lis, peccata mundi dona eis requi - em, _____ dona e - is requiem. _____

re - qui - em, _____

Sempi ternam _____ Sempi ternam _____ Sempi ternam, _____

Calypso TEXTURES

"Mary Ann" is a well-known calypso song from the West Indies. Calypso music often features percussion instruments such as steel drums, playing syncopated rhythms.

Analyze the harmony of "Mary Ann." What interval is used to create the harmony?

Sing the melody. Then learn to sing the harmony part.

CD 10–10
MIDI 15

Mary Ann

Calypso Song from the West Indies

All day, __ all night, Miss Ma - ry Ann, __

Down by __ the sea - shore sift - ing sand. __

E - ven lit - tle chil - dren __ join in the band, __
Young __ and _____ old, come __ join in the band, __
Ev - 'ry - bod - y, come and __ join in the band, __

Down by __ the sea - shore sift - ing sand. __

Scales Have Chords

A chord can be built on every note of a scale. The harmony for the song "Mary Ann" uses chords built on the first, second, and fifth note of the scale (F, G, and C). These chords are called the I, ii, and V_7 chords.

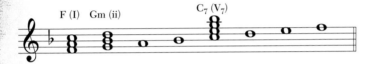

Play the three chords for "Mary Ann" on hand chimes, resonator bells, or mallet instruments.

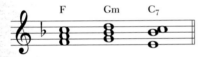

Each chord has three notes—a low note, a middle note, and a high note. **Play** an accompaniment for the song using these notes and one of the following rhythms.

 Electronic Keyboard Use the auto-accompaniment feature of your MIDI keyboard to play one-finger accompaniments to "Mary Ann." Experiment with different musical styles.

Mellow Movements

People in the West Indies like to move to music.
Sometimes they follow specific patterns or steps.

Learn this basic calypso step with your partner. **Perform** the calypso step to the music of "Mary Ann." Move in a relaxed manner. When you are ready, **improvise** and **create** your own calypso steps.

▲ Count 1: Step right foot in front of left, with a small twist

▲ Count 2: Step left foot in place

▲ Count 3: Step right foot next to left foot

▲ Count 4: Step left foot in place

Mellow Percussion

Calypso rhythms can be played on mallet and percussion instruments. Learn these percussion parts. When you are ready, **play** the percussion accompaniment with "Mary Ann."

A Calypso Ensemble

This orchestration adds mallet instruments to accompany "Mary Ann." Learn the orchestration and when you are ready, **perform** both ensembles to accompany the song.

Glockenspiel

Alto Metallophone

Bass Xylophone

MIDI Use the MIDI song file for "Mary Ann" to explore calypso textures. Create arrangements using the mallet and percussion accompaniments.

Review, Assess,

What Do You Know?

1. Read the rhythms below. Identify the rhythms that contain syncopation.

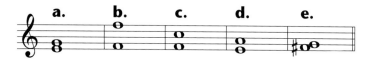

a.   b.

c.   d.

e.   f.

2. Select the correct name for each musical interval.

- octave
- fourth
- second
- fifth
- third

What Do You Hear? 5A

 CD 10–13

Timbre

Listen to *Vocal Timbres Around the World*, page 170. Match the most appropriate description to each musical style.

Musical Style	Description
1. country-western	**a.** folksy and rough vocal timbre, blues progression, guitar accompaniment
2. folk blues	**b.** solo vocal answered by three-part response, drum accompaniment
3. vocal imitation	**c.** solo vocal with vocal inflections, three-part harmony in refrain, country sound
4. African call and response	**d.** voice imitates instruments

Perform, Create

What Do You Hear? 5B

CD 10–17

Form

Listen to *Variations on "The Carnival of Venice,"* page 161. Identify the most appropriate description for each excerpt.

Excerpt	Description of Variation
1. _____	**a.** fast descending notes
2. _____	**b.** main theme; legato
3. _____	**c.** melody as low notes, plus high notes
4. _____	**d.** many fast notes
5. _____	**e.** theme with just a little ornamentation

What You Can Do

Sing Harmony

Sing either of the following songs in two-part harmony.

"Así es mi tierra," page 172
"Habemos llegado," page 174

Move to Show Expression

Perform the movements to *"Hava nagila,"* page 153. Make your movements expressive. When you hear an *accelerando*, match your movements to the pace of the music. Then create new movements that can be used with the song.

New Native American Drumming

Native American music has a rich tradition of drumming. Contemporary Native Americans are creating new versions of traditional music.

Listen to this contemporary rendition of *Dinéh Round Dance* performed on Native American instruments.
Then listen to an interview with the performer.

CD 10–22
Dinéh Round Dance

**Traditional Navajo Dance
as performed by Valerie Dee Naranjo**

A marimba, hoe blade, alto log drum, water sounds, claves, and *kechua* flute are the instruments that accompany the voice in this piece.

CD 10–23
**Interview with
Valerie Dee Naranjo**

M·U·S·I·C M·A·K·E·R·S

Valerie Dee Naranjo

Valerie Dee Naranjo is a performer, singer, and educator proficient in the music and drumming styles of Native American and African cultures. She began singing with her family at an early age in the Southwest and in Mexico. She learned to play Native American musical instruments.

Naranjo has performed with Philip Glass, David Byrne, Selena, and Tori Amos. She has played in Broadway's *The Lion King* and in NBC's *Saturday Night Live Band*.

Making Music Our Own

"Night Hawk Singers" drum group, Crow Reservation
▼

Make Your People Proud

Sing "Go, My Son." How can the words of the song be put into action?

Russell Means
An actor and activist of Native American rights. First National Director of the American Indian Movement.

Wilma P. Mankiller
Principal Chief of the Cherokee Nation.

CD 10–24

Go, My Son

Words and Music by Burson-Nofchissey

Spoken: "Long ago an Indian war chief counseled his people in the ways that they should walk. He wisely told them, education is the ladder to success and happiness. Go, my son, and climb that ladder. . . ."

1. Go, my son,   go and climb the lad-der.   Go, my son,
2. Work, my son,   get an ed-u-ca-tion.   Work, my son,
   on the lad-der   of an ed-u-ca-tion, You can see to

go and earn your fea-ther.   Go, my son,   make your peo-ple proud of
learn a good vo-ca-tion and climb, my son,   go and take a loft-y
help your In-dian na-tion and reach, my son, and lift your peo-ple up with

Graham Greene
Film, stage, and television actor. Nominated for an Oscar in *Dances with Wolves* (1990).

Ben Nighthorse Campbell
United States senator and congressman from the state of Colorado.

1. D♭   2. D♭   3. D♭   E

you. _____   view. _____   3. From you. _____

A

Go, my son, go and climb the lad - der. Go, my son,
on the lad - der of an ed - u - ca - tion, You can see to

F♯m   *Last time to Coda*   D

go and earn your fea - ther. Go, my son, make your peo-ple proud of
help your In - dian na - tion, and

A   *Coda*   D   *rit.*   D/C♯   Bm₇   A

you. _____ From reach, my son. Lift your peo-ple up with you.

Flowing Tempos

We often use similes to express ourselves. We talk about being as "happy as a clown" or "running like the wind." In this song, similes are used to express feelings of peace, joy, and love.

Sing the spiritual "Peace Like a River." Notice the steady beat of the accompaniment. Later, learn the harmony part and **perform** the song in homophonic style.

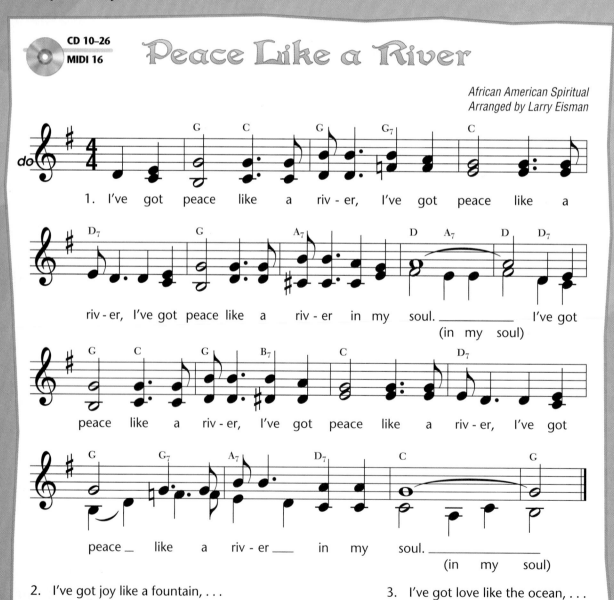

CD 10–26
MIDI 16

Peace Like a River

African American Spiritual
Arranged by Larry Eisman

1. I've got peace like a riv-er, I've got peace like a riv-er, I've got peace like a riv-er in my soul. _____ I've got (in my soul) peace like a riv-er, I've got peace like a riv-er, I've got peace _ like a riv-er _____ in my soul. _____ (in my soul)

2. I've got joy like a fountain, . . .

3. I've got love like the ocean, . . .

Arts Connection

▲ *Sculling at Sunset*
by Phoebe Beasley, 1983

You're the Conductor!

Practice this conducting pattern and **conduct** "Peace Like a River" as you sing.

Use the same pattern to conduct the introduction to "Peace Like a River." Does the pattern "fit" the music?

To demonstrate **rubato** when conducting, you should clearly indicate changes in tempo.

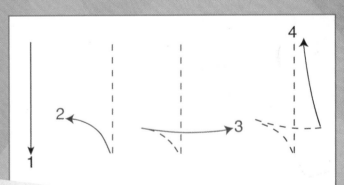

With **rubato,** the tempo of a piece of the music pushes ahead and/or pulls back slightly to allow greater expression.

And a One, a Two, a Three . . .

Here is the conducting pattern for meter in 3. Practice this pattern as you **listen** to *Minuet.* Count "1, 2, 3" to yourself as you conduct.

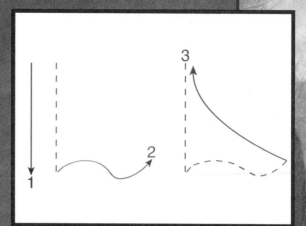

CD 10–28
Minuet

from *Orchestral Suite No. 2* by Johann Sebastian Bach

In this selection, bass and harpsichord accompany the melodic line played by the flute and strings. This is a common accompaniment in Baroque music.

Listen to the famous waltz *The Blue Danube.* Try to keep a steady beat while you conduct this waltz. Notice the different tempo changes and *rubato* as you conduct.

CD 10–29
The Blue Danube

by Johann Strauss, Jr.

Johann Strauss, Jr. (1825–1899) was a famous Austrian composer known for his waltzes. *The Blue Danube* (1867) was featured in the classic "sci-fi" movie *2001: A Space Odyssey* (1968).

Johann Strauss, Jr. ▶

Tune In

The Danube is a river that flows from Germany's Black Forest to the Black Sea.

A Poem of Similes

This poem, written by a seventh-grade student in Gettysburg, Pennsylvania, uses similes. Find the references to similes. Then _____ them to those in "Peace Like a River."

Autumn

by *John Hayden*

Copper-colored leaves
cascade
Down the trees,
Alight
on the ground.

Caught suddenly
by an autumn breeze,
some sprint
across the countryside
like magnificent Olympic runners.

Some dance
a delicate ballet.
Others drift
lazily,
like aimless pigeons
from forest
to forest.
The fiery oranges,
emerald greens,
velvety reds,
radiant golds,
twist
in the air.

Finally
stilled
by the first
wet covering of snow.

ADJUST THE ACCENTS

In $\frac{4}{4}$ time, the first and third beats are usually the strongest beats of the measure. You can group eighth notes with accents on weak beats to create an interesting rhythmic syncopation we call 3+3+2. The $\frac{4}{4}$ pattern is divided into 3 eighth notes + 3 eighth notes + 2 eighth notes.

Perform these rhythms by patting to feel the 3+3+2 groupings.

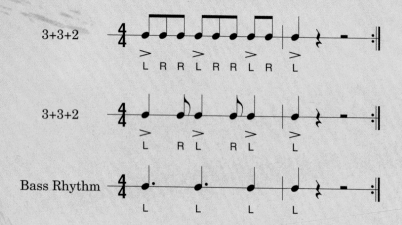

Play this syncopated strum on guitar or Autoharp with Bob Dylan's song "Paths of Victory."

Song of Peace

Bob Dylan was one of the most significant folk songwriters of the 1960s. **Sing** "Paths of Victory," then add the syncopated accompaniments.

▲ Bob Dylan

PATHS OF VICTORY

Words and Music by Bob Dylan

REFRAIN

Trails of trou - bles, ___ Roads of ___ bat - tles, ___ Paths of vic - to - ry, ___

Fine

We shall ___ walk.

VERSE

1. The trail ___ is dust - y, ___ And my road it might be rough, But the bet - ter roads are wait - in', ___ And ___ boys, it ain't ___ far ___ off.

2. I walked down by the riv - er, ___ I turned my ___ head up high, I saw that sil - ver li - nin' ___ that was hang - in' in ___ the ___ sky.

D. C. al Fine

3. The gravel road is bumpy,
   It's a hard road to ride,
   But there's a clearer road a-waitin'
   With the cinders on the side.
   Refrain

4. That evening train was rollin',
   The hummin' of its wheels,
   My eyes they saw a better day
   As I looked across the fields.
   Refrain

Meters Move

Meter is made from groupings of beats. Most commonly, beats are grouped by two, three, or four. If the quarter note gets the beat, the resulting meters would be $\frac{2}{4}$, $\frac{3}{4}$, and $\frac{4}{4}$.

Mixing Song Meters

Composers occasionally mix meters in songs. "New Hungarian Folk Song" is an example of a mixed meter song. **Create** your own movements to show the mixed meter as you **listen** to "New Hungarian Folk Song."

Sing "New Hungarian Folk Song" and conduct as you sing.

CD 10–35

New Hungarian Folk Song

English Words by Jean Sinor

Words and Music by Béla Bartók

Oh, how high, green for - est, spread your high - est tree?
High a - bove the corn a lark now earth-ward flies.

How long since its lat - est leaf fell si - lent - ly?
Sad her heart, for - lorn a - midst the emp - ty skies.

How long since its lat - est leaf fell si - lent - ly?
Shel - tered, hid - den un - der shade of leaf and flower,

Now a lone bird seeks her mate so mourn - ful - ly.
Still she mourns the mate who left her lone - ly here.

Arts Connection

Sopron by John Nemeth (1924–1987). Hungarian landscape ▶

Show What You Know!

Perform these patterns that use syncopation and mixed meters. Then **compose** your own rhythms, using mixed meters, and **perform** them on a nonpitched percussion instrument of your choice.

Adjust the Meters

When we perform or listen to music, we expect the beat to stay the same. Syncopation creates changes that make music more interesting. Contemporary music, with syncopation and changing meters, makes the rhythm even more distinctive.

In the example below, the meter shifts from $\frac{6}{8}$ to $\frac{3}{4}$. The first measure gets two beats, the second measure gets three beats.

The eighth notes in these two measures form a 3+3 pattern followed by a 2+2+2 pattern.

Play the pattern above by tapping or clapping the rhythm.

Playing Mixed Meter

Play the pattern above on a mallet instrument, using only the pitch G. Using the pitches G and D, add a bass line to the pattern.

Create additional rhythms to accompany this pattern. Use other mallet instruments and percussion to create more layers of ostinatos.

Iguala pottery from Mexico ▶

▲ Ceramics from Mexico

Spanish Mixed Meters

Aaron Copland uses changing meter in this rhythmic phrase from *El Salón México*. Note that the changing meter is shown in a single measure—§ ¾— followed by ⅜.

Listen to *El Salón México* and follow the strong beats and changing meters. Watch out for the *ritardando* (slower tempo) in measures 2 and 5. The *ritardando* changes where you feel the beat.

CD 10–40

El Salón México

by Aaron Copland
as performed by the New Philharmonia Orchestra, Aaron Copland, conductor

El Salón México (1936) uses Mexican folk melodies, changing meters, and syncopated rhythms to create its rhythmic excitement.

Now **listen** to another composer's use of mixed meter. In this selection, Spanish composer, Joaquín Rodrigo, uses a § ¾ § mixed-meter pattern for his main theme. As you listen, **conduct** this pattern.

CD 10–41

Concierto de Aranjuez

by Joaquín Rodrigo
as performed by Kazuhito Yamashita and the Jean-François Paillard Chamber Orchestra

Concierto de Aranjuez begins with a *rasgueado*-like strumming pattern. It is one of the most popular guitar concertos of the twentieth century and requires virtuosity from the guitar soloist.

Through-Composed Songs

Most music has sections or phrases that repeat and sections or phrases that are different. Some examples of these forms are:

A **B** ("*Vive l'amour*")

A **B** **A** ("Skye Boat Song")

A **B** **A** **B** **A** ("Worried Man Blues")

Repeated sections of music provide unity in a song.

"Through-composed" music is unified in other ways:

• Composers can use repeating rhythmic or melodic motives. Can you find any motives in "Your Friends Shall Be the Tall Wind"?

• Composers can also use the same through-composed melody for additional verses.

Sing "Your Friends Shall Be the Tall Wind," a through-composed song.

Your Friends Shall Be the Tall Wind

Words by Fannie Stearns Davis

Music by Emma Lou Diemer

1. Your friends shall be the tall wind, the riv - er and the tree; The sun that laughs and march - es, the swal - lows and the sea. Your prayers shall be the mur - mur of grass - es in the rain; The song of wild wood thrush - es that makes God _____ glad a - gain.

2. And you shall run and wan - der, and you shall dream and sing of brave things _____ and bright things be - yond the swal - low's wings. And you shall en - vy no man, nor hurt your heart with sighs; For I will keep you sim - ple, that God may make you wise, That God may make you wise, that God may make you wise.

An Evening Dance

A *chaconne* is a form of music in a slow meter in 3. Originally the *chaconne* was a dance in the seventeenth century. A *chaconne* is distinguished by a **ground bass.** When one, two, or three melodies are added above the ground bass, a thicker musical texture is created.

A **ground bass** is a bass line that continuously repeats throughout a composition.

Listen Before Performing

Listen to "Evening Chaconne" before performing it. Focus on the bass ostinato and the way each melody is constructed. Does it use repeated notes, steps, or leaps?

Playing Tips

Look at the music for "Evening Chaconne." Read the repeating bass part and other melodic ostinatos. Practice each ostinato by singing it. Then play the ostinatos on instruments.

CD 11–3

Evening Chaconne

Music by Konnie Saliba

An Evening Performance

Perform "Evening Chaconne." Begin with the bass instruments and then layer the other parts.

Lumberjack Intervals

A lumberjack's life in the 1800s was dangerous work. Lumberjack crews cut and hauled the huge trees used to build houses, farms, and factories all across our country. Lumberjack stories and songs were created about these colorful characters. **Sing** the lumberjack song "Blue Mountain Lake."

What's the Interval?

As you **listen** to "Blue Mountain Lake," follow the notation on page 205. Make a list of the intervals in the song by counting the distance of each interval. A repeating note is called a unison (interval = 1). What interval is shaded orange? What interval is shaded blue?

Sing "Blue Mountain Lake" with the spirit of a lumberjack.

Show What You Know!

Analyze the notation of "Blue Mountain Lake" on page 205. Draw an interval chart of the intervals that are used in the song and indicate the interval (melodic distance) between each pair of pitches.

'round a melody

"*Kyrie*" is from the Greek language. The words for "*Kyrie*" are used in the Mass and are translated *Lord, have mercy.*

Analyze the melody of the three-part round "*Kyrie.*" What is the key signature? With your teacher's help, write all of the pitches on a musical staff from low to high. **Read** and **sing** the pitches using hand signs and pitch syllables. Notice that the tonic is *la.* In the melody, notice that *so* is raised one half step to *si.*

CD 11–11
MIDI 17

Kyrie

Round from Suriname

Ky - ri - e, ky - ri - e   e - lei - son.

Ky - ri - e, ky - ri - e   e - lei - son.

Ky - ri - e, ky - ri - e___   e - lei - son.

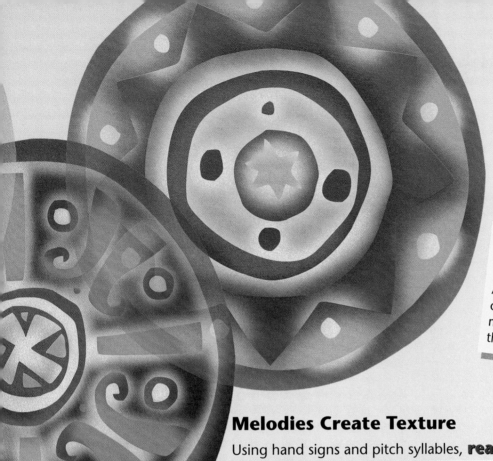

A **monophonic** texture consists of a single melodic line.

A **polyphonic** texture consists of two or more melodic lines that occur at the same time.

Melodies Create Texture

Using hand signs and pitch syllables, **read** and **sing** each part of *"Kyrie"* in *a cappella* unison—a **monophonic** texture.

Then, **sing** *"Kyrie"* as a three-part round. The musical texture is now **polyphonic.**

Another way to perform a round is to sing each part of the song as an ostinato. Group 1 begins and sings Part 1. Group 2 sings Part 2 and Group 3 sings Part 3. Groups 1 and 2 repeat their parts until Group 3 has sung its part twice.

Bell Choirs

Bell choirs are musical groups that play bells that range in size from very small to very large, and from high to low pitch. Bell choirs are often used in churches, but they also play concert music that is written or arranged specifically for them. **Listen** to the melody and texture in *Trepak*.

Tune In

Suriname is a South American country located north of Brazil on the Atlantic coast.

CD 11–16
Trepak

from *The Nutcracker Suite*
by Piotr Ilyich Tchaikovsky
as performed by the Sona Handbell Choir

The ringing of bells takes coordination and concentration in order to play in time.

Take A Chance

In the twentieth century, some composers gave performers and audiences a role in creating the music. This idea is somewhat like improvisation, where performers compose on the spot as they perform.

Jackson Pollock in his studio ▶

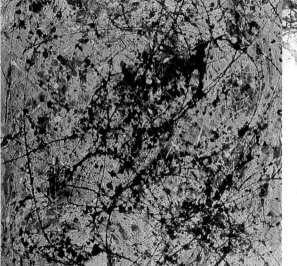

Arts Connection

◀ *Reflections of the Big Dipper* by Jackson Pollock (1912–1956). Composers in the twentieth century considered "action painting," by artists like Pollock, to be similar to chance music.

Chance Music

John Cage was the leader among composers who created chance, or "aleatoric," music.

In *Concert for Piano and Orchestra*, Cage did not create a typical score. **Listen** to this music by Cage.

CD 11–17
Concert for Piano and Orchestra

by John Cage

This piece can be played by any number of players and singers, performing any page in any order.

Tune In

"Which is more musical, a truck passing by a factory or a truck passing by a music school?"
– John Cage

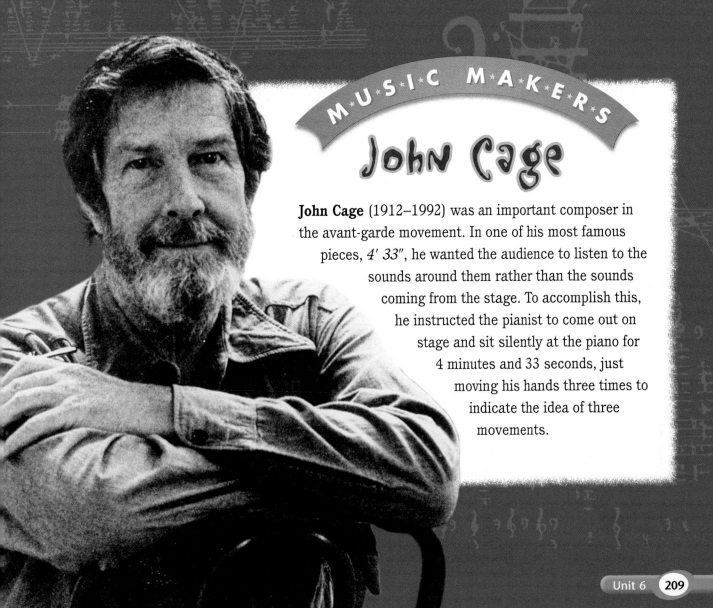

MUSIC MAKERS
John Cage

John Cage (1912–1992) was an important composer in the avant-garde movement. In one of his most famous pieces, *4′ 33″*, he wanted the audience to listen to the sounds around them rather than the sounds coming from the stage. To accomplish this, he instructed the pianist to come out on stage and sit silently at the piano for 4 minutes and 33 seconds, just moving his hands three times to indicate the idea of three movements.

Choir Sounds

You have heard the timbres of instruments, vocal styles, and twentieth-century music. Music sung by choirs also has a distinct timbre—the choral sound.

Choral music is usually written for four different voice parts. The voice parts are called *soprano, alto, tenor,* and *bass*—or SATB, for short. Here is the standard range (or highest and lowest notes) each voice sings:

Soprano   Alto   Tenor   Bass

Listen to an SATB arrangement of *Lo, How a Rose E'er Blooming.* Do any of the voice parts sing alone?

CD 11–18
Lo, How a Rose E'er Blooming

by Michael Praetorius
as performed by the Cambridge Singers
and Orchestra

This is a good example of *a cappella* singing. *A cappella* singing is unaccompanied, or literally, "in the style of the church."

Baroque Choirs

Listen to *Gloria in excelsis* for SATB chorus and orchestra by Antonio Vivaldi.

CD 11–19
Gloria in excelsis

by Antonio Vivaldi
as performed by the Robert Shaw Chorale and the
Atlanta Symphony Orchestra

Many works by composers such as Bach and Handel, as well as contemporary composers, use the combination of SATB chorus with orchestra.

Tune In

When Vivaldi was 15 years old, he began his training to become a priest. In his later years, he concentrated on music as a career.

An SATB Musical Score

Here is an example of printed SATB music. As you **listen** to the first phrase of *Lo, How a Rose E'er Blooming*, follow the voice parts in the score. What term describes this musical texture?

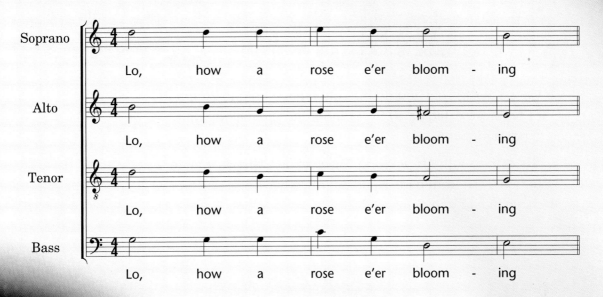

Soprano — Lo, how a rose e'er bloom - ing

Alto — Lo, how a rose e'er bloom - ing

Tenor — Lo, how a rose e'er bloom - ing

Bass — Lo, how a rose e'er bloom - ing

MUSIC MAKERS

Antonio Vivaldi

Antonio Vivaldi (1678–1741) was a famous composer, conductor, and violinist of the eighteenth century. He wrote a great deal of music in his lifetime—more than 750 musical pieces. Vivaldi, known as the "Red Priest" because of his auburn hair, composed operas, masses, hymns, and other types of choral music.

One of Vivaldi's most famous works, *The Four Seasons,* is known as "program music," or music that tells a story. *The Four Seasons* is a musical description of the four seasons of the year.

Vivaldi is remembered for his development of the violin concerto, a musical piece for solo violin with orchestra. Vivaldi spent many years teaching music in a school for orphaned girls. Many of his compositions were written for the students to play.

African Choir Sounds

Choral music from South Africa often has a unique sound, or timbre, created partly by harmonizing the melody with thirds and sixths.

Sing the South African song "*Siyahamba*." First, learn it in unison, then learn parts 2 and 3. Which two vocal parts move together rhythmically?

CD 11–20
MIDI 18

Siyahamba

Traditional Freedom Song from South Africa
Arranged by Rick Baitz

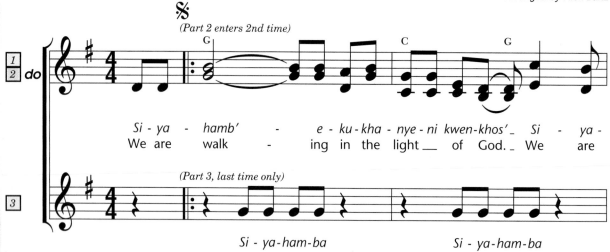

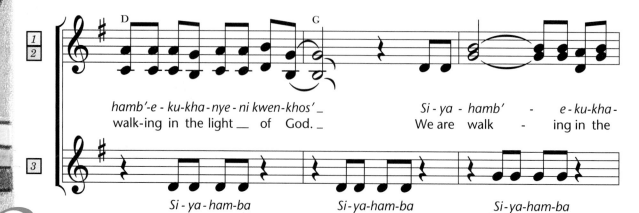

Signing for "*Siyahamba*"

Learn to sign the word "*siyahamba*." Then **perform** it as you sing.

we

▲ *Si-ya*

walk

▲ *-ham-ba*

nye-ni kwen-khos' _ Si - ya - hamb'- e - ku-kha - nye - ni kwen-khos' _
light _ of God. _ We are walk-ing in the light _ of God. _

Si - ya -

Si - ya-ham-ba   Si - ya - ham-ba   Si-ya-ham-ba

ham-ba ___   Si - ya-ham-ba ___

Si - ya-hamb'- e - ku-kha-nye - ni kwen-khos' _
We are walk-ing in the light _ of God. _

Si-ya-ham-ba   Si-ya-ham-ba   Si - ya-ham-ba

Bernstein's Textures

You have learned three musical textures: monophonic (a single melody line), homophonic (a melody line supported by harmony), and polyphonic (two or more melody lines, moving at the same time). Texture is important in the music of Leonard Bernstein. What is the texture of the music on this page?

Listen to *Responsory: Alleluia* to hear how Bernstein uses changes in texture to add interest to the work. Follow the listening map on page 217 as you listen. What two textures do you hear?

The assembled performers from a production of *Mass* ▶

Leonard Bernstein (Adapted)

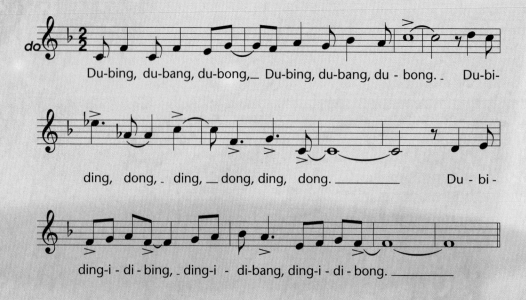

Du-bing, du-bang, du-bong,_ Du-bing, du-bang, du - bong. _ Du-bi-

ding, dong, _ ding, _ dong, ding, dong. _____ Du - bi -

ding-i - di - bing, _ ding-i - di-bang, ding-i - di - bong. _____

from *Mass*
by Leonard Bernstein

Bernstein's *Mass* premiered in 1971 for the opening of the John F. Kennedy Center for the Performing Arts in Washington, D.C.

RESPONSORY: ALLELUIA
LISTENING MAP

Here are the two themes for *Responsory: Alleluia.* Point to each theme as you hear it. When do you hear a theme in canon? What happens at the end?

"Du-Bing Du-Bang Du-Bong" Theme

"Alleluia" Theme

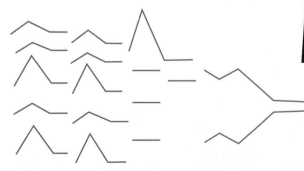

▲ Leonard Bernstein

Bernstein as Conductor

Leonard Bernstein was first known as a conductor. He had a brilliant career with the New York Philharmonic Orchestra and the New York City Center Orchestra. He was a guest conductor for many international orchestras.

Bernstein as Teacher

Bernstein was a gifted teacher of both adults and children. His *Philharmonic Concerts for Young People* appeared on television in 1958 and continued for 15 years.

A Textured Overture

The *Overture to Candide* is another example of Bernstein's use of melody and texture. **Listen** to *Overture to Candide* and its melodic themes.

CD 11–26
Overture to Candide

by Leonard Bernstein
Bernstein uses many short themes and motives that include a brass fanfare, a lively comic melody, and a beautiful *legato* theme played by strings.

Now **listen** to an excerpt from the same piece, in which Bernstein uses a section of the melody below as a canon. Follow this theme on the listening map. Describe the musical textures you hear.

Bernstein's *Candide*

CD 11–27
Overture to Candide

by Leonard Bernstein

Bernstein wrote the *Overture to Candide* in 1956. The second voice of the canon enters when the first voice starts the second measure.

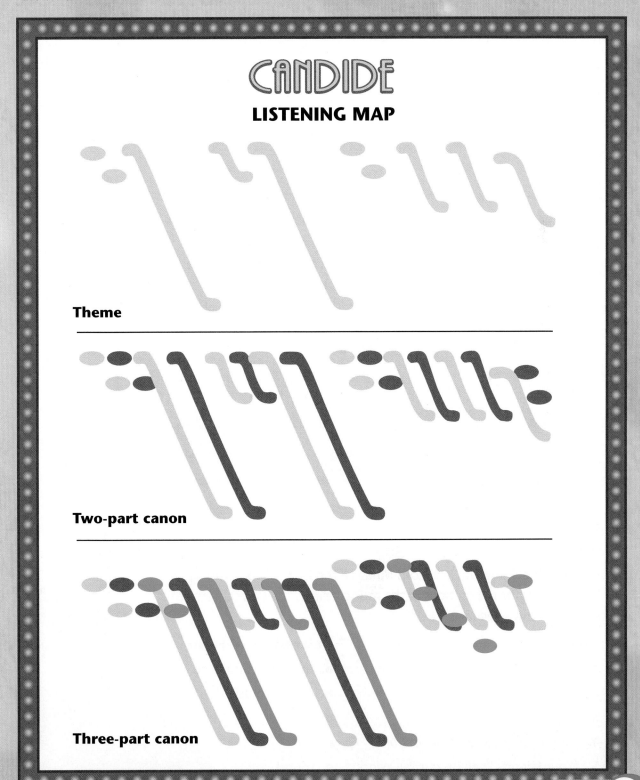

CANDIDE

LISTENING MAP

Theme

Two-part canon

Three-part canon

Review, Assess,

What Do You Know?

1. Identify the intervals of a fourth and fifth.

a.   b.   c.   d.   e.   f.

_____ _____ _____ _____ _____ _____

2. Match each term with its definition.

Term	Definition
a. through-composed	• a change in tempo in which the music pushes ahead and/or pulls back slightly to allow greater expression
b. *a capella*	• a musical piece in which the musical sections do not repeat
c. *rubato*	• a musical texture in which two or more melodic parts occur at the same time, creating layers of harmony
d. polyphonic	• vocal music performed without instrumental accompaniment

What Do You Hear? 6A

 CD 11–28

Form

Listen to the following selections. Analyze the form of each, using letter names for the sections in the music. Match the correct form to each listening selection.

Selection	Description of Form
1. "Skye Boat Song"	**a.** through-composed
2. "*Kyrie*"	**b.** chance music
3. "*Vive l'amour*"	**c.** ABA
4. *Concert for Piano and Orchestra*	**d.** AB
5. "Your Friends Shall Be the Tall Wind"	**e.** round

Perform, Create

CD 11–33

Timbre

Listen to the following choral selections. Point to the description of the timbre that best describes each listening selection.

Selection	Description of Timbre
1. *Gloria in excelsis*	**a.** African chorus
2. *Lo, How a Rose E'er Blooming*	**b.** chorus and orchestra
3. "*Siyahamba*"	**c.** *a cappella* chorus
4. "America, the Beautiful"	

What You Can Do

Analyzing Texture

Review the use of texture in your choice of *Responsory: Alleluia* on page 217, or *Overture to Candide* on page 218. You may wish to listen to the recording you choose. Then, describe the texture of your selection using the words *homophonic* or *polyphonic*.

Play Syncopated Rhythms

Play the rhythm parts on page 197, following the notation. First perform the rhythms using body percussion and then again using percussion instruments.

Perform with Expression

Select a song from this unit. Decide where to use *rubato* in the song. Perform the song with the class, using *rubato* to add expression to the music. Discuss the effect of *rubato* on the character of the song.

PATHS TO
Making
Music

Musical Give and Take

America's music influences music around the world. America's music, in turn, is influenced by music and cultures from around the world.

Country–Western Sound

Country music is everywhere and is enjoyed by many people throughout the world.

Listen to *I've Been Everywhere*, a classic country tune performed by Hank Snow.

CD 11–37
I've Been Everywhere

by Geoff Mack
as performed by Hank Snow

Hank Snow recorded over 100 albums and sold more than 70 million records. He performed at the Grand Ole Opry in Nashville, Tennessee, for more than 46 years.

HANK SNOW
Hank Snow was one of the most famous country music artists of all time.

BIG BILL BROONZY
Big Bill, "the father of Chicago blues," was a country blues guitarist of the 1930s.

America's Music
by Will Schmid

America's Music—A Gift Received

An African rhythm, a European ballad;
Immigrants all, we took our treasures
And formed them into what measures
Larger than any sound ever known.

America's Music—A Gift Given

Blues, Jazz, Country, Rock;
Not pure metals, but sounds fired
In a cauldron of heat inspired
By the mixture of peoples and races.

Exploring America's Music

America's music is a rich tapestry of sound. We can be proud of our diverse cultures, our wonderful country, and exciting music that is ours to listen to and sing.

CHARLIE "BIRD" PARKER
Charlie Parker, the founder of "bebop" jazz, was a legendary jazz saxophonist of the 1940s.

Tune In
Hank Snow discovered a talented young singer in the 1950s and invited him to perform as his opening act, and later at the Grand Ole Opry. This young singer was Elvis Presley.

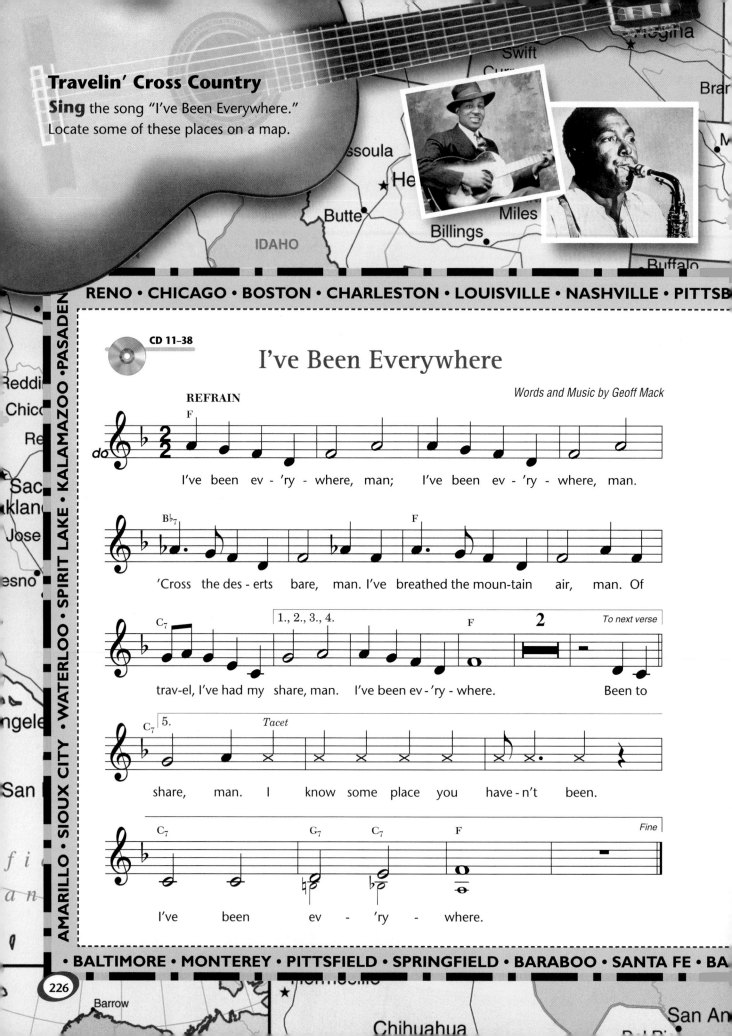

Travelin' Cross Country

Sing the song "I've Been Everywhere."
Locate some of these places on a map.

CD 11–38

I've Been Everywhere

Words and Music by Geoff Mack

REFRAIN

I've been ev - 'ry - where, man;   I've been ev - 'ry - where, man.

'Cross the des - erts bare, man. I've breathed the moun-tain air, man. Of

1., 2., 3., 4.   To next verse

trav-el, I've had my share, man.   I've been ev - 'ry - where.   Been to

5.   *Tacet*

share,   man.   I   know some   place   you   have - n't   been.

Fine

I've   been   ev - 'ry   -   where.

VERSE

F

1. Reno, Chicago, Fargo, Minnesota, Buffalo, Toronto,
2. Boston, Charleston, Dayton, Louisiana, Washington, Houston,
3. Louisville, Nashville, Knoxville, Ombabika, Shefferville, Jacksonville,
4. Pittsburgh, Parkersburg, Gravelburg, Colorado, Ellensburg, Rexburg,

F $B\flat_7$

Winslow, Sarasota, Wichita, Tulsa, Ottawa, Oklahoma,
Kingston, Texarkana, Monterey, Ferriday, Sante Fe, Tallapoosa,
Waterville, Costa Rica, Pittsfield, Springfield, Bakersfield, Shreveport,
Vicksburg, El Dorado, Larrimore, Atmore, Haverstraw, Chattanika,

F C_7

Tampa, Panama, Mattawa, La Paloma, Bangor, Baltimore,
Glen Rock, Black Rock, Little Rock, Oskaloosa, Tennessee, Hennessey,
Hackensack, Cadillac, Fond Du Lac, Davenport, Idaho, Jellicoe,
Chaska, Nebraska, Alaska, Opelika, Baraboo, Waterloo,

C_7 F *D.C.*

Salvador, Amarillo, Tocopilla, Barranquilla, and Padilla, I'm a killer.
Chicopee, Spirit Lake, Grand Lake, Devil's Lake, Crater Lake, for Pete's sake.
Argentina, Diamontina, Pasadena, Catalina, see what I mean-a.
Kalamazoo, Kansas City, Sioux City, Cedar City, Dodge City, what a pity.

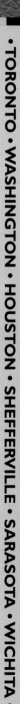

A New World

CD 12–1

The Water Is Wide

Folk Song from England

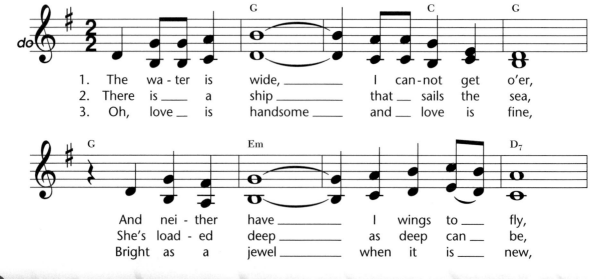

1. The wa - ter is wide, _____ I can - not get o'er,
2. There is ___ a ship _____ that ___ sails the sea,
3. Oh, love ___ is handsome _____ and ___ love is fine,

And nei - ther have _____ I wings to ___ fly,
She's load - ed deep _____ as deep can ___ be,
Bright as a jewel _____ when it is ___ new,

Even before our country became an independent nation, European immigrants were bringing their favorite songs with them to America.

Sing "The Water Is Wide," an early folk song from Great Britain. What is the message of this song?

Tune In

Lyric songs and ballads tell about love, war, home, and heroes. Before the days of television and recordings, such songs provided a source of entertainment after a long day at work.

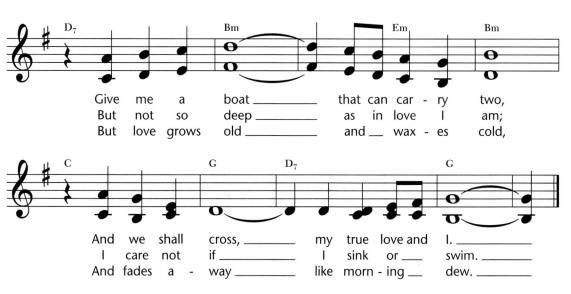

D₇   Bm   Em   Bm

Give me a boat _____ that can car - ry two,
But not so deep _____ as in love I am;
But love grows old _____ and __ wax - es cold,

C   G   D₇   G

And we shall cross, _____ my true love and I. _____
I care not if _____ I sink or __ swim. _____
And fades a - way _____ like morn - ing __ dew. _____

Songs of West Africa

West Coast Africans from countries like Ghana, Ivory Coast, Sierra Leone, and Nigeria brought their songs and their rhythms with them to America. These songs often took the form of **call and response.**

Listen to and then **sing** the Nigerian song *"Ise oluwa"* in the call-and-response style. What instruments do you hear on the recording?

Call and response is a style of performance in which a leader sings a call and a group responds.

CD 12–3

Ise oluwa

Yoruba Folk Song from Nigeria

I - se _____ o - lu - wa _____ ko le ba - je - oh; _____

I - se _____ o - lu - wa _____ ko le ba - je - oh. _____

Ko - le ba - je - oh, _____ ko le ba - je - oh. _____

I - se _____ o - lu - wa _____ ko le ba - je - oh; _____

I - se _____ o - lu - wa _____ ko le ba - je - oh. _____

Sounds of West Africa

Play the following rhythm accompaniment for *"Ise oluwa."*

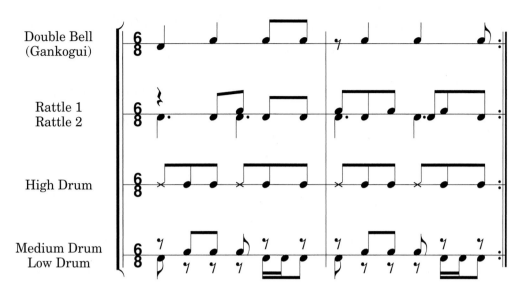

Double Bell (Gankogui)

Rattle 1
Rattle 2

High Drum

Medium Drum
Low Drum

The traditional West African instruments pictured here can be heard on the recording of *"Ise oluwa."*

Djembe [JEHM-beh] ▼

Donno [DOH-noh] ▼

Gankogui [gahn-KOH-gwee] ▼

Shekere [sheh-KEE-reh] ▼

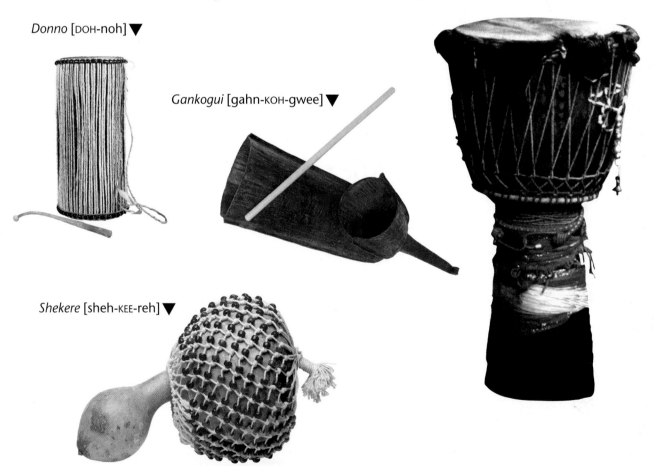

CD-ROM Use *Band-in-a-Box* to create an arrangement of *Ise oluwa* using the African style.

Spiritual and Gospel

Between 1800 and 1861 (the start of the Civil War), African American spirituals came to be an important part of America's musical heritage. These songs expressed slaves' longing for freedom. After 1920, a new style, called **gospel**, grew out of the spiritual tradition.

Sing this arrangement of "This Little Light of Mine," which combines the traditional spiritual with a contemporary gospel style.

Gospel combines jazz rhythm and blues singing with religious music. It may be accompanied by hand clapping, swaying, foot stomping, and other movements.

CD 12–6

This Little Light of Mine

African American Spiritual
Arranged by Linda Twine and Joseph Joubert

Gently

This lit-tle light of mine, ___ I'm gon-na let it shine.

This lit-tle light of mine, ___ I'm gon-na let it shine.

This lit-tle light of mine, ___ I'm gon-na let it shine, Let it shine, _

let it shine, _ let it shine. _____

Joyous

This lit-tle light of mine, _ I'm gon-na let it shine. _
Ev - 'ry - where I go, ___ I'm gon-na let it shine. _

This lit-tle light of mine, _ I'm gon-na let it shine. _____
Ev - 'ry - where I go, ___ I'm gon-na let it shine. _____

This lit - tle light of mine, __ I'm gon-na let it shine. _
Ev - 'ry - where I go, ___ I'm gon-na let it shine. _

1.
____ Let it shine, _ let it shine, _ let it shine. _____
____

2.
____ Let it shine, _ let it shine, _ Let it shine, _ let it shine, __

____ Let it shine, _ let it shine, _ let it shine. _____

Spirituals Live On

Listen to another African American spiritual, performed in gospel style.

CD 12–8
The Battle of Jericho

African American Spiritual
as performed by the Moses Hogan Chorale

The Moses Hogan Chorale is one of the premier choirs in the nation. They specialize in singing traditional African American spirituals and contemporary gospel arrangements.

Read about the Fisk Jubilee Singers below and then listen to this early historical recording of another spiritual.

CD 12–9
Swing Low, Sweet Chariot

African American Spiritual
as performed by the Fisk Jubilee Singers

The "scratches" you hear on the recording are from old vinyl records that have been played many times.

M·U·S·I·C   M·A·K·E·R·S

The Fisk Jubilee Singers

The Fisk Jubilee Singers were organized in 1871 at Fisk University in Nashville, Tennessee. They were named after the biblical "year of jubilee," a time when all slaves were freed. (All of the original singers were former slaves.) The singers traveled throughout America and Europe and were a star attraction at the 1872 World Peace Jubilee. Their concert included both popular songs of the day and spirituals. As a permanent institution at Fisk, the current Jubilee Singers are continuing this vital choral tradition.

Golden Gospel

Listen to *Jonah,* a gospel song about the man who was swallowed by a whale.

CD 12–10
Jonah

Traditional Gospel Song
as performed by the Golden Gate Quartet

Gospel quartet singing was popular in the 1930s and 1940s. It laid the foundation for many African American popular styles that emerged after World War II.

MUSIC MAKERS

The Golden Gate Quartet

The **Golden Gate Quartet** was a gospel/pop quartet of the 1930s and 1940s. Their smooth harmonies allowed them to cross over into pop music as well. They began recording for RCA/Victor in 1937. This was followed by national radio broadcasts. An appearance on a 1938 "Spirituals to Swing" concert at Carnegie Hall made them coast-to-coast favorites.

▲ The Golden Gate Quartet and guitar accompanist

TIMBRE on the Move

At the end of the Civil War (1861–1865), Texas had nearly five million longhorn cows—some running wild and some in herds. Texans such as Charles Goodnight realized that they could round up and brand the cows. They then herded them up to the railroads in Kansas, or the northern grasslands of Wyoming or Montana, and sold them for a good profit. Thus began the heyday of the cowboy. In 1867 cattle drives sent 35,000 cows northward. By 1871 the number of cows herded north had grown to 600,000.

Listen to country music artist, Charlie Daniels, sing about life on a Chisholm Trail cattle drive. The Chisholm Trail was named for Scottish-Cherokee trader, Jesse Chisholm.

CD 12–11
The Old Chisholm Trail

**Traditional Cowboy Song
as performed by Charlie Daniels**

Charlie Daniels begins this song with a narrative about cowboys on the trail. What timbres and sound effects set the mood of being on the trail?

Chisholm Trail Timbres

Analyze the notation of "The Old Chisholm Trail." What instrument might a cowboy play to accompany his singing? How might that influence the melody?

Sing "The Old Chisholm Trail."

Cowboy Life

The typical cowboy was a 19 to twenty-year-old American Civil War veteran who was seeking adventure in the new American West. On the trail, the cowboy was awakened at first light by the chuck wagon trail cook yelling to come get his bacon, beans, and biscuits. Herding cows on the trail and across rivers all day was a dusty, wet, and dangerous business. It was tough work, earning cowboys just a dollar a day.

Buffalo Bill Historical Center, WY; 7.69

Arts Connection

▲ *Trail Herd to Abilene* (1923) by W. H. D. Koerner (1878–1938) depicts a cattle drive.

CD 12–12

THE OLD CHISHOLM TRAIL

Cowboy Song from the United States

VERSE

1.　　Come　a - long, boys, and　lis - ten　to　my　tale,　I'll
2.　I　woke　up　one　morn - in'　on　the Chis-holm Trail,　A
3.　　Ten ____ dollar horse and a　for - ty　dol - lar saddle　I'm
4.　I　jumped __ in the saddle and　grabbed __ the __ horn, ___

tell　you 'bout my trou - bles　on　the　old　Chis-holm Trail.　Com　a
rope __　in　my　hand __　and　a　cow　by　the　tail.
read - y　for ____　punch - in' ____　Tex - as ____　cattle.
Best __　ole __　cow - boy　that　ever　was __　born.

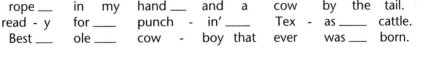

ti　yi　yip-py, yip-py　yay, yip-py yay, Com a　ti　yi　yip-py yip-py　yay.

5. My seat's in the saddle and saddle's in the sky;
   And I'll quit punchin' cows in the sweet by and by.　*Refrain*

A Cowboy Dance

After all their hard work, cowboys were happy to have a break. They enjoyed music, dancing, stories, or poetry. Instruments such as the guitar, harmonica, concertina, banjo, mandolin, and fiddle were popular. Those instruments were also easy to carry on the trail. A man who could tell a good story was a valued companion in the cowboy bunkhouse or the lumberjack shanty.

Listen to Michael Martin Murphy perform his version of *Cowboys' Christmas Ball*. Notice how Murphy and the band end the recording with a number of dance tunes including *Good King Wenceslas*, *Under the Double Eagle*, *Redwing*, and *Oh, Them Golden Slippers*. What instruments do you hear in the band?

CD 12–14
Cowboys' Christmas Ball

**Traditional Cowboy Song
as performed by Michael Martin Murphy**

Larry Chittenden, a New York writer turned cowboy poet, wrote the poem *Cowboys' Christmas Ball* after attending a cowboy Christmas dance in the 1880s.

Dancing Cowboys

Around Christmas time, cowboys were invited down to the main ranch house for a festive dinner and dance. If no women were present, some of the men put on aprons and danced the woman's part. **Sing** "Cowboys' Christmas Ball," which describes the dance.

Arts Connection

▲ *Cowboy Dance*, or *Fiesta de Vaqueros*, by Jenne Magafan (1915–1952) shows a festive cowboy dance.

CD 12–15

COWBOYS' CHRISTMAS BALL

Lyrics from a poem by Larry Chittenden (1893)   *Cowboy Song from the United States*

1. Way   out   in west - ern   Tex - as,   where the   Clear Fork's wa - ters
2. The   mus - ic was   a   fid - dle   and a   live - ly   tam - bour -
3. The   lead - er was   a   fel - ler   that ___   came from Swen-son's
4. "Sa - loot   yer love - ly   crit - ters,   now ___   swing and   let 'em

flow,   Where the   cat - tle   are   a - brows - in'   and the
ine,   And   a   vi - ol came,   im - port - ed   by the
ranch,   They ___   called   him Win - dy   Bil - ly   from ___
go;   Climb   the grape - vine   round 'em;   now ___

Span - ish   po - nies   grow;   Where the   an - te - lope   is
stage from   Ab - i - lene.   The ___   room   was   togged out
Lit - tle   Dead Man's   Branch,   His ___   rig   was   kind - a
all   hands   do - si - do;   You ___   mave - rick,   join   the

graz - in'   and the   lone - ly plov - ers   call,   It   was
gor - geous   with ___   mis - tle - toe   and shawls,   And the
care - less,   big ___   spurs   and high - heeled boots;   He ___
round - up.   Now ___   rope   and bal - ance   all!"   Hi! ___

there that   I   at - tend - ed   the   cow - boys' Christ - mas ball.
can - dles flick - ered fes - tious   a - round the   air - y   hall.
had   the   rep - u - ta - tion   that   comes when fel - lers shoot.
It   was   get - tin' ac - tive   at the   cow - boys' Christ - mas ball.

The Blues Feeling

The **blues** is sometimes described as a feeling, such as "I'm feeling down and out. My baby has just left me." Feelings of loneliness or sadness were also expressed in earlier African American musical styles, such as spirituals and work songs.

Sing the spiritual "Sometimes I Feel Like a Motherless Child." Then **create** your own verses about how you feel.

The **blues** style of music usually has emotional lyrics; slow, offbeat rhythms; and improvised singing and playing.

Tune In

The 12-bar blues form is also used in classic blues, urban blues, boogie woogie, and rock 'n' roll.

CD 12–17

Sometimes I Feel Like a Motherless Child

African American Spiritual

1. Some-times I feel like a moth-er-less child,
2. Some-times I feel like I'm al - most gone,

Some-times I feel like a moth-er-less child,
Some-times I feel like I'm al - most gone,

Some-times I feel like a moth-er-less child,
Some-times I feel like I'm al - most gone,

long way ____ from home, ____

long way ____ from home.

The 12-Bar Blues

Early country blues recorded in the 1920s was simply one singer accompanied by a guitar. Many country blues artists used a form called 12-bar blues (12 measures long), which had three phrases in an **a** **a** **b** lyric structure. "Sun Gonna Shine," on the next page, is a good example of this traditional blues form.

◀ Memphis Minnie (left) and Ma Rainey (top right, with her band) were among blues' most important female artists.

Let the Sunshine In

No matter how blue you may feel, you know that the sun will come out and shine again. It's a good feeling. **Sing** "Sun Gonna Shine." Then **play** an accompaniment on guitar and **create** some of your own blues verses using the 12-bar blues **a** **a** **b** lyric structure.

CD 12–19
MIDI 19

Sun Gonna Shine

Traditional Blues

a A₇

1. Sun gon-na shine on my back door some-day, __
2. Goin' to Chi - ca - go, leavin' on the morn - in' train, _
3. Blues in the mornin' and blues all through the night, _

a D₇   A₇

Sun gon-na shine on my back door some-day, __
Goin' to Chi - ca - go, leavin' on the morn - in' train, _
Blues in the mornin' and blues all through the night, _

b E₇   D₇   A₇

Wind gon - na rise up and blow my blues a - way. __
You can miss me ba - by, But I won't be back a - gain. __
Play those __ blues 'til the ear - ly morn - in' light. __

4. River is deep, and the river sure is wide,
   River is deep, and the river sure is wide,
   Gal (man) I love is on the other side.

5. You used to be my sugar, but you ain't too sweet no more,
   You used to be my sugar, but you ain't too sweet no more,
   You've got another baby hangin' round your door.

Keyed to the Blues

Sing "Key to the Highway," an urban blues popularized by Big Bill Broonzy. Is this song a 12-bar blues? To **play** along on guitar, place your guitar capo on fret 1 to play in E, or on fret 3 to play in D.

by Big Bill Broonzy and Charles Segar as performed by Big Bill Broonzy

Broonzy's music reflects the gospel style of his Southern roots. Between 1928 and his death in 1958, he made more than 300 recordings.

Listen to *Key to the Highway* sung by Big Bill Broonzy.

You "GOT COUNTRY"

In the 1920s, "country" folk music could be heard in Appalachia and throughout the Southern states. Nashville's *Grand Ole Opry* radio show helped create a large audience for country music. Country-western music was born.

Sing the Louisiana Cajun-style song "Jambalaya," a big hit by the country-western artist Hank Williams. Then **play** an accompaniment on guitar using a "down-up down" rhythmic strum.

CD 13–1

Jambalaya
(On the Bayou)

Words and Music by Hank Williams

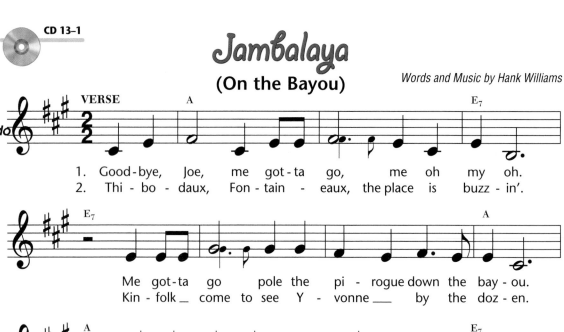

1. Good-bye, Joe, me got-ta go, me oh my oh.
2. Thi-bo-daux, Fon-tain-eaux, the place is buzz-in'.

Me got-ta go pole the pi-rogue down the bay-ou.
Kin-folk come to see Y-vonne by the doz-en.

My Y-vonne, the sweet-est one, me oh my oh.
Dress in style and go hog wild, me oh my oh.

Son of a gun, we'll have big fun on the bay-ou.

Listen to this Cajun recording of *Jambalaya*, which features the accordion and the fiddle.

CD 13–3
Jambalaya

by Hank Williams
as performed by Jo-El Sonnier

This performance of *Jambalaya* is sung entirely in Cajun dialect.

Tune In

References in the lyrics of "Jambalaya" that may be unfamiliar include:

bayou—An area of shallow, slow-moving water

pirogue—A dugout canoe, usually fashioned from a single log

gumbo—A thick soup, made with okra

Jam - ba - la - ya and a craw - fish pie and fi - let gum - bo,

'Cause to - night I'm gon - na see my *ma cher a - mi* - o.

Pick gui - tar, fill fruit jar, and be gay - o,

Son of a gun, we'll have big fun on the bay - ou.

Happy Trails!

Gene Autry and Roy Rogers were two of the biggest singing cowboy movie stars of the twentieth century. They helped create the "western" part of country-western music.

Sing one of Gene Autry's all-time biggest hits, "You Are My Sunshine." Then **play** an accompaniment on guitar using a "down down-up" rhythmic strum.

◀ Roy Rogers and Trigger

CD 13–4

You Are My Sunshine

Words and Music by Jimmie Davis and Charles Mitchell

REFRAIN

You are my sun - shine, _____ my on - ly

sun - shine; _____ You make me hap - py _____

_____ when skies are gray. _____ You'll ne - ver

know, dear, _____ how much I love you; _____

_____ Please don't take my sun - shine a - way. _____

Country Sunshine

Listen for the "western swing" style of playing in this performance by Autry.

CD 13–6

You Are My Sunshine

**by Jimmie Davis and Charles Mitchell
as performed by Gene Autry**

Jimmie Davis, the composer of "You Are My Sunshine," served two terms as governor of Louisiana.

Gene Autry ▶

VERSE

F

The oth - er night, dear, _____ as I lay

F   B♭

sleep - ing, _____ I dreamed I held you

B♭   F

in my arms, _____ When I a -

B♭   F

woke, dear, _____ I was mis - tak - en _____

G₇   F   C₇   F   *D.C. al Fine*

_____ and I hung my head and cried. _____

Longing for Home

Sentimental country-western ballads sometimes use "home," "mama and papa," or "trains" as their themes. **Sing** "Green, Green Grass of Home" and think of places that are important to you. For a vocal interlude and coda, repeat the last phrase of the refrain.

CD 13–7

Green, Green Grass of Home

Words and Music by Curly Putman

VERSE

1. The old home-town looks the same as I step down from the
2. The old house is still stand-ing, tho' the paint is cracked and

train, and there to meet me is my ma - ma and pa-pa. __
dry, and there's that old oak tree that I __ used to play on. __

Down the road I look, and there runs Ma - ry, hair of gold and
Down the lane I walk with my sweet Ma - ry, hair of gold and

lips like cher - ries. It's good to touch the green, green grass of home.
lips like cher - ries. It's good to touch the green, green grass of home.

REFRAIN

Yes, they'll all come to meet me, arms _ reach-ing, smil-ing

sweet-ly; It's good to touch the green, green grass of home. _____

Country Stars

Listen to the two-part harmony vocals in *Don't Look Down*.

CD 13–9
Don't Look Down

by Wendy Waldman and Steve Buckingham as performed by Sweethearts of the Rodeo

From their hit album in 1988, *Don't Look Down* features the Sweethearts' close vocal harmony and country sound.

Country Dancing

Country music and dance go together like ham and eggs. Country and western dancing is very popular, and many people take country dancing lessons.

Two well-known dances in country music are line dancing and the "two-step." Learn the two-step and **perform** it to "Jambalaya," on page 244.

▲ Country line dancing

MUSIC MAKERS

Sweethearts of the Rodeo

▲ Sisters Janice and Kristine Oliver of Sweethearts of the Rodeo

Sweethearts of the Rodeo are another in the long line of sister or brother duets in country music dating back to the 1930s. Janice and Kristine Oliver grew up in southern California. After Janice taught herself how to play guitar, she and Kristine started to sing harmony together. The Sweethearts of the Rodeo took their name from the Byrds' 1968 recording by the same name. They cut their debut album in 1986 and have recorded several other albums.

Jazz: Made in America

American jazz was born from African and European roots. New Orleans was one of the first jazz hotspots. The heart of jazz is improvisation—taking a song and making your own version of it on the spot. There are many styles in the jazz genre, including Dixieland, boogie woogie, big band, swing, bebop, and other contemporary styles.

Sing the jazz standard "Summertime" from George Gershwin's opera, *Porgy and Bess*.

CD 13–10

Summertime

Words by Dubose Heyward

Music by George Gershwin

Sum - mer - time and the liv - in' is eas - y.

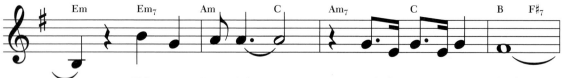

Fish are jump-in' and the cot - ton is high.

Oh, your dad-dy's rich and your ma is good - look - in'.

So hush, lit - tle ba - by, don't you cry.

One of these morn-in's you goin' to rise __ up sing - in', __

Then you'll spread your wings __ and you'll take __ the

sky. _____ But till that morn-in', ____ there's a-noth-in' can

harm you _____ With Dad - dy and Mam - my

stand - in' by. _____

MUSIC MAKERS

George Gershwin

George Gershwin (1898–1937) achieved fame as both a Tin Pan Alley songwriter and as a concert hall composer. Born in Brooklyn, Gershwin wrote many of his best songs with his brother, Ira. His well-known major works that included jazz elements are *Rhapsody in Blue* and *An American in Paris* for orchestra, and the opera *Porgy and Bess*. Gershwin died at the young age of 39 during an operation for a brain tumor.

Play an Improvisation

Learn how to **improvise** using the chords below. Most of the melody for "Summertime" uses notes in the blues minor pentatonic (*la, do, re, mi, so*). You will use these notes (E, G, A, B, and D) to improvise.

Play along on a keyboard. Each slash is worth one beat and tells you to keep playing the same notes. If you play the whole note, you are playing the "root" of the chord. Add the extra notes when you are ready and improvise new rhythms.

la   do   re   mi   so

Summertime, Jazz Style

Listen to this jazz interpretation of *Summertime* by the great trumpet player Miles Davis as you follow the listening map on page 253. You will hear the melody played first, followed by improvisations based on the tune and the chords.

CD 13–12

Summertime

**by George Gershwin
as performed by Miles Davis**

On this recording, Davis uses a Harmon mute to color the sound of the trumpet.

CD-ROM Make your own jazz arrangement and explore improvisation using *Band-in-a-Box.*

Summertime

LISTENING MAP

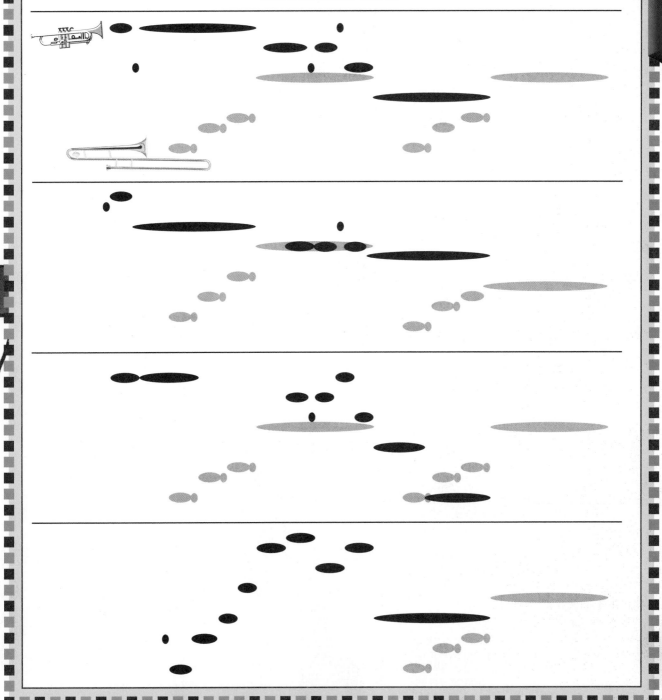

Let's Rock!

Rock 'n' roll burst onto the popular music scene in 1955 and was much influenced by African American rhythm and blues. Electric guitars, bass, saxophones, piano, and drums gave rock 'n' roll a new excitement that electrified teenagers.

Sing and **play** "Don't Be Cruel," one of Elvis Presley's early hits.

MUSIC MAKERS
Elvis Presley

Elvis Presley (1935–1977) was one of the biggest pop music stars of all time. Born in Tupelo, Mississippi, he later settled in Memphis, Tennessee. Between 1956 and 1962, Elvis had 17 Number-1 hits on the Top 100 pop charts. His recording of *Hound Dog* was in the top spot on the charts for 11 weeks. Elvis's musical style was influenced by gospel, country and western, and rhythm and blues.

Tune In

Graceland, Elvis's home in Memphis, is probably the most famous private home in America. In 1991 it was placed on the National Register of Historic Places.

254

CD 13–13

Don't Be Cruel

Words and Music by Otis Blackwell and Elvis Presley

1., 3. You know I can be found _____ sit - ting home all a -
2. Baby if I made you mad for some-thing I might have

lone. If you can't come a - round, at least, please tel - e - phone. Don't be
said. Please let's forget the past, the future looks bright a - head. Don't be

cruel to a heart that's true. _____
cruel to a heart that's

2., 3.

true. _____ I don't want no oth - er love,

Ba - by, it's just you I'm think-ing of.

Don't be cruel to a heart that's true. _ Don't be

cruel to a heart that's true. _ I don't want no oth - er

love, Ba - by, it's just you I'm think-ing of.

Be a Rock Drummer

The rhythm of rock 'n' roll during the 1950s was based on the uneven shuffle of rhythm and blues. As rock 'n' roll turned into rock of the 1960s, the rhythms became even and had a very different feel. What rhythm creates the "shuffle" feel?

Rock 'n' Roll Shuffle

Move as though you are playing a shuffle on the "air" drum set using your hands and feet. Then **play** the rhythms below on percussion instruments.

Ride Cymbal
High Hat
Bass Drum

Buddy Holly

Ride Cymbal: Play this cymbal pattern with a stick in your dominant hand (you may want to use a pencil). Make the sound with your voice.

Bass Drum: Keep your heel on the ground and tap this rhythm with your dominant foot. Try it with the ride cymbal pattern.

High Hat: Keep your heel on the ground and tap this rhythm with your other foot. Add this to the bass drum rhythm.

Combining All Three: Start with the bass drum; then add the high hat. When these two are stable add the ride cymbal.

Listen to Buddy Holly's *That'll Be the Day*. Then **perform** the rock 'n' roll shuffle to the music.

CD 13–15

That'll Be the Day

by Jerry Allison, Norman Petty, and Buddy Holly as performed by Buddy Holly

That'll Be the Day was Buddy Holly's first big hit. It topped the charts in 1957.

Even Rock Rhythm

To change the shuffle beat to an even rock rhythm, substitute straight eighth notes for the ride cymbal. **Play** these patterns on percussion instruments.

Ride Cymbal
Snare Drum
Bass Drum

Chubby Checker helped to firmly establish the rock revolution in the 1960s with hits such as *The Twist* and *Let's Twist Again*. These hits are a good example of even rock rhythms.

Listen to *Let's Twist Again*. Then **perform** even rock rhythms with the music.

CD 13–16
Let's Twist Again

by David Appell and Kal Mann as performed by Chubby Checker

Chubby Checker's 1960 hit, *The Twist*, started a new dance craze unlike anything seen before it. *Let's Twist Again* was a follow-up Twist hit.

Britain's Beatles Rock!

One of the most famous rock groups of all time was the Beatles. **Listen** to their hit song *Penny Lane*.

CD 13–17
Penny Lane

by John Lennon and Paul McCartney

Penny Lane was written about a local bus stop in Liverpool, England, near where Beatles Lennon and McCartney grew up.

The Beatles ▶

The British Are Here

Starting in 1964 with the Beatles' first tour, British groups began to dominate the rock scene. In addition to the Beatles, British performers included the Dave Clark Five, the Rolling Stones, and Petula Clark. "Downtown" was one of Petula Clark's biggest international hits.

Listen to and then **sing** "Downtown." Does the song have shuffle rhythms or even rhythms?

CD 13–18

Downtown

Words and Music by Tony Hatch

1. When you're a - lone _ and life is mak - ing you lone - ly, you can
   When you've got wor - ries, all the noise and the hur - ry seems to
2. Don't hang a - round_ and let your prob - lems sur - round _ you, there are
   May - be you know_ some lit - tle pla - ces to go ___ to where they

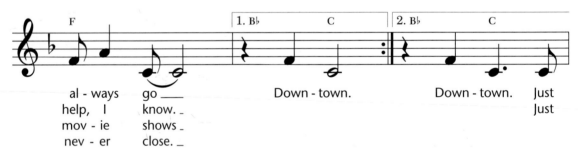

al - ways go ___ Down - town. Down - town. Just
help, I know. _ Just
mov - ie shows _
nev - er close. _

lis - ten to the mu - sic of the traf - fic in the cit - y.
lis - ten to the rhy - thm of a gen - tle Bos - sa No - va.

Ling - er on the side - walk where the ne - on signs are pret - ty. How can you lose? _
You'll be danc - ing with 'em, too, be - fore the night is o - ver, hap - py a - gain. _

CD 13–20

Interview with Petula Clark

M·U·S·I·C M·A·K·E·R·S

Petula Clark

Petula Clark (born 1933) was a star in England at age eight. She sang for British troops in World War II and even starred in a comic strip! Her movie career has spanned almost 30 films. In 1965 she received her first Grammy Award for her recording of "Downtown." Clark has appeared on Broadway and London's West End in *Blood Brothers*, *The Sound of Music*, and *Sunset Boulevard*.

The lights are much bright-er there, you can for - get all your trou - bles for-

get all your cares. So go Down - town. Things-'ll be great when you're

Down - town. No fin - er place for sure, Down - town.

Ev - 'ry - thing's wait - ing for you.

The Surfin' Sound

Not all rock music in the early 1960s was sung with a British accent. From Southern California, groups like Jan and Dean, the Surfaris, and the Beach Boys helped produce "surf rock," a new sound that was uniquely American.

The main elements of surf rock are high vocal harmony, carefree lyrics (mostly about beach parties and hot rods), Chuck Berry-like guitar riffs, and a strong drumbeat.

Sing "Surfin' U. S. A.," one of the Beach Boys' biggest hits.

CD 13–21
MIDI 20

Surfin' U.S.A.

Words by Brian Wilson

Music by Chuck Berry

1. If ev-'ry-bod-y had an o - cean __ a - cross the U. S. A., ____
2. We'll all be plan-nin' out a route _____ we're gon - na take real soon. __

Then ev-'ry-bod - y'd be surf - in' ____ like Cal - i - for - ni - a. ____
We're wax-in' down __ our surf - boards, _ we can't _ wait for June. __

You'd see them wear-in' their bag - gies, __ huar - a - chi san-dals too. ___
We'll all be gone for the sum - mer, __ we're on sa - fa - ri to stay. ___

A bush-y, bush-y blond hair - do. __ Surf-in' U. S. A. ____
Tell the teach-er we're surf - in', __ Surf-in' U. S. A. ____

Surf's Up

In addition to the Beach Boys, Jan and Dean were also known for their surf music. **Listen** to the duo's 1962 hit, *Surfin' Safari*.

CD 13–23
Surfin' Safari

by Mike Love and Brian Wilson as performed by Jan and Dean

Love and Wilson were members of the Beach Boys. Until their record companies objected, Jan and Dean and the Beach Boys often appeared on each others' recordings.

The Beach Boys ▶

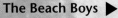

You'll catch 'em surf-in' at Del Mar, ___ Ven-tu-ra Coun-ty Line, ___
At Hag-gar-ty's __ and Swam-i's, ___ Pac-if-ic Pal-i - sades, _

San-ta Cruz and Tress - els, ___ Aus-tra-lia's Nar - a - bine. __
San O-no-fre and Sun - set, ___ Re-don-do Beach, L. A. ____

All o - ver Man - hat - tan, ___ and down Do-he - ny way. __
All o - ver La Jol - la, ____ at Wai - a - me-a Bay. ___

Ev-'ry-bod-y's gone surf - in', ___ Surf-in' U. S. A. ____
Ev-'ry-bod-y's gone surf - in', ___ Surf-in' U. S. A. ____

Latin Pop Is Hot!

Latin pop has been a part of U.S. popular music since the 1930s. In the 1960s, musicians such as Carlos Santana introduced the Latin style into rock music. The hot Latin sound can be heard in the music of Cuban-born Gloria Estefan, Selena (queen of *Tejano* music), Enrique Iglesias, and Ricky Martin, among others.

Latin pop is often filled with exciting rhythms, brass fills, and melodies that are fun to sing. Sing *"Riendo el río corre,"* a rhythmic song with Latin percussion and guitar. This song can also be performed with Drum Ensemble 4, on page 298.

Tito Puente

Gloria Estefan

Enrique Iglesias

Selena

Carlos Santana

Xavier Cugat

Riendo el río corre
(Run, Run, River)

English Words by Sue Ellen LaBelle *Words and Music by Tish Hinojosa*

REFRAIN

Co - rre, co - rre, __ co - rre el rí - o, __ Ri - en-do el rí - o __
Run, run, riv - er, __ Run, run, riv - er, With laugh-ter runs __ the __

Last time to Coda

co - rre. __ Co - rre, co - rre, __ co - rre el rí - o, __ Ri -
riv - er. __ Run, run, riv - er, __ Run, run, riv - er, __ With

VERSE

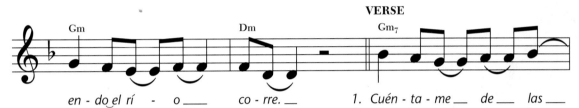

en - do el rí - o __ co - rre. __
laugh-ter runs __ the __ riv - er. __

1. Cuén - ta - me __ de __ las __
2. Sa - bes tú __ de __ la __
1. Tell a - bout __ the __ high __
2. Tell a - bout __ the __ great __

__ mon - ta - ñas __ de tu em - pe - zar, __
__ dis - tan - cia que pien - sas al - can - zar, __
__ moun - tains __ where your jour - ney be - gan, __
__ dis - tance you've gone to reach the __ sea, __

Cuén - ta - me __ de __ pie - dra y pe - na __
Co - mo sue - ño __ de __ la lu - na que
Tell a - bout __ the __ pla - ces __ you __
Whis - p'rings of __ your __ tra - vels __ seem

D.C. al Coda ✛ Coda

que lle - vas __ al __ mar. __ en - do el rí - o __ co - rre. __
me das para __ so - ñar. __ laugh-ter runs __ the __ riv-er. __
passed a - long __ the __ way. __
like a dream __ to __ me. __

Tish Hinojosa

Tish Hinojosa [ee-noh-HOH-sah] (born 1955), the composer of *"Riendo el rió corre,"* was born in San Antonio, Texas, the youngest of 13 children. Hinojosa grew up listening to and singing Mexican ballads and pop songs. She was also influenced by American rock, country, pop, and other Latin styles, including the rich *conjunto* musical tradition. As both a singer and guitarist, Hinojosa has maintained a strong connection with her Mexican American roots.

▲ Maracas

Latin Percussion

Percussion instruments used in Latin pop music include the *guiro*, claves, maracas, *timbales*, cowbell, and congas. **Listen** to the Latin percussion instruments in *Ayer* on page 266.

Conga Drum ▶

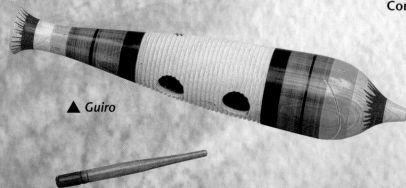

▲ *Guiro*

Latin Moves

Dancing to Latin music is hot! Many people take lessons to learn how to dance to Latin music. In the 1930s Xavier Cugat, known as the "King of the Rumba," helped popularize many Latin American dances such as the *cha-cha, rumba, tango,* and *samba.* Today, there are many modern styles of Latin dance.

Salsa Step

One of the most popular styles of Latin music and dance is *salsa,* which comes from Puerto Rico. Like the Spanish sauce that shares its name, *salsa's* rhythm and style are spicy.

Perform the *salsa* step to "*Riendo el río corre.*"

The *salsa* step ▶

CD-ROM Use *Band-in-a-Box* to create your own Latin pop song.

Latin Sounds

Latin music is sometimes influenced by a combination of musical styles. Two important styles found in Latin music are those of *salsa* and Cuban music.

Salsa, a well-known Latin sound, is a style that emerged in the 1940s. *Salsa* is energetic and vibrant. It uses syncopated bass rhythms, horn sections, and expanded percussion.

Cuban music's distinct sound features continuous eighth-note rhythms, percussion textures, guitar, vocal harmonies, and brass punctuation.

Listen to Gloria Estefan's performance of *Ayer.* It shows Cuban and *salsa* musical influences.

CD 14–1

Ayer

by Juanito R. Marquez
as performed by Gloria Estefan

Ayer (Yesterday) begins in the style of Cuban music. After the *accelerando,* the song takes on a *salsa* style.

Read and **play** the rhythms below on the conga and *timbale* drums. When you are ready, perform them with the recording.

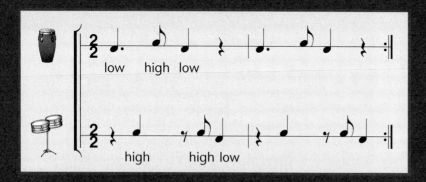

Take It to the Net Visit *www.sfsuccessnet.com* to discover more about Latin music.

266

Venezuela's Treasures

Venezuela is a country of mountains, forests, vast plains, mighty rivers, Caribbean beaches, and vibrant cities. It is a land rich in natural resources and rich in its musical heritage.

Among Venezuela's musical treasures is singer and songwriter Franco de Vita. He is internationally known for his music and vocal recordings. De Vita often writes in a contemporary pop style that combines pop and Latin musical elements.

Listen to de Vita's hit ballad, *Si tú no estás* (If You're Not Here). Which musical elements give the song its Latin character?

CD 14–2
Si tú no estás

written and performed by Franco de Vita

The Latin flavor of *Si tú no estás* comes from its blend of guitar, exciting rhythms, and a brass section.

MUSIC MAKERS

Franco de Vita

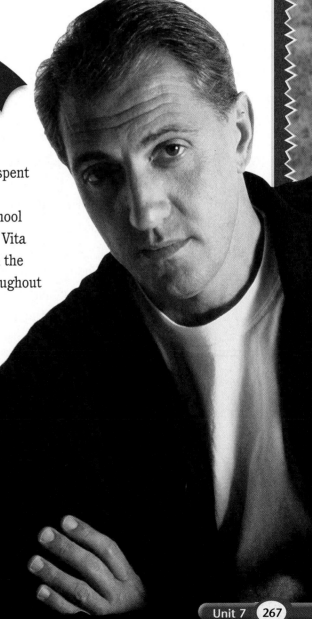

Franco de Vita (born 1954 in Caracas, Venezuela) spent his childhood in Italy but returned to Venezuela as a teenager. He began musical training after high school and studied formally at the Music Conservatory. De Vita first achieved success as a singer and songwriter in the 1980s. His albums have sold millions of copies throughout the world.

Franco de Vita achieved international fame when he wrote Ricky Martin's first single, *Vuelve* (Come Back). De Vita is also known for his songs and lyrics on social issues. His ballad *Lluvia* (Rain), was written about floods that took many lives in Venezuela. The *cuatro* and *tonado* rhythms in *Lluvia* are traditional in Venezuelan music (see page 332).

WORLD MUSIC

"World beat" is a musical style created by the merger of American pop styles and vocal and instrumental elements from Africa, Latin America, Australia, and other parts of the world.

Listen to *The Same*, a good example of "world beat" music. The rhythm patterns, which are influenced by African and Caribbean drumming, are accompanied by pop harmonies and instruments.

CD 14–3
The Same

by Youssou N'Dour and Habib Faye as performed by Youssou N'Dour

The lyrics of *The Same* tell how much of the world's music is "the same."

MUSIC MAKERS

YOUSSOU N'DOUR

Youssou N'Dour (born 1959) was born in Dakar, Senegal. As a child, he learned to sing from his mother, a *griot* (storyteller). N'Dour performs and tours with artists around the world and has collaborated with musicians such as Peter Gabriel and Paul Simon. He wrote the music for the World Cup Soccer anthem and his album *Eyes Open* received a Grammy nomination. N'Dour performs and writes music in a world music style.

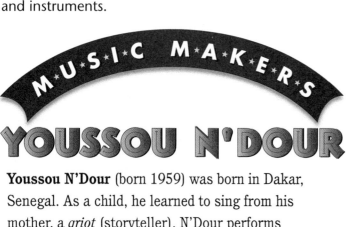

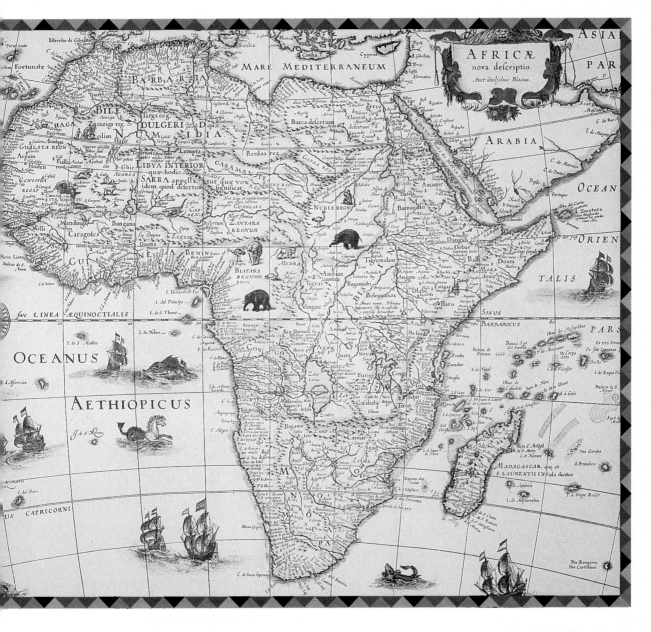

Go to the Source

African and aboriginal music are a source of ideas and inspiration to musicians, such as Herbie Hancock. **Listen** to a recording of the Ba-Benzélé pygmies.

CD 14–4

Hindewhu (whistle) solo

**Traditional pygmy voice and whistle solo
by the Ba-Benzélé pygmies**

This delightful combination of whistle and voice can give
you ideas about how to experiment with your own voice.

Pygmy Inspired Music

Listen to a classic jazz recording by Herbie Hancock that was inspired by the Ba-Benzélé pygmy vocal style on page 269. Hancock used this African inspiration to help create a new jazz style called fusion.

Burning Sky ▼

CD 14–5
Watermelon Man

written and performed by Herbie Hancock

Hancock uses a pygmy theme at the beginning and end of the piece. He builds typical African layered patterns that go with the theme.

Herbie Hancock
▶

Sky Sounds

Listen to the Native American group Burning Sky perform *Watchers of the Canyon*. The guitar, bass, flute, drums, rattles, and the African *djembe* drum are featured in this selection. **Identify** the musical instruments that sound Native American.

CD 14–6
Watchers of the Canyon

written and performed by Burning Sky

Burning Sky combines Native American, African, and popular influences to create a unique sound of Native American instrumental music.

◀ CoCo Lee

Afropop Meets Rap

Listen to CoCo Lee perform *Colours of the World*. This selection is in a typical world beat style. It features Afropop, hip-hop, DJ background, and an emcee rap.

CD 14–7
Colours of the World

**by Jing-Ran Zhu and Qui-Hong Her
as performed by CoCo Lee**

CoCo Lee sings with a big pop sound over a powerful rhythmic background. This sample of Afropop style shows a world music influence.

Aboriginal Sounds

Listen to the bird sounds in *Brolga*. The piece begins with a recording of the Aborigines on Elcho Island, north of Australia. The sound imitates the Brolga bird, crying as it beats its wings on the water of the sacred water hole.

▲ Aborigine playing a *didgeridoo*

CD 14–8
Brolga

**by Graham Wiggins, Mark Revell, and Ian Campbell
as performed by Dr. Didg and Outback**

Brolga uses traditional Australian Aboriginal instruments, including *didgeridoos* and clapping sticks.

Tune In

The *didgeridoo* is a long hollow tube played with the breath and vibrating lips in a fashion much like the tuba. Players use circular breathing (blowing out of the mouth while breathing in from the nose) to sustain long drone tones.

Welcome to World Drumming

There is an explosion of interest in "world drumming"—the drumming styles and music from around the world.

Listen to *Welcome to Our World* by Lebo M. This song combines choral and rhythmic styles of the African continent with contemporary pop style.

CD 14–9
Welcome to Our World

written and performed by Lebo M.

The lyrics of this song are in Zulu, Sethoso, Wolof, and English and are intended to "honor the people of the entire world."

Latin America

South America

Middle East

Africa

Say It with Drums

Popular music in Western countries is being influenced by the rich drumming traditions of African, Asian, and Latin cultures.

Asia

India

Japan

Indonesia

Life and Pride

Lebo M. uses elements of African and contemporary popular musical styles in *Rhythm of the Pride Lands,* an album inspired by *The Lion King.*

Sing "It's Time," from *Rhythm of the Pride Lands.*

CD 14–10

It's Time

Words and Music by Lebo M.,
John Van Tongeren, and Jay Rifkin

VERSE

1. The sun is shin - ing, The chil - dren laugh-ing, play - ing,
   They all re - mind me When I was a lit - tle girl,
2. Some-times I won - der Why peo - ple al - ways seem to
   Look out your win - dow, Be grate - ful for this day and

(To next stanza after each verse)

Full of dreams to find.
Full of life and pride.
turn a - round and lose their way.
make a change. It's o - kay.

They look so peace - ful,
To be so peace - ful, (My bro - ther, be hap - py.)

So sweet and grace - ful,
And to be hope - ful, (My sis - ter, cel - e - brate.)

They're all so hope - ful, And there is
It's sweet and grace - ful, (My bro - ther, be hap - py.)

274

no need for cry - ing, ___   No need for fight - ing. ___

REFRAIN

It's time.
(Oh, ___)   Let's cel-e-brate.   (Oh, ___)   Let's cel-e-brate.

(Oh, ___)   Let's cel-e-brate.   (Oh, ___)   Let's cel-e-brate.

A Rhythm Celebration

Learn to **play** one of the percussion parts below.
Then perform it with the refrain of "It's Time."

REFRAIN *(Play 4 times)*

Low Drum

Bell

High Drum

Drums Around the world

All over the world, people play drums of many different types. The materials the drums are made from depends on what is available locally. People living in a rainforest make large log drums because wood is plentiful. People in Alaska or northern Canada, where trees are scarce, make frame drums of bone or other nonwood materials.

Dholak [DO-lahk] A Chinese hour-glass-shaped, double-headed drum played with sticks. *Dholaks* are also played in Japan and Korea (below). ▼

Bodhrán [BO-rahn] An Irish wooden frame drum played with a small double-ended stick ▶

▲ **Kendang** [KEN-dang] An Indonesian barrel-shaped, double-headed drum. It plays a leading role in the gamelan ensemble.

276

Listen to the recording of *Drums from Around the World*. Some drums are played with hands; others are played with sticks.

This montage features the Japanese *taiko* drum, the Irish *bodhrán* drum, and the Ghanaian *sogo* drum.

◀ **Kpanlogo** [pahn-LOH-go] A barrel-shaped drum found among the Ga people of Ghana, West Africa

Tabla [TAH-blah] Principal drums used in the classical music of northern India. They are a relative of the Western orchestral timpani (kettledrums). ▼

Odaiko [oh-DIE-ko] drum One of several Japanese drums played in the tradition of *taiko* ▼

Say It with Drums

Get the Beat on West African Drumming

Drumming in West Africa often includes rattles and bells. It is usually done in groups sitting in a circle.

The circle is a symbol of equality. Within the circle you will find respect—for the drums, for each other, and for yourself.

▲ To play an open tone (called "high") on a conga-type drum, start by laying all of your fingers on the drum, as shown.

▲ To play a bass tone (called "low"), place your hand on the drum, as shown.

Echo Drumming

Play this drum pattern by following the leader.

Keep your hands relaxed and bounce off the drum head (one hand after the other) as if it were a hot stove. This may also feel a little like dribbling a basketball.

Question and Answer

Start this activity by speaking the questions and answers.

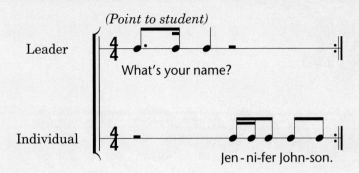

Leader *(Point to student)*

What's your name?

Individual

Jen - ni-fer John-son.

Now, speak and **play** the question and answer on your drum.

Try a different question, first by speaking, then by both speaking and playing the drum. When playing, bounce off the middle of the drum with the whole hand relaxed.

Leader *(Point to student)*

What's for din-ner?

Individual

Ham-bur-ger, French fries.

When you are ready, try **question-and-answer drumming** with drums only. As the leader plays the same question over and over, answer with any two-beat pattern.

Question-and-answer drumming is an African style of playing rhythms. A leader plays a phrase, which is answered by other phrases from the group.

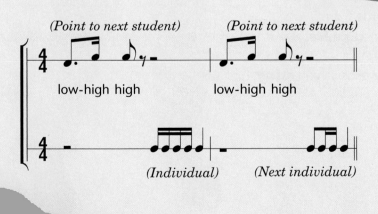

(Point to next student) *(Point to next student)*

low-high high   low-high high

(Individual)   *(Next individual)*

MUSICAL TEAMWORK

In West African drumming, the bell (sometimes called the *gankogui*) often plays a repeated pattern called the **time line.** The time line anchors the whole drum ensemble. A cowbell may be used to play the bell part.

A **time line** is an African rhythm in which a pattern repeats and becomes the main beat that holds the music together.

To play the bell, hold it in your weak hand. With your other hand, strike the edge of the opening with the side of a stick. ▶

Play this time line rhythm on the bell. If you have trouble keeping a steady beat, you might try saying "beat and-a beat and-a beat and-a beat . . . " and then play on the word "beat."

Bell

4/4

(play on edge)

Shake, Rattle, and Play!

The *shekere* [SHEH-keh-reh] is a gourd rattle from West Africa. Let's add the *shekere* to our ensemble.

The *shekere* plays this pattern. Say the words as you **play**.

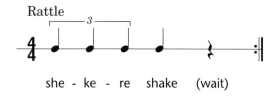

Rattle

4/4

she - ke - re   shake   (wait)

It Takes Teamwork!

Drum Ensemble 1 depends on teamwork. As you **analyze** the score, notice how each part complements the other layered parts. For example, the low drum plays on beats 1 and 2 while the high drum plays on beats 3 and 4—they fit together like a jigsaw puzzle.

Play and speak the low drum part. When this part is stable, bring in the high drum part.

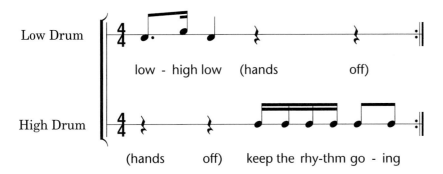

Drum Ensemble 1

Before you **play** Drum Ensemble 1, can you find a new part in the score and **describe** its rhythm?

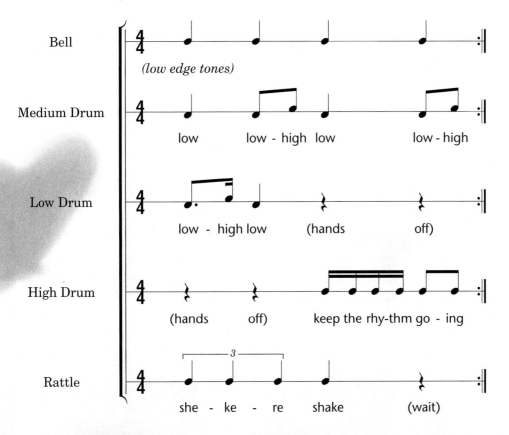

Play and Sing

Drum ensembles in West African countries such as Ghana, Sierra Leone, Ivory Coast, and Liberia are often combined with singing and dancing.

Sing "*Nana Kru*" while some members of the class **play** Drum Ensemble 1. Then, choose a rhythm part and play and sing at the same time. Which parts are the easiest to play while you sing?

CD 14–13

NANA KRU

Traditional Song from the Kou Tribe of Liberia (Adapted)

Na-na,   Na-na Kru,   Na-na,   Na-na, Na-na Kru,

Jump in - to my ca - noe,   Na-na,   you know that I love you.

A Beat of Your Own

To **create** your own drum piece, you will need four or five fellow musicians to play the following instruments.

- bell
- rattle
- two or three drums of different pitches

The bell starts by playing a time line. Then each of the other instruments makes up a part that is complementary. Add one part at a time, coming in only when the other parts are stable.

Listen to *Lost River*, performed by Mickey Hart of the Grateful Dead, along with percussionists and vocalists from all over this planet.

CD 14–15

Lost River

created and performed by Mickey Hart and the musicians of Planet Drum

Lost River uses the following instruments: *djembe, dundun,* drum set, *duggi tarang*, conch shell, cymbals, shakers, wood blocks, floor tom, metal percussion, and voices.

Describe the ways in which *Lost River* sounds like rock music. How has African and other world percussion become part of rock?

Native American DRUMMING

Traditional North American Indian drums come in many different shapes and sizes. These instruments are made from wood, animals, and other local materials.

Historically, the Iroquois Nation were hunters, gatherers, and farmers who lived in one place. The three "life-giving sisters"—corn, beans, and squash—were their primary food. Their longhouses were large structures where they sang, danced, and carried on the life of the community.

Iroquois Mask ►

◄ Iroquois Drum

▼ Iroquois Longhouse

Sounds of the Sioux

In contrast to the Iroquois, the Lakota Sioux were nomadic Great Plains buffalo hunters. Their teepees, made of hides and lodge poles, were easily taken down and transported. The large frame drums were easily carried from place to place.

Listen to the recordings from both the Iroquois and Sioux. What differences do you hear?

CD 14–16
Drums of the Iroquois and Sioux

This montage contains excerpts from the Iroquois *Fish Dance* and the Sioux *Rabbit Dance*.

◀ Lakota Teepee

▲ Lakota Drum

Say It with Drums

Tune In

The Iroquois tradition of one person speaking at a time was introduced to the U.S. Congress by Benjamin Franklin and Thomas Jefferson.

Navajo Celebration

The Navajo were originally nomadic hunters. They later settled in the Southwest and became sheepherders and farmers, somewhat like their neighbors, the Pueblos.

"*Yo-shi nai*" is a circle dance song that means "come and dance." It is a public part of the Navajo Enemy Way, a ceremony honoring the return of Navajo warriors. **Sing** "*Yo-shi nai*." Which part of the melody repeats?

CD 14–17

YO·SHI NAI

Navajo Dance Song

Yo - shi nai, yo - shi nai, yo - shi nai, yo - shi nai,

'e ye _____ ha na, 'a we ya _____ he, 'a

we ya he ye _____ ha na, 'a we ya _____ he.

 **Listen** to another example of traditional Navajo music.

CD 14–19
Jo'ashila

Traditional Navajo Dance Song as performed by Marilyn Hood

Today, Native Americans throughout the country sing and play a wide variety of music that includes styles such as rock, country, and contemporary, in addition to the traditional style above.

▲ Hogan [ho-GAHN], a traditional Navajo dwelling

Marilyn Hood

Marilyn Hood, a Navajo singer, dancer, and painter, was born in Arizona and now lives in a traditional hogan outside Gallup, New Mexico. Hood lives with her four children, teaching them the traditional songs she learned as a child. She feels deeply that the old ways should be honored.

Join the Dance!

The traditional circle dance, called the "round" dance, can be performed to "*Yo-shi nai.*" It is performed "sunwise" (clockwise, to the left), moving to the left with a sideways movement.

◀ Young Navajo dancer

Say It with Drums

RHYTHMS FROM WEST AFRICA

Drum ensembles from West African countries like Ghana play for dancing, singing, and other ceremonies.

Follow the Leader

You learned question-and-answer drumming in Lesson 1. In the next level of playing, the leader plays the question, followed by an individual answer. Then the leader plays the question again, followed by everyone in the group playing an echo.

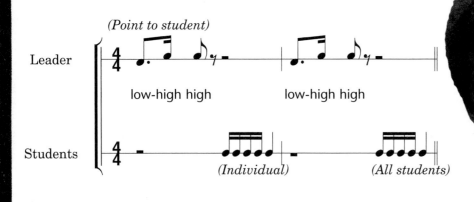

Leader *(Point to student)*

low-high high   low-high high

Students   *(Individual)*   *(All students)*

Tune In

In many West African countries, special drums are made for use on ceremonial occasions when a king or chief is present. This is similar to "Hail to the Chief," which is played for the President of the United States.

288

The Gankogui

Double bells are called by different names in West Africa. Among the Ga people of the city of Accra, capital of Ghana, the name is *gankogui* [gahn-KOH-gwee]. The Caribbean relative of the *gankogui* is the smaller, higher-sounding *agogo* bell.

Drum Ensemble 2

Play Drum Ensemble 2 by adding one part after the other.

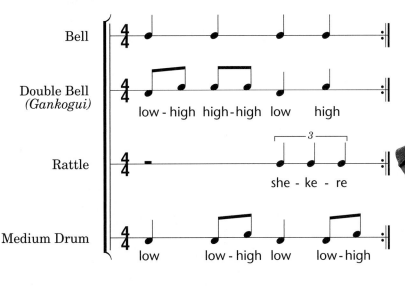

Drum Ensemble 2 uses drum, bell, and rattle patterns. Which parts are the same as in Drum Ensemble 1, on page 281?

If you compare the double bell and the *shekere* (rattle) parts, you will see that they complement each other. When the *shekere* plays, the double bell is less busy.

A Fishing Song

The words of the song "*Kelo aba w'ye*," from the Ga people of Ghana, mean "bring us fish to eat." When you have learned to **sing** it, **perform** it with Drum Ensemble 2.

KELO ABA W'YE

Traditional Song from Ghana

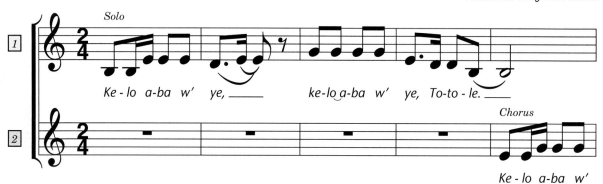

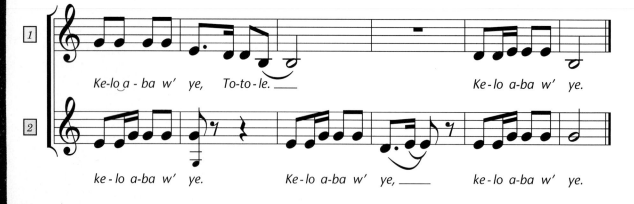

Listen to the Pros

Listen to *Obokete*, traditional royal music from Ghana.

Focus on these features.

- the time line played by the bells (Does it stay the same throughout?)
- different drum parts (How many different drum parts do you hear?)
- the interaction of the drum parts

CD 14–21
Obokete

**traditional royal music from Ghana
as performed by Sowah Mensah**

This recording illustrates drum ensembles, which are an important part of West African culture.

Sowah Mensah

Sowah Mensah is a composer, arranger, ethnomusicologist, and a master drummer from Ghana. He is on the music faculty both of Macalester College and the University of St. Thomas in St. Paul, Minnesota. His compositions have been performed by the Minnesota Orchestra. Mensah enjoys performing throughout North and South America and conducting workshops throughout the United States.

Enjoy a Little Harmony

Sing "Take Time in Life," from Liberia. It can also be **performed** with Drum Ensemble 2.

CD 14–22

TAKE TIME IN LIFE

Folk Song from Liberia

I was pass-ing by, My broth-er called to me, And he said to me you bet-ter
sis - ter she

take time in life. (Bet-ter) take time in life, (Bet-ter) take time in life, (Bet-ter)

take time in life ('cause you got) far way to go. (Bet - ter) far way to go.

For variety, **perform** the chorus parts of "Take Time in Life" in harmony.

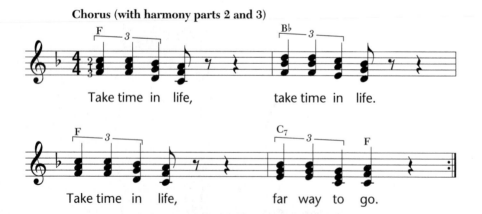

Chorus (with harmony parts 2 and 3)

Take time in life, take time in life.

Take time in life, far way to go.

Play Those Patterns

Show that you understand how African drum ensembles use complementary layered patterns by forming small ensembles of four players (two bells, two drums, one rattle); then **create** and **play** your own rhythms, using the following routine.

- The first bell player starts with a time line. The *gankogui* player enters with a short pattern that repeats many times.

- The rattle player then adds a complementary pattern that fits with the bell.

- The drummers then add complementary parts.

- **Play** your ensemble for the class or record it.

- If time permits, switch instruments and **create** another ensemble.

A TASTE OF THE HIGHLIFE

Highlife music is very popular in cities throughout the continent of Africa.

"*Banuwa*," from Liberia, can be sung with the highlife drumming on the next page.

Highlife combines traditional West African style and jazz. Instruments often include saxophones, brass, electric guitars, and percussion.

CD 15–1
MIDI 21

BANUWA

Folk Song from Liberia

Ba - nu - wa, ba - nu - wa, ba - nu - wa yo. ____

Ba - nu - wa, ba - nu - wa, ba - nu - wa yo. ____

Ba - nu - wa, ba - nu - wa, ba - nu - wa yo. ____ (A-)

(2nd time only)

la - no, neh - ni a - la - no.   A - la - no.   A-

la - no, neh - ni a - la - no.   A - la - no.

Drum Ensemble 3 (Highlife)

Practice Drum Ensemble 3 by first learning to **play** the rattle (*shekere*) part. Then add the bell and drum parts.

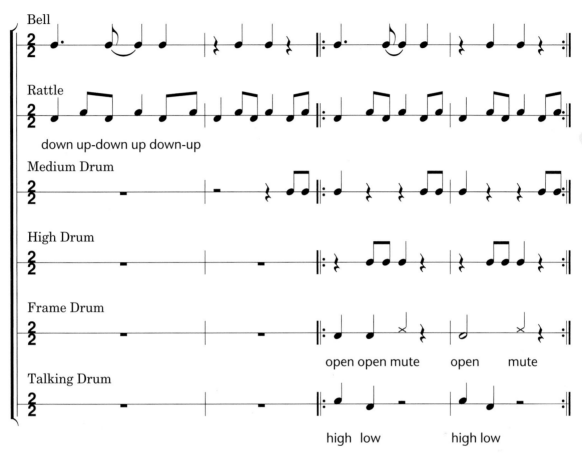

down up-down up down-up

open open mute   open   mute

high low   high low

Give a Hand for Highlife

"Everybody Loves Saturday Night," on page 296, is popular throughout West Africa. **Sing** it with highlife Drum Ensemble 3.

Perform the movements below with Drum Ensemble 3 or *Kpanlogo for 2* on page 296.

• Stand in a circle.

• Keep your left palm up and right palm down; match that up with each person next to you. Clap your neighbor's hands once.

• Turn your hands over and clap again.

• Clap your own hands twice in front.

Repeat this pattern.

Highlife band

EVERYBODY LOVES SATURDAY NIGHT

Folk Song from West Africa

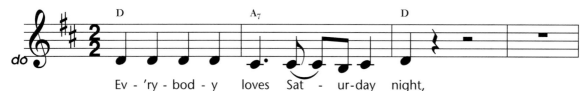

Ev - 'ry - bod - y   loves   Sat - ur - day   night,

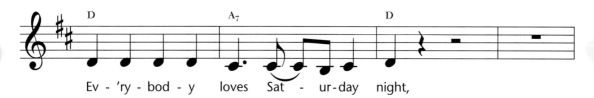

Ev - 'ry - bod - y   loves   Sat - ur - day   night,

Ev-'ry-bod - y,   ev-'ry-bod - y,   ev-'ry-bod - y,   ev-'ry-bod - y,

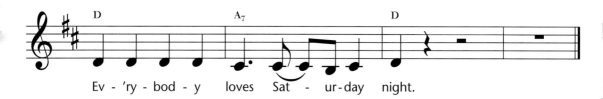

Ev - 'ry - bod - y   loves   Sat - ur - day   night.

Put On Your Listening Cap

Listen to the rhythm of *Kpanlogo for 2*, a social dance of the Ga people. It is similar to highlife.

created and performed by Sowah Mensah
Kpanlogo is the Ghanaian term for highlife.

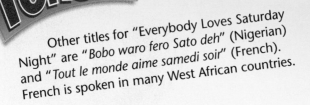

Other titles for "Everybody Loves Saturday Night" are "Bobo waro fero Sato deh" (Nigerian) and "Tout le monde aime samedi soir" (French). French is spoken in many West African countries.

Everybody Loves a *Samba*

Listen to *Evening Samba* as you follow the listening map. Notice how similar this South American *samba* is to the African highlife style.

CD 15–8

Evening Samba

created and performed by Mickey Hart and the musicians of Planet Drum

Many of the world's greatest drummers joined together to make this recording. Performers include Airto Moreira, Babatunde Olatunji, Sikiru Adepoju, Zakir Hussain, and T. H. Vinayakram.

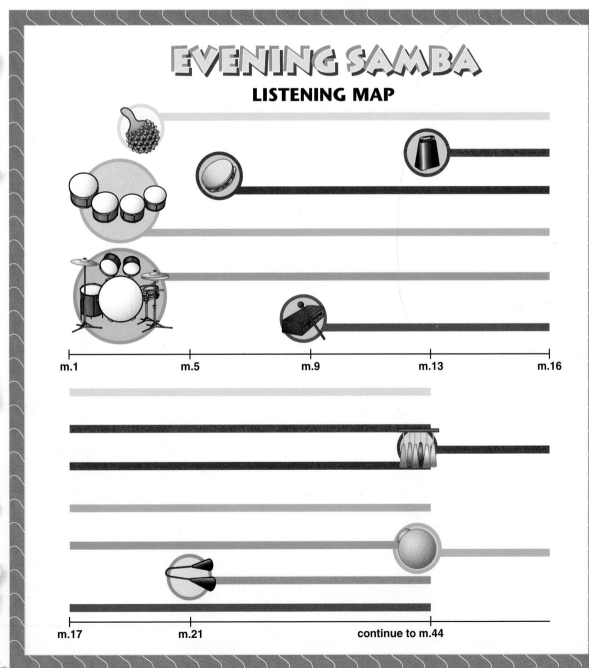

Say It with Drums

CARIBBEAN Connections

The drum ensembles in the Caribbean islands have been influenced by West African and European music. Drum Ensemble 4 feels a lot like West African highlife.

Practice each part. Then **play** as an ensemble, adding one part at a time.

Drum Ensemble 4 (Latin American 2-beat)

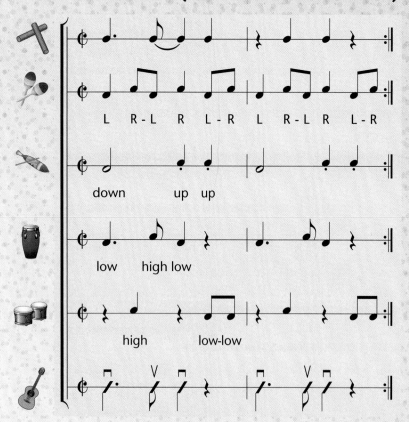

 Video Library Watch the video *Steel Drums* to learn more about steel drums from the Caribbean.

Drums of Steel

The sound of steel drums is unique and recognized by most people as coming from the Caribbean. Steel drums are made from empty oil drums with tops that are shaped to produce musical pitches. Striking a specific area of the drum with a mallet produces a musical note with a timbre that is distinctly "steel drum."

Listen to this steel drum excerpt and the unique sound of this drum.

CD 15–9
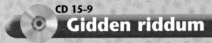
Gidden riddum

by Emile Borde
as performed by the Trinidad Tripoli Steel Band
The music of this steel drum ensemble includes elements of soca, calypso, and reggae styles.

Tune In

The steel drum was developed in Trinidad in the 1930s. There are numerous sizes of steel drums, ranging from bass to tenor.

Sounds of the Caribbean

Sing "Water Come a Me Eye," a calypso song from the
Caribbean island of Trinidad. Then perform it with
Drum Ensemble 4.

CD 15–10

Water Come a Me Eye

Folk Song from Trinidad

VERSE

Call
C

Response
G₇   C

1. Ev-'ry time_ I re-mem-ber Li-za, Wa-ter come_ a me eye,
2. I still wait-in' at home for Li-za,

Call
C

Response
G₇   C

Ev-'ry time_ I think of Li-za, Wa-ter come_ a me eye.
Heart is sore_ but wait-in', Li-za,

REFRAIN

Call
C

Response
G₇   C

Come back, Li-za, come back, gal, Wa-ter come_ a me eye,

Call
C

Response
G₇   C

Come back Li-za, come back, gal, Wa-ter come_ a me eye.

Sing "*Má Teodora.*" In the song, *chopping up the firewood* refers to dancing.

Play Drum Ensemble 4 to accompany "*Má Teodora.*"

CD 15–12

Má Teodora

Folk Song from Cuba

¿Dón - de es - tá la Má Teo - do - ra?
Where, oh where is Ma Teo - do - ra?

Ra - jan - do la ___ le-ña es -
She's chop-ping up ___ the fire -

tá. ¿Con su pa - lo y su ban - do - la?
wood. With her staff and her ban - do - la?

Ra - jan - do la ___ le-ña es -
She's chop-ping up ___ the fire -

tá. ¿Dón-de es - tá que no la ve - o?
wood. Where is Ma - ma, I don't see her?

Ra - jan - do la ___ le-ña es -
She's chop-ping up ___ the fire -

tá. Ra - jan - do la ___ le - ña es - tá. Ra -
wood. She's chop - ping up ___ the fire - wood. She's

jan - do la ___ le - ña es - tá.
chop - ping up ___ the fire - wood.

Say It with Drums

Asian Drums

The music of Japan and Okinawa uses two different pentatonic (five-tone) scales—one that comes from China and one that originates in Japan. **Sing** *"Asadoya."* Which of these two scales is used in the song? **Listen** to the *koto* in the Sound Bank. How can you identify it on the recording?

Chinese

Japanese

Arts Connection

Bridge Across the Moon (artist unknown). Japanese gardening, poetry, and art are sometimes expressed in miniature. Examples include bonsai trees, haiku poetry, and the miniature brush strokes in fine paintings. ▼

Asadoya

English Words by D. G. Britton

Folk Song from Okinawa

あ　あ　さどゅや＿　ぬ＿　く＿や＿ま　に＿
A　A-sa-do-ya＿ nu＿ Ku-ya-ma ni＿
Ah,　House of A-sa-do - ya,＿ Why are you so dear to＿

よ　さ　ゆ　い　ゆ　い　　あ　ん　ちゅ　ら＿＿　さ
yo　sa　yu-i　yu-i,　A-n chu-ra＿ sa
me?　Sa　yu-i　yu-i,　'Tis where Ku-ya　-　ma

な＿　う　ま　り　ば　し＿　お　ま　た　は＿　り　ぬ
na＿ u-ma-ri ba-shi-o. Ma-ta ha-ri-nu
first the light of day＿ did＿ see. And she was my love, my

ちん　だ　ら　か　ぬしゃ　ま　よ＿＿＿＿＿
chin-da-ra, ka-nu-sya-ma yo.＿＿＿＿
dar - ling, and all the world to me.＿＿＿＿

CD 15–17

Martial Drumming

Taiko is a popular and dramatic form of Japanese drumming that relates to martial arts. The drums are played with large dowel-like sticks.

Listen to this example of *taiko* drumming, performed by an ensemble from the Japanese island of Sado.

CD 15–21

Lion

created and performed by Leonard Eto and the Kodo Drummers

Kodo has two meanings: "heartbeat" and "children of the drum." Why, do you think, did the performers choose this name for their ensemble?

Indian Rhythms

In northern India, drummers play a set of drums called *tabla*. Southern Indian drummers play the *mridangam,* a double-headed drum. Drummers from both traditions first learn drum patterns vocally. They use syllables, such as "ta-tika-doom." (See the Sound Bank for more information on the Indian instruments in this lesson.)

Indian Ensembles—North

A typical classical music ensemble from northern India is comprised of the *sitar,* the *tamboura,* and the *tabla.*

Listen to this excerpt, featuring Ravi Shankar, one of the most famous sitar players in the world.

CD 15–22
Máru-bihág

**Traditional Indian Raga
as performed by Ravi Shankar**

Máru-bihág begins with a short, non-rhythmic section played by *sitar* and *tamboura.* This is followed by a longer, rhythmic section in which the *tabla* joins in.

Tune In

The *tamboura* plays sustained tones (drones) using the intervals of the octave and the fifth in the natural harmonic series.

Tabla from northern India ▶

304

Indian Ensembles—South

Classical music ensembles from South India often feature the *veena*—a large, fretted, plucked, string instrument. Other traditional South Indian instruments include the *mridangam, tamboura,* flute, and violin.

Listen to this selection played by a South Indian ensemble. Which instruments do you hear?

CD 15–23
Maha ganapathim

by Muthuswami Dikshitar
as perfomed by Shrimati Rejeswari Pariti and Shri Vadiraja Bhat

Shrimati Rajeswari Pariti, an accomplished *vainika* (*veena* player), performs *carnatic* music—classical music of South India. The *veena,* one of the oldest instruments in the world, dates back to 500 B.C.

Dancing with Sticks

The *raas* is a stick dance from India that is performed during festivals.

Perform the movements of the Indian Stick Dance to the music *Dham dhamak dham samelu.* Be very careful when moving your sticks.

As you move, count in meter in 4 and play each tap on the strong beat—half note.

▲ *Mridangam* drum from South India

CD 15–24
Dham dhamak dham samelu

Stick Dance from the Gujarati Region of India
The Stick Dance is often performed continuously with many songs accompanying it.

Stick Dance

1. "Tap Right"—Move your sticks to the right side of your body. Tap your own sticks together.

2. "Tap Partner Right"—Move your sticks to the center, keeping your sticks parallel to the right. Tap your partner's sticks.

3. "Tap Partner Left"—Keeping your sticks in front of you, "pivot" your sticks to the left (keeping your sticks parallel). Tap your partner's sticks.

4. "Tap Right"—Move your sticks to the right side of your body (as in step 1). Tap your own sticks together.

5. "Tap Single Stick"—Move only your right stick to the center. Tap your partner's stick. Turn.

Say It with Drums

Shades of the Middle East

The Middle East is filled with wonderful culture, traditions, and music. Middle Eastern folk dances are an important part of the region's culture. Songs often have rhythms and melodies that let you both sing and dance to them. *"Alumot"* is one such song.

Sing *"Alumot,"* an Israeli song that celebrates the harvest.

CD 15–26

Alumot
(Sheaves of Grain)

English Words by Sue Ellen LaBelle

Harvest Song from Israel

Ye - la - dim _____ na - gi - la ve - na - sov bim - cho - lot!
Har - vest time has _ come! We'll cir - cle round and dance. Let's re - joice!

Shi - bo - lim _____ hiv - shi - lu. Ne' e - sof a - lu - mot!
Sheaves of wheat are _ ripe, We'll sing a song of joy. Raise your voice!

A - lu - mot shel za - hav, ha - sa - deh ra - chav, ra - chav.
Gold - en sheaves, grain and leaves, We will be the gath - er - ers,

Ba - sa - deh u - va - nir, shi - ru ze - mer la - ka - tsir!
In the field, land's great yield, Let's sing to the har - vest - ers!

An Israeli Hora

The *hora* was a popular Romanian dance that came to Israel in the early twentieth century with Romanian settlers. At that time, the land was called Palestine. Israel later became a nation in 1948. The word *hora* means "circle dance."

The *hora* is danced in a closed circle with your hands joined with your neighbors' hands at your side. It can also be danced with your hands on your neighbors' shoulders. In Israel, the traditional *hora* moves to the left (clockwise). The steps are high and energetic, with leaps and kicks. The movements are similar to those of the Arabic *debke*, which moves to the right.

The basic Israeli *hora* movement is: Step L, step R, step L, lift R, step R, lift L.

Perform the Israeli *hora* to the music of "*Alumot.*"

Israeli *hora* dancers ▼

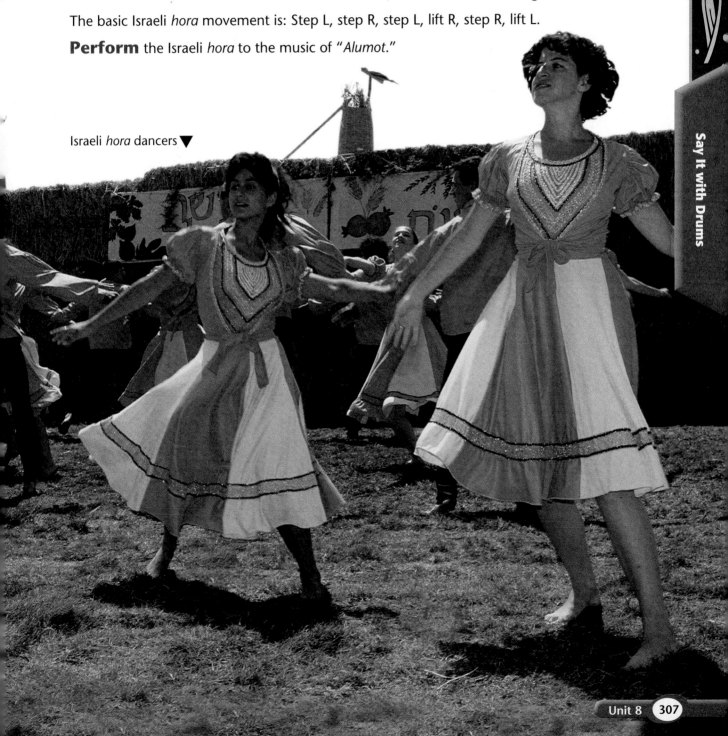

A Palestinian Debke Dance

Sing "*Al yadee*," a Palestinian dance song (*debke*). Afterwards,
learn and **play** the *dombak* rhythm below while you sing the song.

CD 15–32

Al yadee

Words Adapted by Sally Monsour

Ancient Arabic Chant

1. Al ya - dee, ya - dee, ya - dee; ___ Come and take a walk with me;
2. Al ya - dee, ya - dee, ya - dee; ___ Come and take a walk with me;

In the mead-ow we shall see; ___ Birds are fly - ing, fly - ing ___ free.
To the val - ley, near the sea; ___ We will al - ways hap - py ___ be.

Al ya - dee, ya - dee, ya - dee; ___ Come and take a walk with _ me.
Al ya - dee, ya - dee, ya - dee; ___ Come and take a walk with _ me.

Dombak [DOM-bak] A Middle
Eastern goblet-shaped drum; it
has a deep bass and sharp
high tones ▶

Debke Movement

The *debke* (sometimes called *debky*) is one of the most common dances of the Arabic people who live in Lebanon, Jordan, and Syria and of the Palestinian people. *Debke* means "line dance," and traditional *debke* are often done in short lines. Although similar to the Israeli *hora*, the *debke* steps are sharp and powerful and have more up and down stamps and knee movements.

The basic Arabic *debke* is performed moving to the right, hands down at your sides and joined with neighbors' hands. The steps are: Step R, step L, step R, stamp L, step L, stamp R.

The same dance pattern can be found in eastern European and Asian countries. In Bulgaria, it is called *horo*; in Hungary, *kor*; in Serbia and Croatia, *kolo*; in Macedonia, *oro*; and in Greece, *choros*.

Arab *debke* dancers ▼

Listen to this recording of a *dombak* being played with a violin, tambourine, and a Turkish instrument called the *oud* (similar to a lute).

CD 15–36
Yemeni baglamis telli basina

**Traditional Turkish Dance
as performed by Farabi**

The *dombak* has a rich bass tone ("dom") when played in the middle of the drumhead, and a high, sharp tone ("bak") when played near the edge of the drumhead.

African Influences

West Africans were transported as slaves to all parts of the Western Hemisphere. Their drumming and music followed them and survived. Drum Ensemble 5 is an example of African-inspired rhythm. It is from the island of Bequia (beh-kwee) in the Caribbean.

Drum Ensemble 5

Play each part separately. Then put them all together.

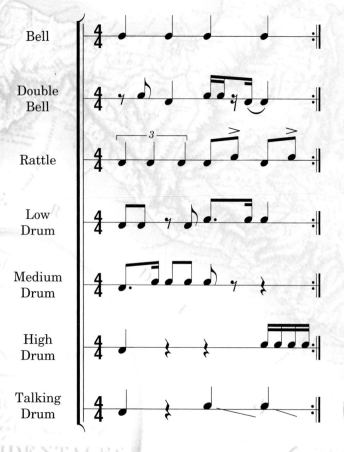

Sing for Freedom

Sing "By the Waters of Babylon." Then **perform** it with Drum Ensemble 5.

CD 16–1

BY THE WATERS OF BABYLON

Words from Psalm 137

Caribbean Folk Song

(Add harmony part on D.C. only)

By the wa-ters of Bab - y - lon, Where we sat down,

And there we wept when we re-mem-bered Zi - on.

But the wick - ed car-ry us a-way cap-tiv - i - ty, Re -

quire of us a song. ___ How can you sing the Lord's _

___ own song ___ in a strange land?

MARTINIQUE

GRENADA BASIN

ST. LUCIA

ST. VINCENT AND THE GRENADINES

BEQUIA

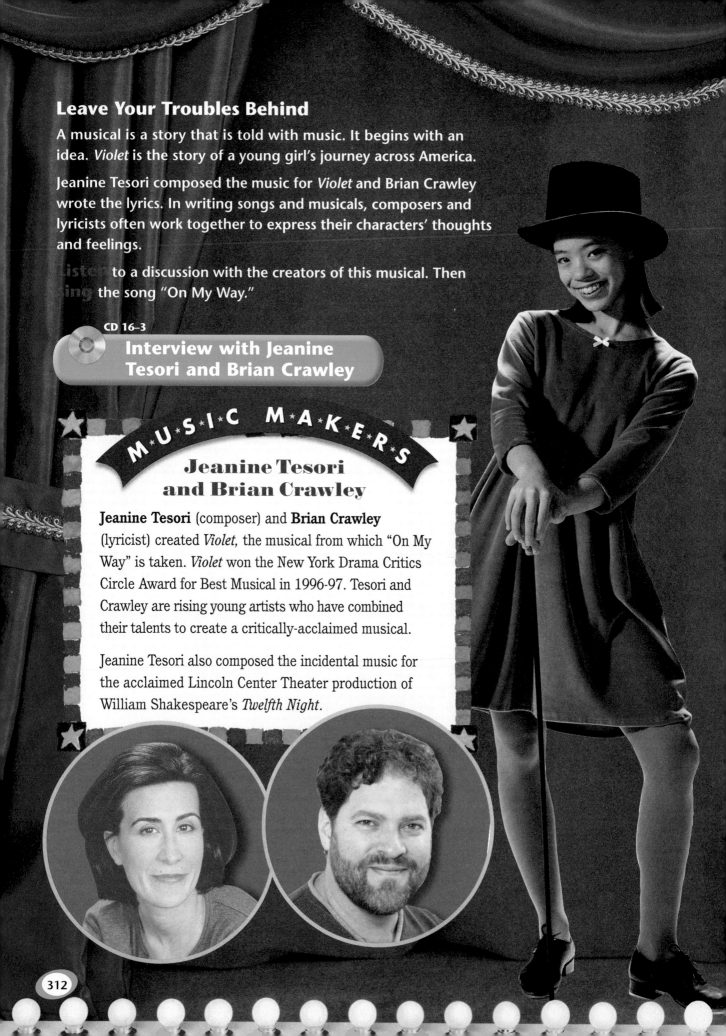

Leave Your Troubles Behind

A musical is a story that is told with music. It begins with an idea. *Violet* is the story of a young girl's journey across America.

Jeanine Tesori composed the music for *Violet* and Brian Crawley wrote the lyrics. In writing songs and musicals, composers and lyricists often work together to express their characters' thoughts and feelings.

Listen to a discussion with the creators of this musical. Then sing the song "On My Way."

CD 16–3

Interview with Jeanine Tesori and Brian Crawley

M·U·S·I·C M·A·K·E·R·S

Jeanine Tesori and Brian Crawley

Jeanine Tesori (composer) and Brian Crawley (lyricist) created *Violet*, the musical from which "On My Way" is taken. *Violet* won the New York Drama Critics Circle Award for Best Musical in 1996-97. Tesori and Crawley are rising young artists who have combined their talents to create a critically-acclaimed musical.

Jeanine Tesori also composed the incidental music for the acclaimed Lincoln Center Theater production of William Shakespeare's *Twelfth Night*.

BE A STAR!

A stage can be anywhere people choose to perform—on Broadway, in film, in concert halls, on music videos, in your own home.

CD 16–4

On My Way

(from *Violet*)

Words by Brian Crawley

Music by Jeanine Tesori
Arranged by Michael Rafter

Be - fore an - oth - er sun - rise ___ wakes me, Be -

fore an - oth - er night is ___ gone, I'll

find out where this high - way ___ takes me, ___ You

know I've got to trav - el ___ on.

A Melody for a King

The Lion King is an original story created by the artists and writers at the Walt Disney Studios. The animated film *The Lion King* became a box office hit and was later adapted for the Broadway stage.

As you experience some of the music of *The Lion King*, keep in mind the story of Simba, the young lion cub, who struggles to return to his rightful place as king of the lions.

Listen to *The Circle of Life*. How does the accompaniment let you know this story takes place in Africa?

CD 16–6
The Circle of Life

by Elton John and Tim Rice
The rhythmic accompaniment and melodic chant are examples of African musical styles used throughout *The Lion King*.

Rhythms and Influences of Africa

African music is known for its complex drumming rhythms, melodies and chants, and performing styles such as call and response. In *The Circle of Life*, you can hear some of these elements and how they influence the character of the music.

Here is a playing activity that can accompany this listening.

Practice and then **play** these rhythms with *The Circle of Life.*

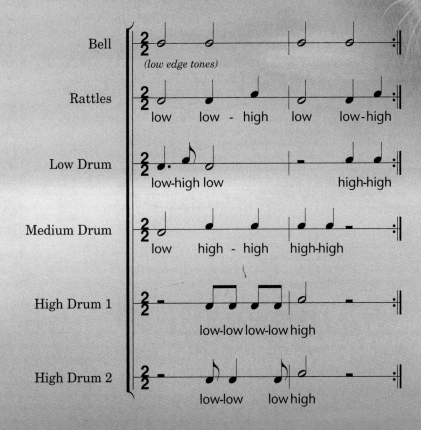

Be a Star!

The African Heritage

When Africans came to America, they brought their musical traditions, songs, and rhythms with them. Thus, the heritage of the music of the African people can be found in African American music as well.

Sing this traditional African American song. As you sing, conduct a two-beat pattern and **listen** to the African-style rhythms that accompany "There Is Love Somewhere."

There is Love Somewhere

Traditional African American Song

CD 16–7

1. There is love _____ some - where, _____ There is love _____ some - where. _____ I'm gon-na reach __ out _____ 'til I find some. _____ There is love _____ some - where. _____

2. There is hope . . .
3. There is joy . . .
4. There is peace . . .

Play the rhythms on page 317. Determine if these rhythms will work with "There Is Love Somewhere." **Analyze** the lyrics and choose which rhythms you will play for each verse. When you are ready, **perform** your accompaniment as the class sings.

Pride Land Rhythms

Performer, singer, and songwriter Lebo M. recorded the album *Rhythm of the Pride Lands,* which contains songs inspired by the music of *The Lion King.*

Listen to *It's Time,* as performed by Lebo M. and an African chorus. The call and response between Lebo M.'s solo and the chorus is just one of many African musical elements.

CD 16–9
It's Time

**from *Rhythm of the Pride Lands*
by Lebo M., John Van Tongeren, and Jay Rifkin
as performed by Lebo M. and chorus**

The positive message of *It's Time* is emphasized by the joyful lyrics and singing of the African chorus.

M·U·S·I·C M·A·K·E·R·S
David "Dakota" Sanchez

Dakota Sanchez (born 1986) played the part of Young Simba in the Broadway production of *The Lion King.* He made his Broadway debut in this musical when he was in seventh grade. Sanchez loves to sing. While in elementary school, the future Broadway performer sang in the school chorus and for school assemblies and celebrations. Sanchez currently attends the Professional Performing Arts School in New York City. He lives in New York with his mother and father and his siblings, Raquel and Nicolas. In his free time, he loves to read science fiction. His ambition is to be a scientist.

Listen to Dakota Sanchez talk about his musical career and his experience with *The Lion King.*

CD 16–10
Interview with David "Dakota" Sanchez

Be a Star!

The Best of 'Dancin' Feet

Dance is often prominent in musicals. Some dancing, such as ballet and tap, requires special shoes. Tap dancing is the most important element in the Broadway show *Bring In Da Noise, Bring In Da Funk*. The show traces the history of tap dancing through many different places and styles.

Perform this chant from *Bring In Da Noise, Bring In Da Funk*.

CD 16–11

Now That's Tap

*Words and Music by
Ann Duquesnay, Daryl Waters, and Zane Zacharoff*

Give em' __ flash, __ Give em' __ style __ and a great big big big

big big _ smile, _ Now that's tap! Make sure your tux is

fit - tin' __ right. __ Be pre - pared _ ta' wing all __ night _ and those

pearl - y whites, _ moon - beam _ bright, _ Now that's tap!

Be a Star!

Dance— a Body Language

Have you ever tried to communicate without using your voice? How would you use body gestures to tell a friend to come and sit by you or to tell a friend goodbye?

In ballet, dancers use gestures and movement to communicate stories. Their movements are very carefully choreographed.

The Ballet Scene

Ballet uses elaborate scenery, costumes, and special music. A composer writes the music, and a choreographer determines how the dancers will move.

Tune In

Did you know that some football players study ballet to help with flexibility and agility?

◀ *Ballet Rehearsal on Set.* Look at this famous painting of ballet dancers by the French artist Edgar Degas [deh-GAH] (1834–1917). How are the ballet dancers portrayed?

M·U·S·I·C M·A·K·E·R·S

George Balanchine

George Balanchine [BAL-an-sheen] (1904–1983) was one of the world's greatest choreographers. He arrived in the United States from Russia in 1933 to open the School of American Ballet. Balanchine also choreographed musicals, making dance an important part of the story. In the late 1940s, Balanchine founded the New York City Ballet. Under his direction the company became world famous. Balanchine's choreography for *The Nutcracker* has been performed by ballet companies all over the world.

Be a Star!

A Holiday Ballet

The Nutcracker is one of the most popular ballets of all time.

The story begins when Marie, a young girl, receives a nutcracker carved in the shape of a little man. When her brother and his friends break it playing roughly, Marie becomes upset. Later that night Marie dreams that the nutcracker comes to life as a gallant soldier. The soldier goes to battle with the king of a gang of mice. When the Mouse King dies, the nutcracker becomes a prince. The prince escorts Marie on a wonderful journey. Eventually they go to a dance where many kinds of sweets, toys, and even flowers dance in their honor.

MUSIC MAKERS

Piotr Ilyich Tchaikovsky

Piotr Ilyich Tchaikovsky [chy-KOHF-skee] (1840–1893) was born in Russia and learned to play the piano as a young child. Before becoming a musician, he worked as a lawyer. Tchaikovsky loved the outdoors and took long walks daily. It is said that many of his beautiful melodies came to him while he was walking through the woods and fields near his home.

A Nutcracker Map

Look at the listening map as you **listen** to "Waltz of the Flowers" from *The Nutcracker.* Follow the map and determine the form as you listen.

CD 16–13
Waltz of the Flowers

from *The Nutcracker*
by Piotr Ilyich Tchaikovsky

The Nutcracker is very popular at holiday time, due to its setting and colorful characters.

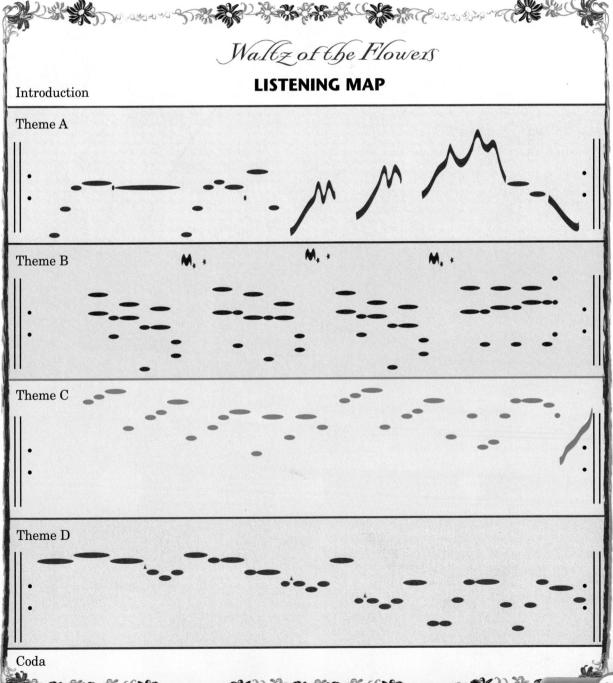

Waltz of the Flowers

LISTENING MAP

Introduction

Theme A

Theme B

Theme C

Theme D

Coda

Dance, Irish Style

Not all stage dance is ballet. Some dancers perform traditional dances of their native country.

Lord of the Dance and *Riverdance* are two shows that celebrate the very best of Irish dancing.

Listen to this medley from *Lord of the Dance.* Identify the sections in which the rhythms are suitable for fast dancing.

CD 16–14

Lord of the Dance Medley

by Ron Hardiman
as performed by Doug Cameron
Doug Cameron performs this special arrangement of *Lord of the Dance* on a Stradivarius violin valued at more than two million dollars.

Irish dancers often compete in dance contests. Every performer in *Lord of the Dance* and *Riverdance* is a dance champion. Some of the characteristics of Irish dancing are:

- Keep your torso very upright.
- Put your arms and hands straight down at your sides. (Hands may also be placed on hips.)
- Point your toes and take small, sharp steps and kicks.

CD 16–15

Paddy Whack

Traditional Irish Jig

Paddy Whack features traditional Irish instruments, including the Celtic harp.

▲ Michael Flatley and dancers in *Lord of the Dance*

Tune In

Riverdance began as a seven-minute TV appearance in 1994 and has grown to a two-hour musical show that is seen all over the world.

"STOMP" Rhythms

Stomp is a musical that uses brooms, trash cans, automobile parts, and other non-conventional instruments. Here is a theater piece called "Sha Sha Sha," similar to one performed in *Stomp*. **Read** the score and then **perform** the piece. Afterwards, **listen** to a selection from *Stomp*.

CD 16–17
Trash Can Stomp

from the musical *Stomp*

The performers use trash cans to produce interesting rhythms and textures.

CD 16–18

Sha Sha Sha

Music by Edward Pearsall

Paint Brush	
Whisk Broom	slap end of table
Broom	strike end of broom bristles on floor
Push Broom	

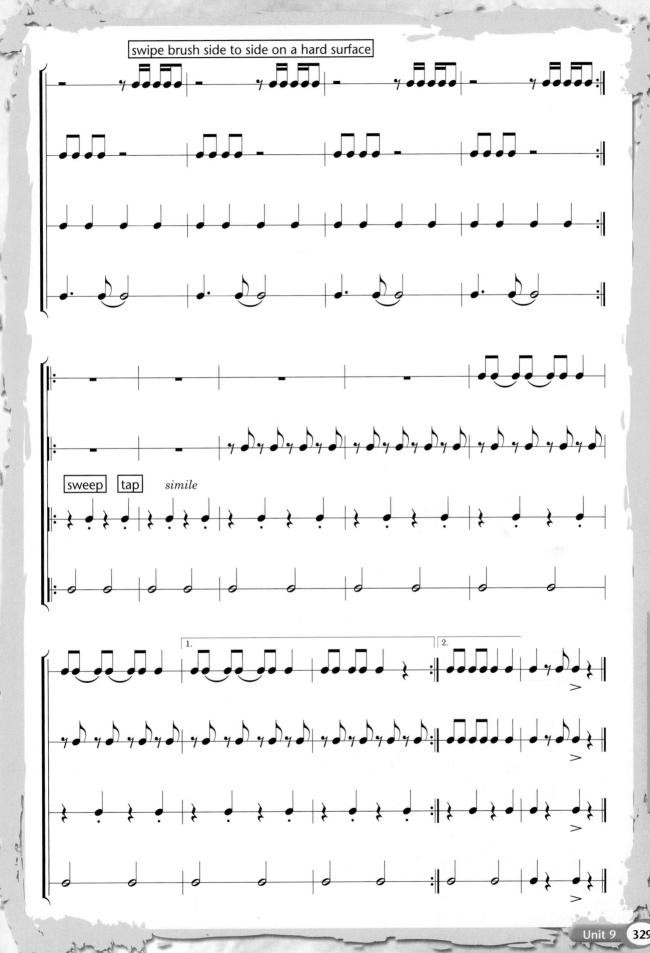

sweep tap *simile*

Good Listening By Design

Concert halls are designed so that the **acoustics** of the hall enhance the sound for a great musical performance.

The Morton Meyerson Symphony Center, in Dallas, Texas, was built for live musical performances. It is the home of the Dallas Symphony Orchestra.

Acoustics is the science of the production, control, and transmission of sound.

▲ The Morton Meyerson Symphony Center was designed by Pei Cobb Freed & Partners

◀ Interior view of the concert hall

The Concert Band on Stage

American composer Ron Nelson has written many works for concert band.

Listen to an excerpt from one such work, performed by the Dallas Wind Symphony and recorded at the Morton Meyerson Symphony Center.

CD 16–19
Rocky Point Holiday

by Ron Nelson
as performed by the Dallas Wind Symphony;
Jerry Junkin, conductor

This recording by the Dallas Wind Symphony demonstrates the excellent acoustics of the Morton Meyerson Symphony Center.

M·U·S·I·C M·A·K·E·R·S

Walter P. Vangreen

Walter P. Vangreen is an Architectural Designer. As a child he studied piano. Vangreen pursued a career in architecture because of his interest in buildings and design. He believes that architecture and music have much in common because both arts are governed by mathematical ratios. Vangreen was one of the architectural designers of the Morton Meyerson Symphony Center.

Be a Star!

Latin Style!

Latin music is currently very popular in the United States. Singers like Marc Anthony, Gloria Estefan, and Jennifer Lopez perform Latin music on stage to large numbers of fans. Latin music comes from a rich tradition that includes many musical styles from Latin America, Spain, South America, and the Caribbean.

Latin Style and Rhythm

Latin music often has similar musical traits—beautiful melodies, guitars, and vocal harmonies. Latin music is often recognized by its distinct and energetic rhythms.

Listen to two excerpts of the song *Lluvia* [YOO-vyah] by the Venezuelan singer Franco de Vita. In each excerpt, listen to the guitar and rhythm patterns.

CD 17–1, 2
Lluvia

written and performed by Franco de Vita

Lluvia (Rain) is first performed with guitar and vocals, and then in an orchestrated version with rhythm instruments.

Latin Dance Rhythms

The rhythms in Latin music are one of the most characteristic elements of its style. Basic rhythms are embellished and layered to create complex and interesting textures.

Read the following rhythms by first using rhythm syllables. **Conduct** in meter in 4 to feel the underlying steady beat. **Play** the rhythm patterns on your favorite percussion instrument. When you are ready, **perform** the rhythms as accompaniment to Tito Puente's *Ti mon bo*, on page 334.

a.

Long   short-short

b.

c.

Long Short-Short

A rhythm pattern that is part of many Latin styles can be described as "long, short-short." This "rhythmic pulse" underlies many Latin dances, such as the *rumba*, *cha-cha*, and *tango*. As shown below, rhythms are embellished and layered on top of this pulse to give each dance its unique character.

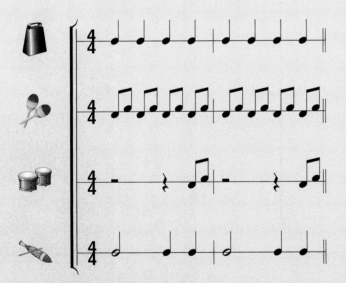

If you go to a wedding and dance, you can dance to many songs by saying to yourself, "long, short-short." The *rumba* is danced this way. **Move** your feet on each syllable, always alternating your feet. Here are the steps:

L	R L	R	L R	L	R L	R	L R
Long	short-short	Long	short-short	Long	short-short	Long	short-short

A Popular Latin Dance

Many people dance socially. The *cha-cha* is a favorite type of Latin social dance. The *cha-cha* rhythm is a variation of the "long, short-short" rhythm. **Play** the *cha-cha* rhythm pattern below as you say "1-2, cha-cha-cha." Then **perform** the *cha-cha* movements to *(Chi Chi Chi) Cha Cha Cha*. When you are ready, **perform** the rhythm accompaniment on page 333 with the music.

Cha-cha

▲ Left-two, cha-cha-cha
Right-two, cha-cha-cha

CD 17–3

(Chi Chi Chi) Cha Cha Cha

**by Marco Rizo and Kevin Morgan
as performed by Xavier Cugat and His Orchestra**

Xavier Cugat, known as "King of the Rumba," brought Spanish and Latin American dance rhythms to the United States. What dance rhythms can you identify in this piece?

334

A Latin Ballad

Latin music also includes ballads and love songs in traditional Latin style and in new contemporary pop styles.

Listen to *You Sang to Me*, a contemporary Latin ballad, and notice the syncopation of the melody.

CD 17–4

You Sang to Me

by Marc Anthony and Mark C. Rooney as performed by Sophia Salguero

You Sang to Me tells of love and emotions that are common themes in many Latin ballads and pop songs.

M·U·S·I·C M·A·K·E·R·S
Marc Anthony

Marc Anthony (born 1968) is one of today's biggest Latin pop stars. He first learned about music from his father, a Latino musician and composer, who encouraged Marc and his seven older brothers to sing and perform. When Anthony was a teenager, he began his career by writing club and dance music. A producer heard Marc's singing and invited him to make an entire album of Latino music. The album, *When the Night Is Over*, featured the work of several famous salsa musicians and marked the beginning of Anthony's interest in Latin and salsa music.

Anthony has performed with Latin salsa stars, including Tito Puente and Ruben Blades. Today, Anthony composes and performs in both the Latin salsa and contemporary pop styles.

Choirs on Stage

All over the world, young people sing in choirs and perform in classrooms, auditoriums, and concert halls.

Jim Papoulis composed "*Oye*" for the children of Acapulco, Mexico. **Identify** the chorus and solo parts in the refrain of the song. As you **sing**, take turns singing the solo part while the rest of the class sings the chorus.

▲ Papoulis conducting a children's chorus

CD 17–5

Oye

Words and Music by Jim Papoulis

VERSE

Bm (Solo)   G   Bm
1. Es - tán só - los,   llo - ran - do   en si - len - cio,
2. Es - cú - cha - los, mí - ra - los   es - cu - cha... lo

G   Bm   G
en la os - cu - ri - dad. __ Es - tán so - ñan - do,   de - se - an - do
que tra - tan... de de - cir. ___ Es - tán en bús - que - da, del ca - mi - no

Bm   G
con es - per - an - za,   por la op - or - tun - i - dad. __ Es - cú - cha - los, __
pe - que - ñas vo - ces, lla - mán - do - te. ___

A
___ es - cú - cha - los, ___ ell - os te lla - man. ___

336

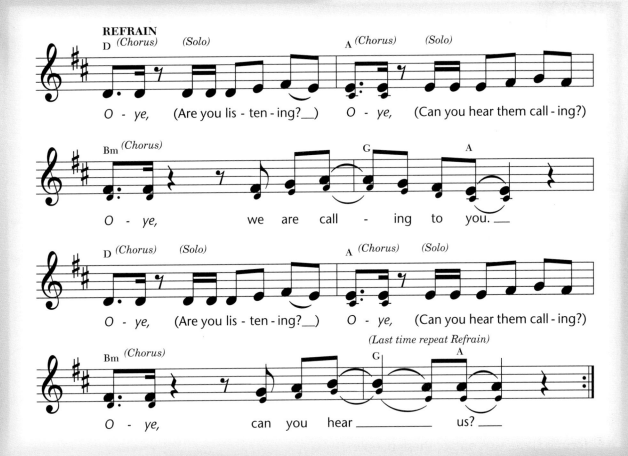

REFRAIN

O - ye, (Are you lis - ten - ing?__) O - ye, (Can you hear them call - ing?)

O - ye, we are call - ing to you.__

O - ye, (Are you lis - ten - ing?__) O - ye, (Can you hear them call - ing?)

(Last time repeat Refrain)

O - ye, can you hear __ us? __

M·U·S·I·C M·A·K·E·R·S

Jim Papoulis

Composer **Jim Papoulis** (born 1957) enjoys writing music for young people. He conducts songwriting workshops for schools and he co-founded *The Foundation for Small Voices* to help children around the globe. His album, *Sounds of a Better World = Small Voices Calling* was premiered at Carnegie Hall and featured The Harlem Boy's Choir, the Norwegian Children's Choir, and the Young People's Chorus of New York. Papoulis hopes his music will inspire people to respect the young people in their care. Papoulis composes in many genres. He scored the music for the 1999 film, *Going Nomad*.

Listen to *Give Us Hope*. What is the message that Papoulis gives to young people with this song?

CD 17–8

Give Us Hope

by **Jim Papoulis, Leo Schass, and Regine Urbach** as performed by The Young People's Chorus of NYC

This choral performance features *a cappella* singing, homophonic texture, and rich vocal harmonies.

Sing a Special Arrangement

Linda Twine's **cantata** *Changed My Name* was inspired by the lives of Sojourner Truth and Harriet Tubman, who were active in helping to fight slavery in the 1800s.

Slaves worked for their masters and were sold among slaveowners as property. Eventually people began to speak out against this practice. Sojourner Truth (1797–1883), a former slave, was one of these people.

Slaves sometimes tried to escape to freedom. When escaped slaves were caught, they were returned to their owners. Eventually people began to organize routes for slaves to escape from the South to the North. These routes became known as the "Underground Railroad." One of the people involved in the Underground Railroad was Harriet Tubman (1821–1913). She helped more than 300 slaves make the journey to freedom.

A **cantata** (kahn-TAH-tuh) is a large dramatic work, sometimes of a religious nature, for choir and instruments. Many cantatas contain solo and chorus sections, with continuous narration (recitative).

◀ Harriet Tubman

▼ Linda Twine

Listen to these recorded excerpts from *Changed My Name*.

CD 17–9
Changed My Name

by Linda Twine
Changed My Name tells the story of the slaves and their fight for freedom through narration and singing.

Escape to Freedom

Sing an arrangement of a song from *Changed My Name*—"Run! Run! Hide!" on page 340. Notice how the rhythms and the alternating text *run, run, hide* produce a type of excitement that describes a desperate attempt to escape from slavery.

Listen to Linda Twine talk about her music in this interview.

CD 17–10
Interview with Linda Twine

Linda Twine's skills as an arranger and a recording artist are also evident in the African American spiritual "This Little Light of Mine," on page 232.

Sojourner Truth with Abraham Lincoln ▶

Run! Run! Hide!

TUBMAN: *There was one of two things I had a right to, liberty or death; if I could not have one, I would have the other; for no man should take me alive.*

Words and Music by Linda Twine
Adapted from the Cantata "Changed My Name"

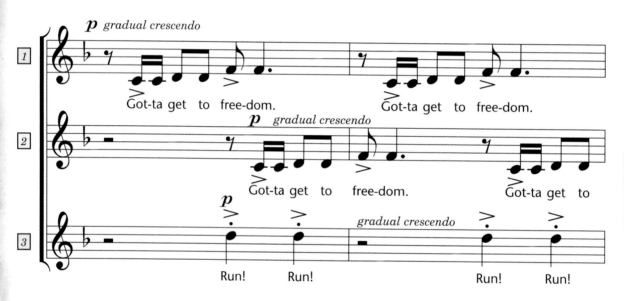

Music in the Movies

Music plays an important role in motion pictures. It heightens the drama and emotion of the film. Filmmakers hire composers to write music to enhance the emotional message of the film. Many songs written for movies become popular hits.

The Perfect Storm is a film based on a true story. Six men sailed into the north Atlantic Ocean aboard the "Andrea Gail" on a fishing expedition. While at sea, the men encountered the worst storm in modern history. The men and their boat were lost at sea in October, 1991.

Listen to *Yours Forever,* the theme song from *The Perfect Storm*. How many times does the composer use this motive, based on the interval of a fifth?

▲ Movie poster from the film *The Perfect Storm*

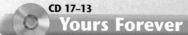

CD 17–13
Yours Forever

by James Horner, John Mellencamp, and George Green as performed by John Mellencamp

Motives based on the intervals of fourths and fifths are also found in the film music written by James Horner.

Tune In

Early movies had no sound. A pianist or organist performed music live in the theater as the film was projected on the screen. The first motion pictures with sound were called "talkies."

Movie Soundtracks Create Mood

Movie music, called "the soundtrack," helps to create the atmosphere and mood of the scenes that you see on the screen. Imagine watching a movie with no soundtrack, sound effects, or music. How would their absence affect the movie?

Listen to these excerpts from the soundtrack of *The Perfect Storm*. Decide how the composer uses tempo, rhythm, and dynamics to create the expressive qualities of the music.

CD 17–14, 15

Coming Home from the Sea

**from *The Perfect Storm*
by James Horner**

The opening haunting melody can be heard throughout the movie. The second theme is quick, rhythmic, and adds excitement to the action on the screen.

Directing Your Own Movie

Imagine that you are a very famous film director and have received a screenplay from a writer. Your job is to create a video from this script.

Read the screenplay on page 346 and choose an actor to play each part. Discuss scenery and props that would enhance your video. Rehearse the scene and direct your actors to give great performances. When you are ready, record the scene with a videotape camera. View the video and evaluate the performance.

Congratulations! You have directed another hit video.

Video Library Watch the video *Alligator Scene* to see how different musical styles affect the character of a video.

Be a Star!

Screenplay

Beach Scene: A group of students are at a beach playing tug-of-war. One of the students calls attention to a shining stone, and the game stops. Everyone examines the stone. Soon more stones are found, one after another. The students decide to follow the trail created by the stones, which leads to a great cavern with a beautiful pool of water at the bottom. The students look away for a moment; but when they look back, there is a pirate ship in the pool. They whisper in awe. Again they look away for a moment. When they look back, the pirate ship has vanished! Did they really see it? They believe they did, and they make a pact to keep it a secret!

Dialogue: GROUPS OF STUDENTS ARE PLAYING TUG-OF-WAR WHEN SUDDENLY THE GAME HALTS.

Student 1: Hey, you guys! Look at this!
Several students: What? Where?
Student 1: Look at that shiny thing on the ground.

EVERYONE DROPS THE ROPE AND RUNS TO SEE THE DISCOVERY

Student 2: That's the brightest green stone I've ever seen!
Student 3: Look! There's another one!

SOON EVERYONE IS FINDING THESE BRILLIANT STONES

Student 4: It's a trail! Let's follow it!
All students: Maybe it leads to a buried treasure!

EXCITEDLY, THEY ALL HEAD OFF TO FOLLOW THE TRAIL.

Student 5: Whoa! Watch out—it's a cavern!
Student 6: Look way down there! It's a huge pool of water!

THEY LOOK AWAY AND MURMUR AMONG THEMSELVES

Student 8: (LOOKING BACK AT THE CAVERN) It's a pirate ship! A real pirate ship!
Student 9: Hey, isn't that the captain?
Student 10: Captain Hook!
Student 11: Aren't ships supposed to be really huge? This thing is puny!
Student 12: You're right! That's a really small ship!

THE GROUP LOOKS AWAY FOR A MOMENT TO DISCUSS.

Student 13: Hey, you guys! It's *gone!*

THE GROUP MOANS IN DISAPPOINTMENT

Student 14: OK, we cracked! It just wasn't there! We didn't really see it.

Student 1: No, it was there! I know we saw it!

Student 15: Yeah, that's cool! We all know we saw it!

Student 16: Nobody is going to believe us, though.

Student 1: So we don't tell anyone—deal? This stays with us!

THE STUDENTS CHATTER AMONG THEMSELVES AGAIN, AND THEY AGREE TO KEEP THIS A SECRET.

Adding Music to Your Movie

Your movie has been filmed and has spoken dialogue. To add more drama to the film, you need to add a musical score to the film. Here are three different orchestral soundtracks to accompany your film. **Listen** to each soundtrack and decide which one best fits your film.

CD 17–16
One Fine Day

by Edward Pearsall

This orchestral arrangement features string and woodwind melody lines over strings.

CD 17–17
Jungle Beat

by Edward Pearsall

A jungle-like rhythm is the backdrop for unusual chords and mysterious melodic figures.

CD 17–18
Illusions

by Edward Pearsall

This string orchestra piece has a melodic **A** section and a rhythmic **B** section.

▲ A 1970s recording session for a Bernard Herrmann film score

MusicVideos

Music videos of our favorite singers are one of the most popular of all entertainment media today. The music video is a visual performance as important as the concert stage.

Gloria Estefan is one of the most popular female singers to emerge in the pop, rock, and Latino music scenes. With the Miami Sound Machine, she created a blend of Latin rhythms with pop rock that was new and exciting.

Listen to the syncopated rhythms of the Miami Sound Machine's hit song "The Rhythm Is Gonna Get You." Then **sing** the song with rhythmic excitement.

CD 17–19

The Rhythm Is Gonna Get You

Words and Music by Gloria Estefan and Enrique Garcia

Be a Star!

The Spirit of Music

The Olympics brings to the world a spirit of cooperation and sport competition. From its simple origins in ancient Greece, the Olympics has grown into a multimedia event that commands the attention of hundreds of millions of television viewers from around the world.

Music is an important part of the identity of the Olympics, and its opening ceremonies have become spectacular stage presentations. In 1988, the organizers of the Summer Olympics in Seoul, Korea, used two inspirational pieces of music—*Olympic Spirit* and *One Moment in Time.*

Listen to the 1988 Olympic theme, *Olympic Spirit,* from acclaimed composer John Williams.

CD 18–1

Olympic Spirit

by John Williams

The brass fanfare and lyric symphonic theme capture the majesty of the Olympic spirit.

MUSIC MAKERS

John Williams

John Williams (born 1932) is one of the most famous American composers and conductors today. Williams has written music for over 80 films, including *Jaws, E.T., Jurassic Park, Schindler's List,* and all the *Indiana Jones* and *Star Wars* films. He has written the Olympic themes for the 1984, 1988, and 1996 Olympic games.

Williams was the conductor of the Boston Pops from 1980 to 1993. He has won five Academy Awards and 16 Grammy Awards.

Sound Waves

How is sound produced, and how does it travel? In this unit, you will explore the worlds of sound, science, and music.

★ **Giving Our Best**

Sing "One Moment in Time," a song that was performed by Whitney Houston at the Seoul Olympics.

One Moment in Time

CD 18–2

Words and Music by
Albert Hammond and John Bettis

Each day I live, I want to be a day to give the best of
me. I'm on-ly one, but not a - lone. My fin-est day is yet unknown. I broke my heart for ev-'ry gain.
be the ver-y best.
To taste the sweet, I faced the
I want it all, no time for
pain. I rise and fall, yet through it all this much re-mains:
less. I've laid the plans, now lay the chance here in my hands: I want
one mo-ment in time when I'm more than I thought I could be, when
all of my dreams are a heart-beat a-way and the an-swers are all up to
me. Give me one mo-ment in time when I'm rac-ing with des-ti-ny.

Vibration
the basis of sound

Sound is created when something vibrates or oscillates. Vibration in a musical instrument produces sound waves. The faster the vibration of an object, the higher the pitch.

Listen to the timbre of these instruments as you study their waveforms.

CD 18–4
Sound Waves Montage

Recorded are the sounds of a piccolo, bassoon, violin, cello, and string bass.

1 cycle

▲ This is a picture of a flute waveform. One vibration of the waveform is the distance from one peak to the next.

▲ Bassoon

◄ Piccolo

The Three "Ls" of Pitch

Here is a good way to remember how the physical characteristics of a vibrating object affect the pitch. Remember this as the three "Ls."

Longer or Larger or Looser = Lower

- The *longer,* the lower: Which is lower? A piccolo or bassoon?

- The *larger,* the lower: Which is lower? A violin or string bass?

- The *looser,* the lower: What happens when you loosen a string on a cello?

Musical Families

Do the three "Ls" work on all instruments?
Try these experiments and **describe** the results.

The String Family

▶ What happens to the sound when strings are
longer or larger (thicker)? If a violin string is
loosened, what happens to the sound?

◀ Cello

String
Bass ▶

◀ Violin

◀ Saxophone

◀ Flute

Clarinet ▶

The Woodwind Family

◀ When a woodwind instrument
is longer or larger, what
happens to the sound?

Music's Heavy Hitters

The Brass Family

▶ Compare the sound of brass instruments that are longer and larger.

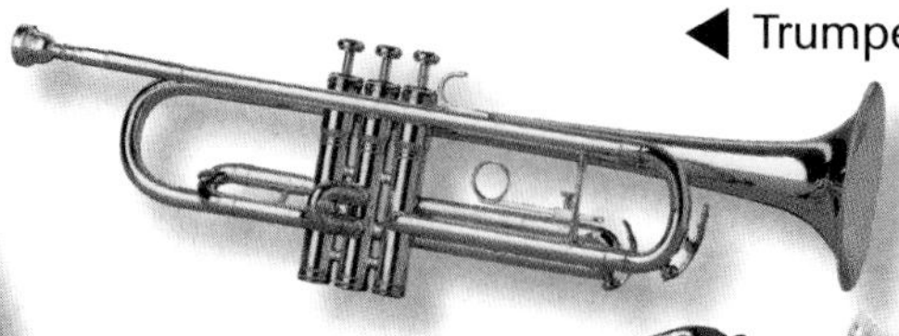

◀ Trumpet

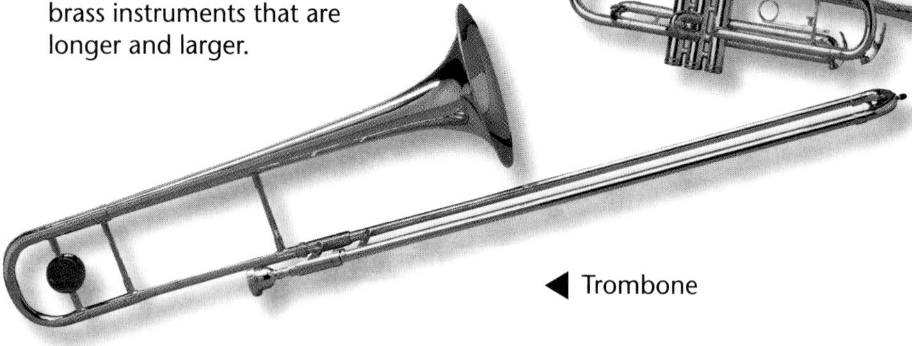

◀ Trombone

▲ French Horn

The Percussion Family

Compare the sound of a larger drumhead to that of a smaller drumhead. What happens to pitch when the pedal on a timpani loosens or tightens the drumhead?

◀ Conga

▼ Xylophone

Timpani ▶

The Electronic Instrument Family

If the sound is electronic and not acoustic, do the three "Ls" apply?

◀ Synthesizer

Electric Percussion

Edgar Varèse (1885–1965) created a unique contemporary musical work with his percussion piece *Ionisation*. This famous work stands as a classic example of twentieth-century *avant-garde* music. In *avant-garde* music, composers often use sound itself as the main element in music.

Listen to *Ionisation* and follow the listening map.

CD 18–5
Ionisation

by Edgar Varèse

Ionisation uses more than 40 percussion instruments to create a variety of musical sounds and events.

IONISATION

LISTENING MAP

Listen to *Ionisation* and **identify** each of the instruments and sounds as you hear them being played.

JUG BAND SOUNDS

Playing in a jug band is a fun way to make music using instruments that are easy to play. Gather together these instruments and learn to play them. Decide which instrument you will play in this jug band song.

Sing "Mama Don't 'Low." Imagine how the jug band accompaniment will sound.

 CD 18–6

MAMA DON'T 'LOW

Folk Song from the United States

1. Ma-ma don't 'low no gui-tar play-in' 'round here,
2. Ma-ma don't 'low no ban-jo pick-in' 'round here,

Ma-ma don't 'low no gui-tar play-in' 'round here,
Ma-ma don't 'low no ban-jo pick-in' 'round here,

I don't care what Ma-ma don't 'low, Gon-na play my gui-tar an-y-how,
I don't care what Ma-ma don't 'low, Gon-na pick my ban-jo an-y-how,

Ma-ma don't 'low no gui-tar play-in' 'round here.
Ma-ma don't 'low no ban-jo pick-in' 'round here.

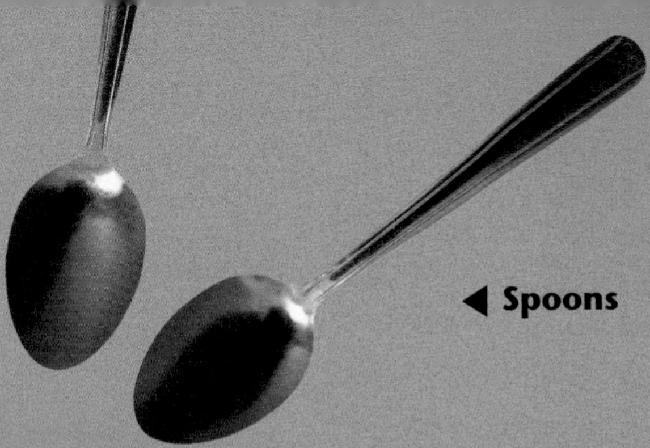

◀ **Spoons**

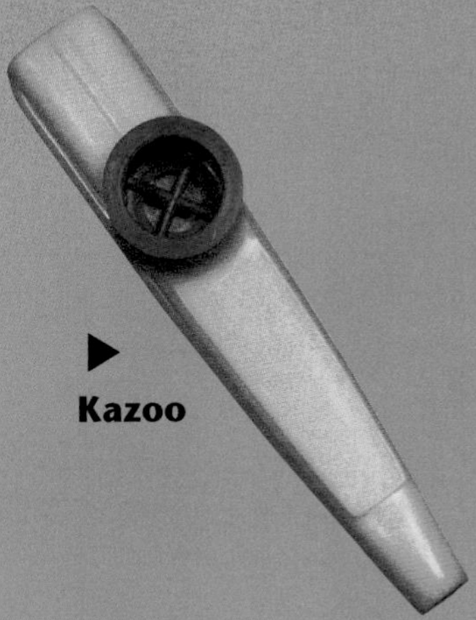

▼ **Washboard**

▶
Kazoo

Jug Band Patterns

Use these patterns to accompany "Mama Don't 'Low."
Improvise new patterns and rhythms to add variety.

Jug

Kazoo *(phrases 1 and 4)*   *(slide)*

Washboard

Spoons

▲ **Jug**

Jug Band Guitar

The song "Mama Don't 'Low" has three basic guitar chords, shown below. **Play** a basic $\frac{2}{4}$ pattern with one strum on each beat.

Autoharp

Learn the G, D_7 and C chords on the Autoharp as part of the jug band accompaniment.

Gutbucket (Washtub Bass)

Making a gutbucket is a project for the adventurous. If you can't make one, you can play the "air" gutbucket. (The technique is the same as the "air" guitar.)

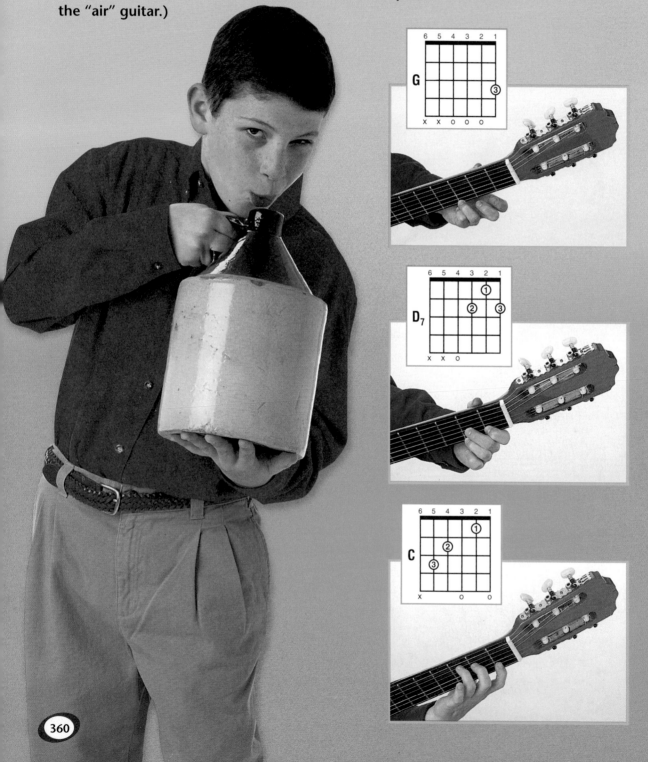

Ready, Set, Play!

Your jug band is now ready.

Play a jug band accompaniment as you **sing** "Mama Don't 'Low." When you are ready, you can add some solos to the accompaniment as well.

Now that you have played in a jug band, **listen** to a professional jug band.

CD 18–9
Jug Band Music

by Geoff Muldaur
as performed by Jim Kweskin and The Jug Band

It is not always easy to hear jug band instruments, since they have no amplifiers.

Types of VIBRATIONS

An interesting way to group most instruments is by how they vibrate or oscillate. What are the ways in which an instrument begins its vibration? Membranophones, aerophones, idiophones, chordophones, and electrophones are all groups of instruments. Use the Sound Bank to look at photos and **listen** to the sound of each instrument.

Listen to the membranophones in *Uma história de Ifá*.

CD 18–10
Uma história de Ifá

by Ytthmar Tropicália and Rey Zulu as performed by Margareth Menezes

Membranophones provide an exciting introduction to this Afro-Brazilian music.

In the **membranophone** family, a stretched membrane or skin vibrates to produce sound. Membranophones include most drums. ▶

Listen to *Galliard battaglia* to hear members of the aerophone family.

CD 18–11
Galliard battaglia

by Samuel Scheidt as performed by the Canadian Brass

This Baroque dance piece features two trumpets, French horn, trombone, and tuba. These instruments form the brass quintet.

◀ In the **aerophone** family, an air column vibrates. Aerophones include woodwinds, brass, organs, and the human voice.

Idiophones and Chordophones

Listen to Mickey Hart and five world-class percussionists play *The Hunt*. This piece uses percussion from around the world, such as *djembe*, jaw harp, drum set, *dundun*, *naal* bells, *tabla*, shakers, *ashiko*, *ngoma*, and *ghatam*.

CD 18–12
The Hunt

by Mickey Hart and the Percussionists of Planet Drum

Woodblocks, bells, chimes, and other idiophones and membranophones are used in this piece.

▲ In the **idiophone** family, the body of the instrument vibrates. There are no strings or membranes. Cymbals, bells, and woodblocks are idiophones.

Listen to Tchaikovsky's "Finale" from *Serenade for Strings in C* to hear chordophones.

CD 18–13
Finale

from *Serenade for Strings in C*, Opus 48 by Piotr Ilych Tchaikovsky

This exciting Russian dance shows off the string orchestra at its best.

◀ In the **chordophone** family, strings vibrate. Chordophones include orchestral strings, guitar, and piano.

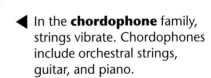

A Working Song

Sing "*Corta la caña*," a Puerto Rican song that uses an interesting mixture of idiophones, membranophones, and chordophones in its accompaniment.
Identify which instruments are used.

CD 18–14
MIDI 22

CORTA LA CAÑA
(Head for the Canefields)

English Words by Aura Kontra

Folk Song from Puerto Rico

Yo ven-go de mon-te a-den - tro de cor-tar ca-ña, ca - ñe -
I work in the su - gar cane - fields, The crop that I bear is heav -

- ro, por más ca - ña que se cor - te nun-ca se ga-na el di - ne -
- y, No mat-ter how much I car - ry it will nev - er bring much mon-

- ro. To-do el mun-do la pro-cla - ma que es muy fá-cil de cor -
- ey. Some say it's an ea-sy liv - ing, cut-ting su-gar all day

tar, cuan-do se ja-la la mo - cha na-die quie-re tra-ba-jar.
long. When-ev-er a hand is need - ed no one wants to come a-long.

Cor - ta la ca - ña, ca - ñe - ro, cór - ta la. ____
Head for the cane - fields each morn-ing, cut them down. _

Cor - ta la ca - ña, ca - ñe - ro, cór - ta la. ____
Head for the cane - fields till sun - set, cut them down. _

Latin Rhythms

Gloria Estefan is one of the premiere performers of Latin music. **Listen** to *Mi tierra* (My Homeland). It is a song about missing the Cuban homeland. **Listen** for the pattern that the *conga* plays.

CD 18–18
Mi tierra

by Estefano
as performed by Gloria Estefan

Mi tierra has the quick tempo, continuous eighth-note rhythms, *conga* rhythms, and brass punctuation characteristic of Latin music.

Conga Rhythms

The *conga* drum is important in Latin music. *Congas* are most often played in pairs (low-high). They provide the rhythmic basis of Puerto Rican and Cuban music. Sometimes these rhythms are similar to *mambo* rhythms.

Learn and **play** the following rhythms in the *mambo* style. When you are ready, **play** along with *Mi tierra*. Later, **create** and **improvise** new *mambo* rhythms on your favorite instrument.

Gloria Estefan ▼

Sequencing Software Input the *mambo* rhythm into the sequencing software. Explore timbre by assigning different instruments to the rhythm.

Electrophones

Electrophones are electronic instruments. Instead of acoustic vibrations, sound is created by an oscillating current. When these waveforms are transmitted through speakers, we hear musical sound.

The electrophone family includes most contemporary electronic instruments such as synthesizers, drum machines, and samplers.

Electronic Music From a Pioneer

"Electronic music" is a genre of music composition that was prominent in the 1970s and 1980s. Composers began to write electronic music because electronic instruments were manufactured by Robert Moog, Donald Buchla, and Arp Instruments. Morton Subotnick is an important composer in electronic music.

Listen to *Wild Bull*, an electronic music composition by Subotnick. What musical timbres do you hear? Discuss how composers created electronic music.

CD 18–19
Wild Bull

by Morton Subotnick

These electronic sounds were created by early electronic instruments (some with no keyboard).

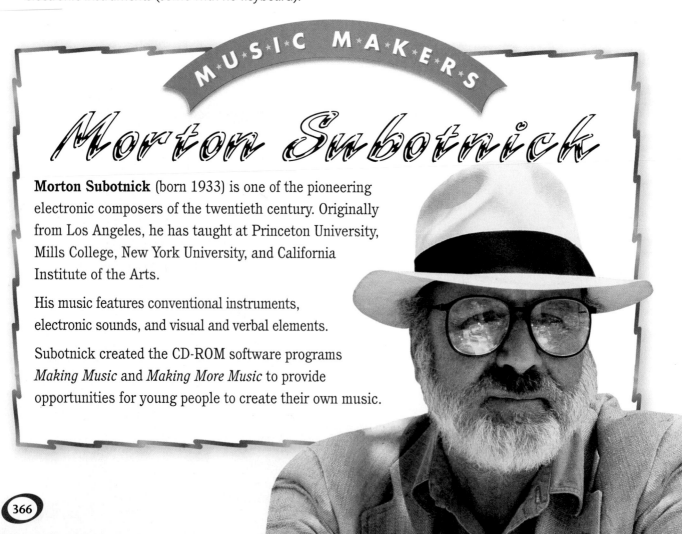

MUSIC MAKERS

Morton Subotnick

Morton Subotnick (born 1933) is one of the pioneering electronic composers of the twentieth century. Originally from Los Angeles, he has taught at Princeton University, Mills College, New York University, and California Institute of the Arts.

His music features conventional instruments, electronic sounds, and visual and verbal elements.

Subotnick created the CD-ROM software programs *Making Music* and *Making More Music* to provide opportunities for young people to create their own music.

New Electronics

Electronic instruments developed from their early beginnings to today's sophisticated synthesizers, keyboards, computers, samplers, and digital music systems. Today, much of the world's pop and commercial music is created using electronics.

Techno and dance music is sometimes created, or mixed, by DJs using electronic equipment. It can also be created in a traditional recording studio using synthesizers and other electronic keyboards. The result is the same—exciting pop electronic music.

Dance and Techno Music

Dance and techno music is a worldwide phenomenon. Singers, musicians, DJs, and producers in countries all over the planet are producing music that has a great beat and is fun to dance to.

Listen to *Think*, an example of techno and dance music. The music is performed by the group Information Society. **Identify** the electronic sounds as they occur in the music.

CD 18–20
Think

by Paul Robb
as performed by Information Society

A recording engineer creating a "mix" in a Nashville recording studio ▼

The steady dance beat, electronic rhythms, and melodic "hooks" are characteristic of dance and techno music.

Dance and TECHNO Beats

"Dance" and "techno" music share similar traits: they both have a strong beat, they are sometimes mixed "live" by DJs, they use repeated patterns called "loops," technology is important (electronic keyboards, sampler boxes, computers, digital audio), and the music is for dancing. Dance and techno evolved from disco in the 1970s and new wave in the 1980s.

The Beat

Dance and techno have these musical elements: a strong emphasis on each beat, accents on beats 2 and 4, powerful bass, and repeated melodic patterns. The backbeat rhythm is the foundation of many dance and techno beats.

Listen to the song *This Is Your Night*. **Identify** the musical elements.

CD 18–21

This Is Your Night

by Amber and the Berman Brothers as performed by Amber

The strong disco-like beat, electronic instruments, and repetitive melody make this music great for dancing and singing.

 A DJ creates a "live" mix.

Loops, Layers, and Rhythms

How do you compose or "mix" dance or techno? One recipe is to take some dance rhythms, loop them so that they repeat, and add a bass line and some melodic motives. Finally, layer them and mix.

Below are some elements used in the mix of *This Is Your Night.*
Perform the rhythms, bass line, melody patterns, and chords on rhythm and keyboard instruments. Then **listen** to the "dance mix" and **describe** how the parts are layered. Finally, **create** a new dance mix from these parts.

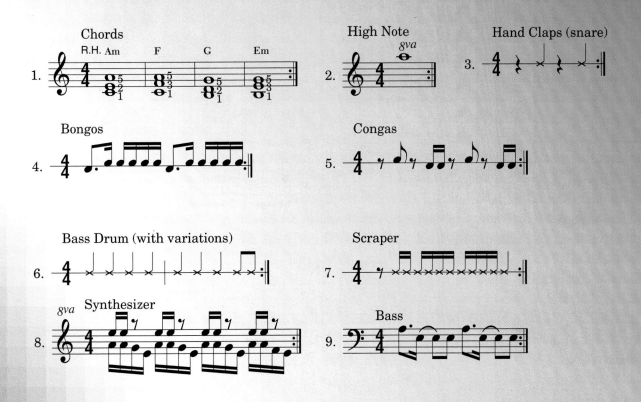

CD 18–22

This Is Your Night (Dance Mix)

as mixed by "Junior" Vasquez

The introduction to this dance number layers the dance rhythms, bass, harmony, and melodic patterns to create a dance mix.

MIDI Sequencing Software Use sequencing software to create a new "dance mix" for *This Is Your Night.*

Recorder Review

Review the finger positions below for the recorder.
Sing and **play** recorder on "Boil Them Cabbage Down." Some of you can **sing** the melody, while others **play** the recorder.

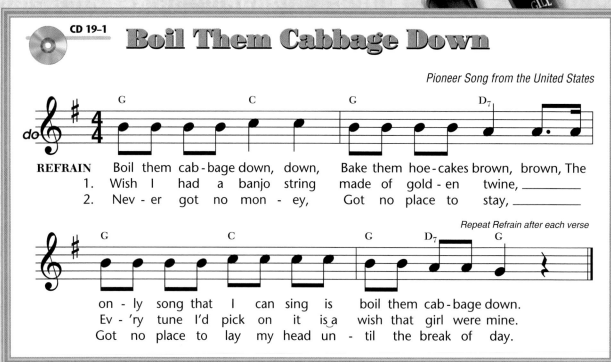

CD 19–1

Boil Them Cabbage Down

Pioneer Song from the United States

do

| G | C | G | D₇ |

REFRAIN   Boil them cab-bage down, down,   Bake them hoe-cakes brown, brown, The
1. Wish I had a banjo string   made of gold-en twine, _____
2. Nev-er got no mon-ey,   Got no place to stay, _____

Repeat Refrain after each verse

| G | C | G | D₇ | G |

on-ly song that I can sing is   boil them cab-bage down.
Ev-'ry tune I'd pick on it is a   wish that girl were mine.
Got no place to lay my head un - til the break of day.

Recorder Fingerings

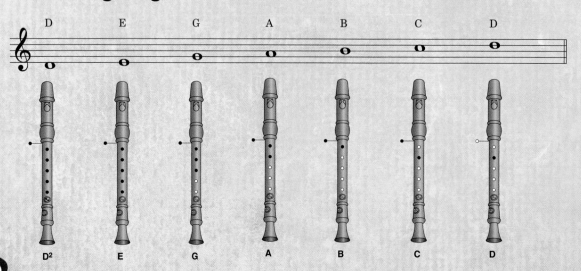

| D | E | G | A | B | C | D |

D²   E   G   A   B   C   D

Dot the Quarter

Sing and **play** "Worried Man Blues," a song about the effect of the Great Depression on people in the 1930s.

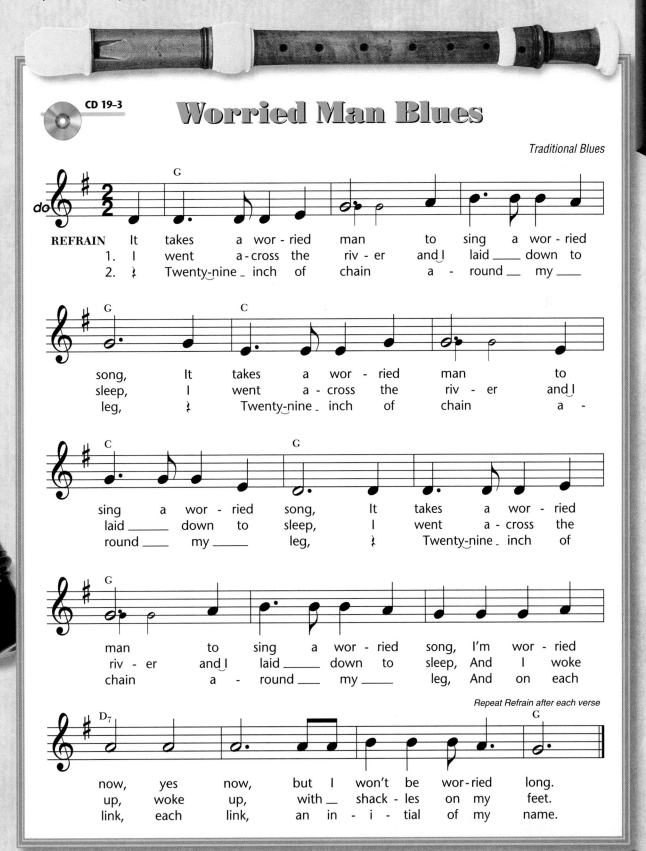

CD 19–3

Worried Man Blues

Traditional Blues

REFRAIN It takes a wor-ried man to sing a wor-ried
1. I went a-cross the riv-er and I laid ____ down to
2. Twenty-nine inch of chain a - round ____ my ____

song, It takes a wor-ried man to
sleep, I went a-cross the riv-er and I
leg, Twenty-nine inch of chain a -

sing a wor-ried song, It takes a wor-ried
laid ____ down to sleep, I went a-cross the
round ____ my ____ leg, Twenty-nine inch of

man to sing a wor-ried song, I'm wor-ried
riv-er and I laid ____ down to sleep, And I woke
chain a - round ____ my ____ leg, And on each

Repeat Refrain after each verse

now, yes now, but I won't be wor-ried long.
up, woke up, with __ shack-les on my feet.
link, each link, an in - i - tial of my name.

Time for $\frac{6}{8}$

Play this warm-up for "Skye Boat Song." Pay careful attention to the rhythms in $\frac{6}{8}$ meter.

Sing and **play** the Scottish "Skye Boat Song."

CD 19–5
MIDI 23

Skye Boat Song

Words by Sir Harold Boulton

Music by Annie MacLeod

REFRAIN

Speed, bon - nie boat, like a bird on the wing;

"On - ward," the sail - ors cry. _____

Car - ry the lad that's born to be king,

O - ver the sea to Skye.

Fine

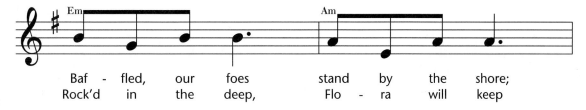

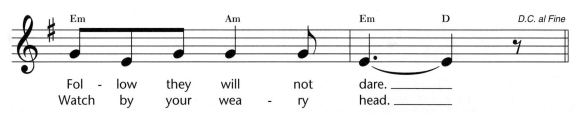

Playing Guitar and Autoharp

The guitar and the Autoharp often accompany singing together. Use the G and D₇ chords to accompany "Tom Dooley," and the D and A₇ chords for "Down in the Valley."

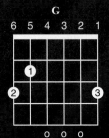
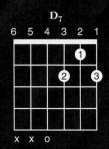
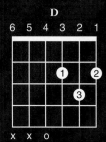
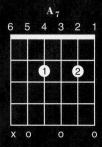

Both the Autoharp and guitar can play a simple "down" strum on each beat.

Sing "Tom Dooley" and **play** along using guitar, Autoharp, and recorder.

CD 19–7

Tom Dooley

Folk Song from the United States

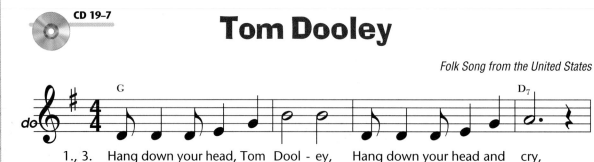

1., 3. Hang down your head, Tom Dool - ey, Hang down your head and cry,
2. This ___ time to - mor - row, Won - der ___ where I'll be?

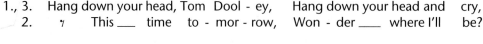

Hang down your head, Tom Dool - ey, Poor boy, you're bound to die.
Down in some lone - some val - ley, Hang-in' from a white oak tree.

Down in the Valley

Folk Song from Kentucky

1. Down in the val - ley, the val - ley so
2. Build me a cas - tle for - ty feet
3. Writ - ing a let - ter con - tain - ing three

low, Hang your head o - ver, hear the wind
high, So I can see you as you pass
lines, An - swer my ques - tion: "Will you be

blow. Hear the wind blow, dear, hear the wind
by. As you pass by, dear, as you pass
mine?" Will you be mine, dear, will you be

blow, Hang your head o - ver, hear the wind blow.
by, So I can see you as you pass by.
mine? An - swer my ques - tion: "Will you be mine?"

Strum Down the Valley

"Down in the Valley" uses the chords D and A₇.
Notice that "Down in the Valley" and "Tom
Dooley" change chords on the rhyming words.

Strum with a "down" stroke three times in each
measure.

Sing "Down in the Valley" and play a guitar or
an Autoharp accompaniment.

Review the G and D7 chords on page 374. Then practice the three chords below. The guitar should play a simple "down" strum on the first beat of each measure in *"Cuando pa' Chile me voy."*

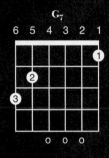
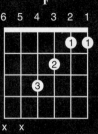

If you are playing Autoharp, find the chords ahead of time. Leave your left-hand fingers on the chord bars even when you are not pressing them. Autoharps should strum on the first beat of each measure, also.

Sing and play guitar and Autoharp on *"Cuando pa ' Chile me voy."*

Cuando pa' Chile me voy
(Leavin' for Chile)

English Words by Aura Kontra

Cueca from Chile

VERSE

1. Cuan - do pa' Chi - le   me voy,   Cru - zan - do la cor - di - lle - ra,
   Y cuan-do vuel - vo   de Chi - le,   En - tre ce - rros y que - bra - das,
1. Leav - in' for Chi - le   a - gain,   I'm cross-ing the high-est moun-tains.
   And when I come home from Chi - le,   I cross o - ver hills and riv - ers.

Cuan - do pa' Chi - le   me voy,   Cru - zan - do la cor - di - lle - ra, La-te el
Y cuan-do vuel - vo   de Chi - le,   En - tre ce - rros y que - bra - das, La-te el
Leav - in' for Chi - le   a - gain,   I'm cross-ing the high-est moun-tains. And my
And when I come home from Chi - le,   I cross o - ver hills and riv - ers. And my

co - ra - zón con - ten - to,　Pues　u - na chi - le - na me̯es - pe - ra. La - te̯el
co - ra - zón con - ten - to,　Pues me̯es - pe - ra　u - na cu - ya - na. La - te̯el
hap - py heart is　sing - ing,　for some-one I know there is　wait - ing. And　my
hap - py heart is　sing - ing,　for　soon I'll be court - ing an - oth - er. And　my

1.

co - ra - zón con - ten - to,　Pues　u - na chi - le - na me̯es - pe - ra.
co - ra - zón con - ten - to,　Pues me̯es - pe - ra　u - na cu -
hap - py heart is　sing - ing,　for some-one I know there is　wait - ing.
hap - py heart is　sing - ing,　for　soon I'll be court - ing an -

2.　　　　　　REFRAIN

ya - na.　　Vi - van el bai - le　y la dan - za, vi - van la
oth - er.　　Long live the mu - sic　of the dan - za, long live the

cue - ca y la zam - ba,　　Dos pun - tas tie - ne̯el ca - mi - no y̯en las dos
cue - ca and zam - ba.　　At jour-ney's end or at　jour-ney's be - gin - ning,

1.　　　　　　　　　　　　　2.

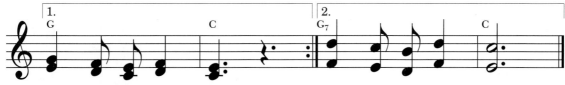

al - guien me̯a - guar - da.　　　al - guien me̯a - guar - da.
some - one　a - waits　me.　　　some - one　a - waits　me.

2. *En Chile bailo la cueca,*　} 2 times
   En Cuyo bailo la zamba,

   En Chile con las chilenas,　} 2 times
   Con las otras en Calingasta.

   Vida trist, vida alegre,　} 2 times
   Es la vida del arriero,

   Penitas en el camino,　} 2 times
   Y risas al fin del sendero.

Refrain

2. I dance the *cueca* in Chile,　} 2 times
   In Cuyo I do the *zamba.*

   Dancing with the girls from Chile,　} 2 times
   Or with the ones from Calingasta.

   Days can be happy or sad,　} 2 times
   The life of an *arriero.*

   Troubles face me on my journey,　} 2 times
   But laughter awaits me at nightfall.

Refrain

THE LIFE OF A SOUND

When you listen to a live cellist perform, you are listening to acoustic sound. When you listen to a CD of the cellist, you are listening to recorded sound. Think of acoustic and recorded musical sound as having a life.

Acoustic Sound

Motion and vibration start the sound. An instrument's body amplifies and colors the sound. The sound travels and is heard by listeners. Follow the acoustic sound played by a cello.

1. Motion and vibration Drawing a bow across the string starts the vibration. The string vibrates and creates a waveform, a musical note, or pitch.

2. Amplification The body of the cello acts as an amplifier. The waveform is changed by the cello body. The sound's timbre and volume level are defined.

3. Transmission As the cello makes the sound, its sound waves travel through the air.

4. Perception If a listener is present in the room, the sound waves reach the listener's ears. The listener's brain identifies the sound as a cello.

Recorded Sound

Recording sound saves it so that you can play it back at a later time. Follow the path of sound as it is recorded and played back.

1. Recording sound Acoustic sound is recorded by a microphone. The microphone converts sound waves to electrical impulses. A tape recorder preserves the microphone's signals onto tape.

2. Playing sound The magnetic information on the tape is converted to electrical energy.

3. Hearing the sound This energy drives the tiny speakers in the headphones.

Use Your Instrument

Sing the African American spiritual "Ezekiel Saw the Wheel." As you sing, think about how the sound of your voice travels to the listeners' ears.

CD 19–16

Ezekiel Saw the Wheel

African American Spiritual

E - ze-kiel __ saw the wheel, 'Way up in the mid-dle of the air, E -

ze-kiel __ saw the wheel, 'Way in the mid-dle of the air. Now the

big wheel turn by faith, And the lit - tle wheel turn by the

grace of God, It's a wheel in a wheel, 'Way in the mid-dle of the air.

1. Some go to church for to sing and shout, 'Way in the mid-dle of the air, Be -
2. One of these __ days 'bout __ twelve o' - clock, 'Way in the mid-dle of the air,

fore six months they're shout-ed out! 'Way in the mid-dle of the air.
This old world gonna reel and rock! 'Way in the mid-dle of the air.

Sequencing Software Use the digital audio features of your sequencing software to record live sounds into the computer. Explore changing the timbre of each sound.

Percussion instruments make many different sounds. A mallet striking a wooden xylophone and a mallet striking a metal glockenspiel produce different sounds. A tambourine makes its sound using both a membrane and metallic jingles. The solid body of a triangle produces its distinctive sound.

Play this accompaniment to "Ezekiel Saw the Wheel." As you play, think about how each instrument produces its sound.

Arranged by Julie Scott

Sequencing Software Record a trumpet using digital audio recording software. Then view the trumpet's waveforms and wavelengths with the software.

Whacky Music

Plastic tubes like Boomwhackers® are fun to play. You can use them to make background patterns that go with songs. They come in different lengths to make a range of pitches. They illustrate one of the Three "Ls" of Pitch described on page 354—The Longer, The Lower. **Describe** the timbre of a Boomwhacker® or other tuned tube.

Play each of these rhythms by hitting the tube(s). Start with the first rhythm and then add each pattern until all of the parts are playing together. When you are ready, **perform** "The Whacky Wheel" with the recording of "Ezekiel Saw the Wheel" on page 379.

The Whacky Wheel Ensemble

Music by Will Schmid

1st Boomer

Bass Boomer (optional)

2nd Boomer

3rd Boomer

4th Boomer

Tune In

On the Caribbean Island of Trinidad, musicians play "Bamboo Tamboo" using different lengths of bamboo tubes hit on the ground to create a variety of rhythm patterns.

Create Your Own Hose-a-phone

To do this experiment, you will need a trumpet mouthpiece, a six- to eight- foot length of rubber hose that just fits over the mouthpiece end, and a small funnel that will also fit into the hose.

Demonstrate the three parts of a bugle or trumpet tone.

1. Motion: Buzz the lips alone; then buzz them with the mouthpiece.

2. Vibration: Insert the mouthpiece into the hose and play as many tones as you can. Play different pitches by tightening and loosening the tension of your lips. For extra theatrical effect, swing the end of the hose around or wrap it around your body like a Sousaphone.

3. Amplification: Insert the funnel in the end of the hose and play again, noting the change of tone.

Nature's INSTRUMENTS

No matter where people live in the world, they make musical instruments out of whatever local materials are available.

Rattles from around the world show how people use different materials. Here are some examples.

Listen to *Llactamanta*, an Ecuadorian folk tune from the Andes mountains. It uses locally made instruments—the *ch'ajch'as* (llama toenail rattles) and the bamboo panpipes (see pages 46–47). Make your own rattle from available materials gathered from your house. Then, **create** a rhythm accompaniment to *Llactamanta*.

CD 19–18
Llactamanta

Ecuadorian Folk Tune

Other Andean instruments include winds: *quena, flauta, zampoñas;* strings: guitar, *mandolina,* and *charango;* percussion: *ch'ajch'as, guiro,* and bongos.

▲ Gourd rattle from Latin America

Basket rattles from Africa ▶

Bean maracas from the Caribbean ▶

Bamboo Instruments

Bamboo grows easily in warm and wet parts of the world, such as South America, much of Asia, and the South Pacific. Many musical instruments are made of bamboo. **Listen** again to the bamboo panpipes in *Llactamanta*.

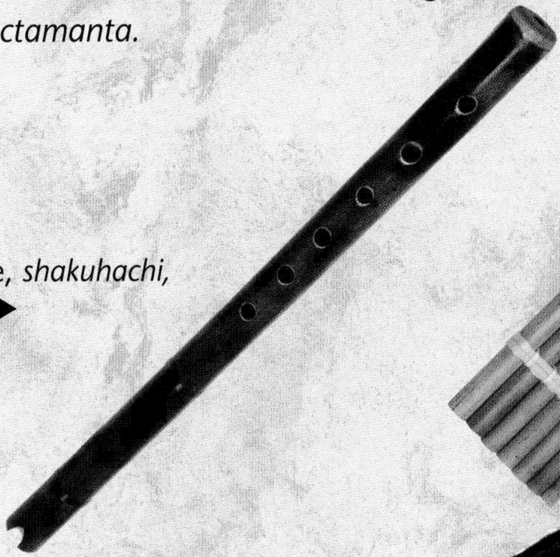

Bamboo flute, *shakuhachi*, from Japan ▶

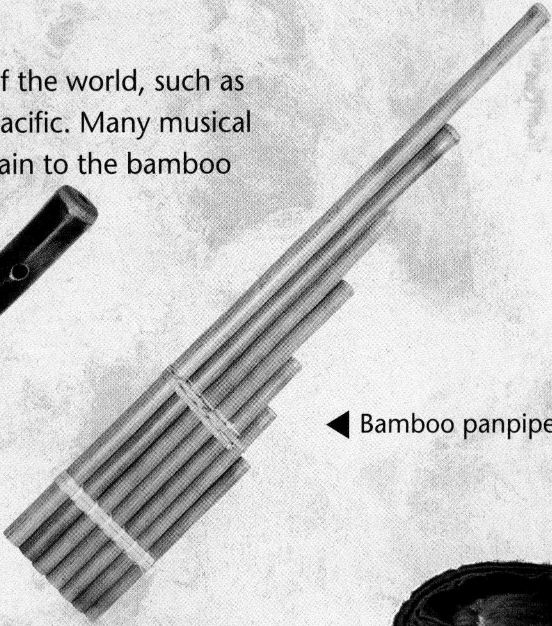

◀ Bamboo panpipes

▲ Chinese *sheng*

Tune In

Some ancient Asian cultures had eight basic categories for musical instruments: Earth (pottery), Wood, Stone, Bamboo, Metal, Gourds, Skin, and Silk.

Gamelan Orchestras

The people of Bali and Java play in gamelan orchestras.

The Indonesian **gamelan** consists of percussion, winds, and bell instruments that play as an orchestra. The gamelan is unique in its sound. The *gamelan angklung* is a smaller and lighter gamelan orchestra that plays in processions.

Listen to this example of *gamelan angklung*.

A **gamelan** is an Indonesian orchestra consisting primarily of gongs, gong-chimes, metallophones, and drums.

CD 19–19
Gamelan angklung

This music uses the five-tone *gamelan angklung* of northern Bali.

A Gamelan from Bali

Gamelans from the small island of Bali are generally more energetic than the gamelans of the island of Java. **Listen** for the variety of percussion instruments in *Kebjar teruna*, a piece for Balinese gamelan.

CD 19–20

Kebjar teruna

The *kebjar* is a dramatic Balinese dance in which a dancer interprets the different moods played by the gamelan.

▲ Terraced rice fields in Bali, Indonesia

Tuned Percussion

Select a variety of percussion instruments that play pitches. Xylophone, glockenspiel, bells, and all pitched Orff instruments would be good choices.

When you have assembled a tuned percussion ensemble, you can **play** your instrument in a creative way.

- Explore your instrument. How do you create a sound? **Create** interesting rhythms with your instrument.

- Experiment with combining different timbres. When everyone is ready to start, one person may begin playing. Others should gradually join in and play together with what is already going on.

- After some time, stop the ensemble and **discuss** how to make it sound better; then **play** again.

Singing the Blues Away

Here is a special form of jazz singing called "scat." Scat singing is a jazz style that uses cool-sounding nonsense syllables. The idea is to make your voice sound like a jazz instrument.

One of the most important jazz singers to adopt and use scat singing as part of his style was Mel Tormé [tohr-MAY].

Listen to Tormé's classic scat singing in *It Don't Mean a Thing If It Ain't Got that Swing*.

CD 19–21

It Don't Mean a Thing (If It Ain't Got That Swing)

by Duke Ellington
as performed by Mel Tormé

This performance also features jazz solo improvisations by the members of Mel Tormé's band.

M·U·S·I·C M·A·K·E·R·S

Mel Tormé

Mel Tormé (1925–1999) was one of the most famous jazz singers of all time. His incredible talent at scat singing was one of his trademarks. Tormé began his career early. He was a radio star at age 4, a composer at age 15, and a movie actor at age 18. Although he appeared in many films and TV sitcoms, Tormé is remembered for his legacy of smooth, sophisticated jazz performances.

STRIKE UP THE CHORUS

Millions of people enjoy
singing in choirs. Choirs
perform in all styles—
from folk to rock and
from classical to jazz.

Sing 'n' Snap

Singing the blues doesn't mean you have to be sad.

Sing "Just a Snap-Happy Blues," a song that is sung entirely with scat syllables.

CD 19–22
MIDI 24

just a snap-happy blues

Words and Music by Norma Jean Luckey

Dee bah   doo ___ bop   a dop,   Dee bah   doo ___

___ bop   a dop,   Dee bah   doo ___ bah dee bah dah bah doo bah ___

___   Doo bah   doo bah doo wah ___   dool'-ya doo bah dee bah,

doo bah doo bah ___   dee   doo bah doo bah doo wah ___

Dah bah doo bah ___ bah ___   bah dah   Dah bah doo bah ___   bah ___

dop   Dah bah doo bah ___   bah ___   bah dah,

Snappy Moves

Create some jazzy moves for the blues tune "Just a Snap-Happy Blues." **Move** when you are singing. Freeze when the music rests.

A Gospel Gift

"A Gift to Share" is a gospel song. Gospel music grew out of the African American spirituals of the 18th and 19th centuries. Gospel can be fast or slow, but it is always full of expression.

Sing "A Gift to Share" with expression.

Singing Tips

Sing the vowels of each word as if the vowels stand very tall inside your mouth. Find the green color box in measure 5. Imagine a warm and resonant tone quality as you sing with the shape of an *ah* vowel.

Reading Music Tips

The opening melody appears not to stop or rest until measure 20. How will you decide where to breathe? Use phrase endings and punctuation marks to help you decide.

Knowing the Score

A phrase is a small group of notes that has a definite melody or shape. The first phrase of this song is highlighted in yellow. Notice that there are many phrases in this song—some are long, and others are short. Find measures 33–44. Do the rests interrupt the phrases, or are they part of it?

A Gift to Share

Words and Music by Rollo A. Dilworth

Rhythm Train

Many songs are about trains. African Americans once used trains to symbolize the Underground Railroad—the train to freedom.

Sing "The Gospel Train."

Singing Tips

Enunciating the first consonant of each word adds to the rhythmic vitality of this song. It is important not to slide in and out of pitches. A crisp, rhythmic delivery of the words will capture the style of "The Gospel Train."

Reading Music Tips

The pickup is a rhythmic motive that appears throughout "The Gospel Train." (See the color box on page 398.) **Analyze** the rhythm in this motive. How does it suggest the rhythmic motion of a train?

Knowing the Score

The form of this song is a series of **A** (Refrain) and **B** (Verse) sections. The dynamics vary from f in the first refrain to pp in the first verse. **Analyze** the words to figure out why there is such a large contrast in dynamic levels.

Play these rhythm patterns on a mallet instrument. **Create** ostinatos to accompany "The Gospel Train" by combining the patterns in new ways.

𝒜rts Connection

▲ *Harriet and the Freedom Train* by Barbara Olsen. This mixed-media collage celebrates the life of Harriet Tubman (1821–1913), the anti-slavery activist and a "conductor" on the Underground Railroad. Olsen, who created the art illustrations throughout this lesson, has said her main inspiration has always been "women who have made a difference."

The Gospel Train

African American Spiritual

Arranged by Shirley W. McRae

A

Lit - tle chil-dren, lit - tle chil-dren,

Get on board, lit - tle chil-dren, get on board, lit - tle chil-dren, get on

Lit - tle chil-dren, lit - tle chil-dren,

B

lit - tle chil - dren, Room for man-y a more.

board, lit - tle chil - dren, There's room for man-y a more. 1. The

lit - tle chil - dren, Room for man-y a more.

All a - board!

gos-pel train is com-in', I hear it just at hand, I hear the wheels a -

Train is com - in', hear it just at hand, wheels a -

A Cajun LULLABY

The Acadians were French people who settled in the eastern part of Canada. They were exiled from Canada in the 1750s, and many eventually settled in Louisiana. In Louisiana, the name "Acadian," pronounced "A-ca-jun," was shortened to "Cajun."

Sing the Cajun lullaby "*Fais do do.*"

Singing Tips

Listen to "*Fais do do.*" Notice that it is written in $\frac{3}{4}$ meter, but you will feel it as one beat per measure. As you **sing**, emphasize the strong beat at the beginning of each phrase. Remember that, although the harmony parts are important, they should be sung a little softer than the melody.

Reading Music Tips

When learning a song in another language, approach reading each phrase as follows: first practice the rhythm of the words, using rhythm syllables, then **sing** the melody, using pitch syllables. Next, speak the French words in rhythm before you sing.

Knowing the Score

How many times is the first phrase repeated? In what measure does the second phrase begin?

Cajun accordion ▶

FAIS DO DO
(Go to Sleep)

English Words by Sue Ellen LaBelle

Acadian Folk Song
Arranged by Susan Brumfield

Fais do do, 'co - las, mon p'tit frè - re,
Go to sleep, my dear lit - tle broth - er,

fais do do, t'au - ras du lo lo.
Go to sleep, wake to a new day.

Fais do
Go to

Fais do
Go to

Tune In

A *fais do do* was a community dance. It got its name because parents put their children to bed at the dance. Men and women at a *fais do do* danced the waltz and the two-step.

A SONG OF PEACE

The expression *shalom aleichem* is a Hebrew greeting that means "peace be with you." The song "*Shalom aleichem*" is a song of praise sung by Jewish families on Friday evenings before their Sabbath meal.

Sing *"Shalom aleichem."*

Singing Tips

Sing Part 1 on a legato *loo*, connecting every note. Every time you encounter a pair of eighth notes, stress and lengthen the first note ever so slightly.

Use the recorded Pronunciation Practice to learn the Hebrew lyrics. Then **sing** the Hebrew words, stressing and lengthening the first note in each pair of eighth notes. Pay close attention to the accidentals and pitches that give the song its minor sound.

Reading Music Tips

Identify the F-sharps and F-naturals in the song. Notice what pitches are before and after these notes.

Knowing the Score

Analyze the score to determine where in the music both voice parts are singing the same notes. Where are the parts singing in harmony?

SHALOM ALEICHEM

Traditional Jewish Song
Arranged by Allan E. Naplan

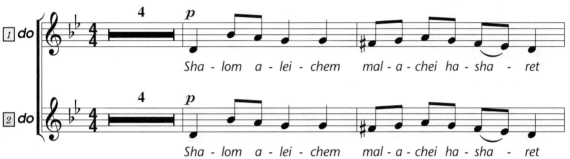

Sha - lom a - lei - chem mal - a - chei ha - sha - ret

Sha - lom a - lei - chem mal - a - chei ha - sha - ret

mal - a - chei el - yon mi - me - lech

mal - a - chei el - yon mi - me - lech

mal - a - chei ham - la - chim ha - ka - dosh ba - ruch hu.

mal - a - chei ham - la - chim ha - ka - dosh ba - ruch ___ hu.

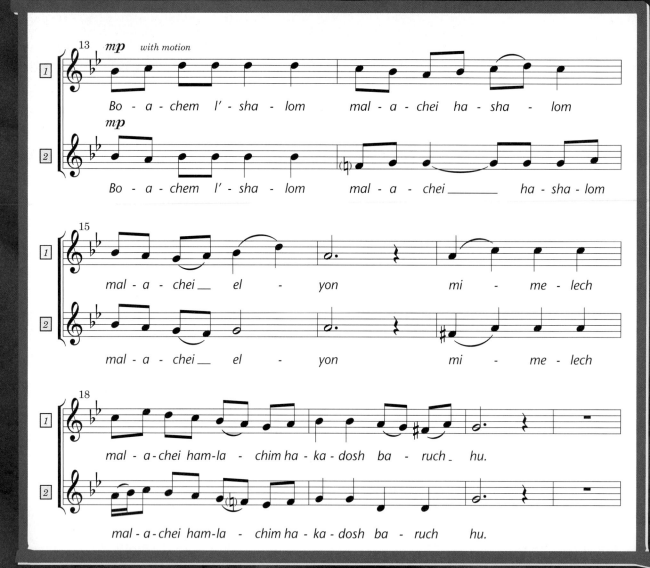

Bo - a - chem l' - sha - lom mal - a - chei ha - sha - lom

Bo - a - chem l' - sha - lom mal - a - chei _____ ha - sha - lom

mal - a - chei __ el - yon mi - me - lech

mal - a - chei __ el - yon mi - me - lech

mal - a - chei ham-la - chim ha - ka - dosh ba - ruch _ hu.

mal - a - chei ham-la - chim ha - ka - dosh ba - ruch hu.

A Gift of Song

A group of singers and musicians banded together in 1985 to record "*Cantaré, cantarás.*" All the proceeds from the song went to help needy children in Latin America, the Caribbean, and Africa. "*Cantaré, cantarás*" has become well known throughout the world.

Sing "*Cantaré, cantarás.*"

Singing Tips

A good warm-up can help you get ready to sing your best. Try singing *so, mi, fa, re, do* in a slow tempo. Concentrate on good pitch and tone quality. Examine measures 1–6. Then **sing** them using pitch syllables. **Listen** to the Pronunciation Practice to learn the Spanish words. Then **sing** "*Cantaré, cantarás.*"

Reading Music Tips

Composers often use sequences to make a melody more interesting. A sequence repeats a pattern, beginning on a different note of the scale. Notice how the notes in measures 3–4 are repeated in measures 5–6 (down a whole step). Sight-read the sequence patterns in measures 11–14.

Knowing the Score

"*Cantaré, cantarás*" is in **A** **B** **A** **B** form. **Describe** the "roadmap" of the sections. In the refrain, what intervals do the two voice parts most frequently sing to create harmony?

Cantaré, cantarás
(I Will Sing, You Will Sing)

English Words by Eileen Mahood-José

Words and Music by Albert Hammond and Juan Carlos Calderón
Arranged by Richard Kaller

A VERSE

F₇   B♭   F₇

Te da - ré __ cuan - to pue - do dar, __
I will give __ all that I can give, __

D₇/F♯   Gm   E♭   F

Só - lo sé can - tar __ y pa - ra tí es me can - to __
I can on - ly sing, __ and this song is my gift. _____

F₇   B♭   F₇

__ Y mi voz __ Jun - to a los de - más, __
__ And my voice __ to - geth - er with the rest, __

D₇/F♯   Gm   E♭   F

En la in - men - si - dad __ se es - tá __ es - cu - chan - do.
ech - oes through the world __ un - til __ it __ finds __ suc - cess.

Strike Up the Chorus

B REFRAIN

17 F7 Bb Eb

Can - ta - ré _____ can - ta - rás _____
Ca - da vez _____ so - mos más _____
I will sing, _____ you will sing, _____
If you hold _____ out a hand, _____

21 F7 Bb

Y e - sa luz _____ al fi - nal _____ del sen - de - ro.
Y si al fin _____ nos da - mos la ma - no
And a song _____ will bring ___ us to - geth - er.
And you nev - er let go _____ of your dream, _____

25 Bb Gm C7

Bri - lla - rá _____ co - mo un sol _____ Que i - lu - mi -
Siem - pre ha - brá _____ un lu - gar _____ Pa - ra to -
And our hopes _ and our prayers, _ We will make _
We'll make sure ___ there's a place ___ For ___ ev -

30 Cm7 Dm Eb **1.** F7 **2.** (Last time
F7 repeat refrain ad lib)

- na el mun - do en - te - ro.
- do ser _____ hu - ma - - no.
____ them _ last ____ for - ev - er.
- 'ry hu - man __ be - - ing.

414

*A*rts Connection

▲ *Calla Lily Vendor* by Mexican artist
Diego Rivera (1886–1957)

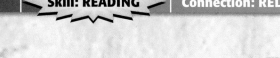

A Sailing Song

"*Vem kan segla?*" ("Who Can Sail?") is a choral arrangement of a folk song from Finland. Finland is a northern European country that borders Russia. Other countries in this region, such as Sweden and Norway, also claim versions of this song. Look carefully at the words of the song. What do you think they mean?

Sing "*Vem kan segla?*"

Singing Tips

Pay careful attention to your breathing technique. This will help you change dynamics and sing *crescendos* and *decrescendos*. **Sing** measures 1–8 in one breath.

Reading Music Tips

Rhythm Look at the rhythm pattern in measures 1 and 2 of Part 2. Find the other places in the song where this rhythm occurs. This is an important motive in "*Vem kan segla?*"

Melody At the start of the song, notice that the melody of Part 3 echoes Part 2. Where else does this occur?

Dynamics Find the dynamic markings in the score. What do the letters p and mp stand for? Find the *cresc.* marking. What does *crescendo* mean?

Knowing the Score

All the parts for "*Vem kan segla?*" are printed, including the keyboard accompaniment.

Choral music printed this way is called an *octavo*. A pianist uses the *octavo* score to play the accompaniment.

Arts Connection

Carved memorial stone (*stele*) with a ship of Vikings (7th century) ▼

Vem kan segla?

(Who Can Sail?)

English Words by Gunilla Marcus-Luboff

Folk Song from Finland
Arranged by Carl-Bertil Agnestig

Keyboard

Arts Connection

▲ Two Norse ships at sea (Hand-colored woodcut)

Playing the Recorder

Adding a recorder accompaniment to a choral piece adds
variety to the vocal parts. Practice and then **play** this recorder
part for "*Vem kan segla?*"

▲ *Thor's Hammer.* A Viking
amulet from Iceland
(10th century)

The Gokstad Ship. A Viking
ship (9th century) ▶

◀ A Scandinavian gilded bronze
padlock (7th century)

Midnight Melodies

The story of Christmas includes many carols about angels singing in the sky on Christmas night. "Hark the Herald Angels Sing," "Angels We Have Heard on High," and "It Came Upon a Midnight Clear" are examples of carols in which angels sing about important news for all people of the world.

Sing "Angels on the Midnight Clear."

Singing Tips

Sing the words that have half notes with a feeling of length accompanied by a slight *crescendo*. **Sing** the countermelody a little softer and in a flowing style when accompanying the melody.

Reading Music Tips

Analyze and **sing** the pick-up notes and the following downbeats in the color boxes. Emphasize the words on the downbeats, as in *it CAME*.

Knowing the Score

Identify the main melody and the countermelody. How often are the melody and countermelody sung separately and together? **Identify** the *fermata*. What is its musical purpose?

Angels on the Midnight Clear

Words by Edmund H. Sears

Music by Richard S. Willis

It came up - on __ the mid - night clear, That glo - rious

song __ of old, _____ From an - gels bend - ing near the

earth, To touch their harps __ of gold: _____ "Peace on the

earth, __ good - will to men, From heav'n's __ all gra - cious

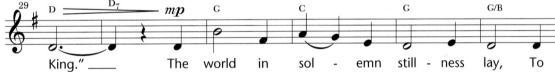

King." ____ The world in sol - emn still - ness lay, To

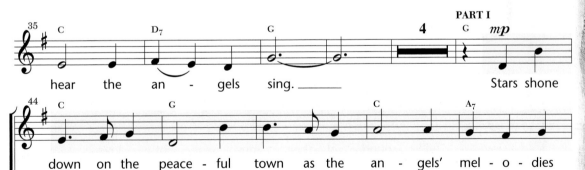

hear the an - gels sing. _____ Stars shone

down on the peace - ful town as the an - gels' mel - o - dies

Nobody knows for certain when "Ding Dong! Merrily on High" was written. The composer is unknown. So, we call it a traditional Christmas carol. In medieval times, the word *carol* meant a type of dance. By the 16th century, a joyous song for Christmas became the definition of carol.

Sing "Ding Dong! Merrily on High."

Singing Tips

The tempo of the song is fast and lively, so sing crisp consonants to make sure listeners can understand the words. Words such as *ding*, *dong,* and *ringing* provide a perfect opportunity to imitate the sounds of bells. To sound like bells, enunciate the consonants with energy.

Reading Music Tips

"Ding Dong! Merrily on High" is in verse-refrain, or **A** **B** **A** **B** **A** **B** form. The refrains are a little different each time and should be practiced. The refrain of the second verse (measure 35) is sung as a sequence, alternating between the voice parts on the word *Gloria.* Notice that the ending pitch of each part is the same as the beginning pitch of the next part.

Knowing the Score

The half notes in measures 17–18 and 56–60 imitate bells. The key signature changes before Verse 3 (measure 48). Why would a composer change keys at this point in the song? Find the *fermata* sign and the term *poco a poco cresc.* What are these words telling the singer to do?

Ding Dong! Merrily on High

Arranged by Howard Cable
Edited by Henry Leck

Take a Little Trip

"Goin' to Boston" is an American folk song. Until the twentieth century, folk songs were usually not written down. People sang them and had to remember them in order to pass them from one generation to the next. Hearing and singing songs in this way—by ear—is called the "oral/aural tradition."

Sing "Goin' to Boston."

Singing Tips

Listen carefully when you sing harmony. The harmony should be strong, but just a little softer than the melody. Use crisp consonants, good vowel shapes, and your best breathing skills to make the words in the refrain sound clear to the listeners.

Reading Music Tips

When learning "Goin' to Boston," focus on melodies and rhythms that repeat. For example, when you learn the phrases *Goodbye, girls, I'm goin' to Boston* and *Won't we look purty in the ballroom,* you will know much of the song.

Look over the pitch patterns in Verse 1 before you **sing** the song. Do they move mostly by step or by skip? Find the rhythm pattern in measures 9 and 10. Where does it repeat in the rest of the song? **Listen** to the first refrain as you follow the music. Which pitch gives the song a bit of an unusual sound?

Knowing the Score

Look for a meter change. Why do you think the song's arranger did this? "Goin' to Boston" has five verses. How are they similar? How are they different?

Goin' to Boston

Folk Song from the United States
Arranged by Shirley W. McRae

Good - bye,   girls. _____

1. Good-bye, girls, I'm   goin' to Bos - ton,   good-bye, girls, I'm   goin' to Bos - ton,

good-bye, girls, I'm   goin' to Bos - ton,   ear - lye in   the   morn - in'.

Won't we look pur-ty in the ball - room,   won't we look pur-ty in the ball - room,

won't we look pur-ty in the ball - room,   ear - lye in   the   morn - in'.

2. Come on, girls, and   let's   go with 'em,   come on, girls, and   let's   go with 'em,

come on, girls, and   let's   go with 'em,   ear - lye in   the   morn - in'.

Won't we look pur-ty in the ball - room, won't we look pur-ty in the ball - room,

won't we look pur-ty in the ball - room, ear - lye in the morn - in'.

(Clap)

(Pat)

(Clap)

3. Right and left will make it bet - ter, ____

mf

(Clap)

right and left will make it bet - ter, __

mf

right and left will make it bet - ter, ear - lye in the morn - in'.

____ ear - lye in the morn - in'.

Won't we look pur-ty in the ball - room, won't we look pur-ty in the

Won't we look pur-ty in the ball - room, won't we look pur-ty in the

ball - room, won't we look pur-ty in the ball - room,

ball - room, won't we look pur-ty in the ball - room,

ear - lye in the morn - in'.

ear - lye in the morn - in'.

5. Get out the way, you'll get run o - ver, get out the way, you'll get run o - ver,

get out the way, you'll get run o - ver, ear - lye in the morn - in'.

(Clap) Won't we look pur-ty in the ball - room, won't we look pur-ty in the

ball - room, won't we look pur-ty in the ball - room, ear - lye in the

morn - in'. Won't we look pur - ty in the ball - room,

won't we look pur - ty in the ball - room, won't we look pur - ty in the

ball - room, ear - lye in the morn - in'!

Everybody's a Body

Our differences are what make us all wonderful and unique. Music helps us realize that all people are equal and deserving of respect.

The "Body" Song is in calypso style and reminds us that we are all somebody important.

Listen to *The "Body" Song* and its important message.

CD 21–1
The "Body" Song

**by Brenda Russell
as performed by Al Jarreau
and Brenda Russell**

The calypso style and steel drums create an exciting rhythmic beat in *The "Body" Song*.

Celebrate the Day

Our planet is home to many different cultures. We are many peoples, alike in many ways and different in many ways. Let's sing and celebrate together.

A Single Sun

We live under a single sun on a single planet.

Sing "Under the Same Sun," a song with another powerful message.

Words and Music by Clifford Carter

CD 21–2

Under the Same Sun

REFRAIN

Though we dance to __ the beat   of   a dif - f'rent drum, we can

Last time (Repeat ad lib.)
Fine

learn to live _ to-geth - er ___ un - der _ the same _ sun. ___

VERSE

1. Some-times it's hard _____   to un - der - stand _____
2. From town to town, _____   from shore to   shore, _____

our   bro-thers _ and sis - ters _____   from a dis-tant _ land. _
there's a big-ger _____   world _____   out - side your _ door. _

____   Try to em-brace   an - oth - er view,
____   Op - en your heart   to some-one new,

Last time to next strain

a brand new world   is call-ing out   to   you. _____
the love   you give   will _ come back to   you. _____

440

A World United

The United Nations was formed on October 24, 1945, to promote world peace and preserve human dignity. Its headquarters, though in New York City, is actually international territory. Fifty-one countries signed the original charter. Today more than 185 countries are members of this worldwide organization.

Russian composer Dmitri Shostakovich wrote the melody to this song. Harold Rome, an American teacher, later added the lyrics. **Sing** the song "The United Nations."

Tune In

The United Nations has its own flag, its own post office, and its own postage stamps.

Arts Connection

▲ This stained glass window in the UN building was designed by the French artist Marc Chagall as a memorial to Dag Hammarskjöld. Hammarskjöld, the second secretary-general of the United Nations, died in a plane crash in 1961 while on a mission of peace. The window contains several symbols of peace and love.

The United Nations on the March

Words by Harold Rome

Music by Dmitri Shostakovich

VERSE

1. The sun and the stars all are ring-ing, _____ With song ris-ing
2. Take heart all you na-tions swept un-der, _____ With pow-ers of
3. As sure as the sun meets the morn-ing, _____ And riv-ers go

from the ___ earth. _____ The hope of hu-man-i-ty
dark-ness that ride, _____ The wrath of the peo-ple shall
down to the sea, _____ A new day for all is ___

sing-ing, _____ A hymn to a new world in birth.
thun-der, _____ Re-lent-less as time and the tide.
dawn-ing, _____ Our chil-dren shall live proud and free!

REFRAIN

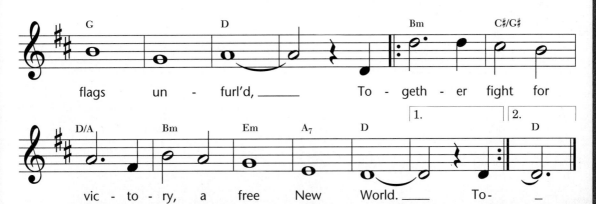

U-ni-ted Na-tions on the march with

flags un-furl'd, _____ To-geth-er fight for

1. **2.**

vic-to-ry, a free New World. _____ To- _

CD 21–4

Celebrating People

Native Americans celebrate harmony among people and with the universe through music and dance, as shown by the example on page 445. The song on page 446 expresses a similar message of peace, love, and unity.

Celebration Through Dance

The Native American round dance is a social dance commonly performed at pow-wows. The singers may use lyrics or vocables (syllable sounds).

Listen to *Round Dance.* The rhythm is in meter in 3 with accents on the strong beats. What instruments accompany the singers?

CD 21–6
Round Dance

Traditional Round Dance
as performed at the Kihekah Steh Pow-wow, Skiatook, Oklahoma

This pow-wow round dance is in the tradition of the Plains Indians and uses a leader-response style.

▲ An intertribal group of Native Americans demonstrating and teaching a friendship round dance to schoolchildren

Moving to the Round Dance

Perform the following round dance movements as you listen to the music again.

- Form a circle.

- Join hands or place your hands on your neighbors' shoulders.

- Move to the left (clockwise) with a side-stepping movement. Move your feet on each strong beat—left-together.

The round dance is known by many different names. "Circle dance," "friendship dance," "Mother Earth dance," and "owl dance" are just a few.

No Voice Is Small

"I Am But a Small Voice" is a song with a message of peace and love.

Sing the song and reflect on the hope for peace in the world.

CD 21–7

I Am But a Small Voice

Original Words by Odina E. Batnag

English Words and Music by Roger Whittaker

Countermelody

Give us peace, _ pros-per-i-ty, ___ And love for all man-kind.

Melody

Peace, pros-per-i-ty, ___ And love for all man - kind.

I am but a small voice, _ I have but a

small _ dream: _ To smile up-on the sun, Be free to dance _ and sing, Be

free to sing _ my song to ev - 'ry - one.

Signing a Message

Learn the three signs for the phrase, *I am but a small voice*. **Perform** the signs as you sing the song.

▲ *I am but a*

▲ *small*

▲ *voice.*

HALLOWEEN TREAT

For many people, Halloween is a time to wear costumes and gather treats. "The Purple People Eater" is an early pop song that made fun of the flying saucer scares of the 1950s. Join in the nonsense while you **sing** this song.

CD 21–9

THE PURPLE PEOPLE EATER

Words and Music by Sheb Wooley

1. Well, I saw the thing a-com-in' out of the sky, __ It had
2. Well, he came down to Earth __ and he __ lit in a tree, __ I said,

one long horn and one big eye. __ I com-menced to shak-in' and I
"Mister Purple People Eater, don't eat me." __ I heard him __ say __ in a

said, "Ooh - wee, __ it looks like a pur-ple peo - ple eat - er to me." __
voice so gruff, __ "I wouldn't eat __ you __ 'cause __ you're __ so tough." __

REFRAIN

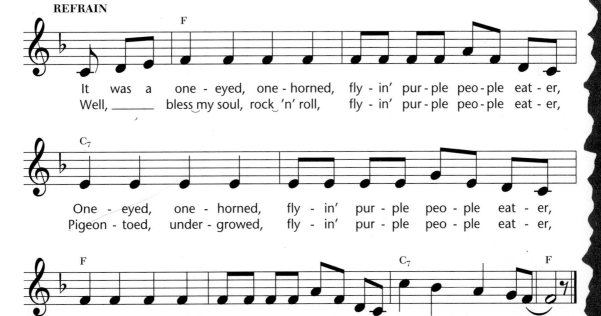

F

It was a one - eyed, one - horned, fly - in' pur - ple peo - ple eat - er,
Well, _____ bless my soul, rock 'n' roll, fly - in' pur - ple peo - ple eat - er,

C₇

One - eyed, one - horned, fly - in' pur - ple peo - ple eat - er,
Pigeon - toed, under - growed, fly - in' pur - ple peo - ple eat - er,

F   C₇   F

One-eyed, one-horned, fly - in' pur-ple peo-ple eat-er, Sure looked strange to me. _
He wears short shorts, friend-ly lit - tle peo-ple eat-er, What a sight to see. _

Thai Full Moon

In Thailand, people observe *Loigratong*, a celebration of the full moon, in November. *Loigratong* originated in the fourteenth century as a request to the water spirits to forgive any offenses against them.

Listen to the recorded Pronunciation Practice to learn the Thai words, then **sing** the song.

In many Asian cultures, Western harmonies are used today to accompany songs. **Perform** an accompaniment to "*Loigratong*," using the I, IV, and V_7 chords. Accompany the song with a keyboard, guitar, or Autoharp.

Festival participants holding "*Loigratong* boats"—small rafts in the shape of a lotus flower ▼

Loigratong

English Words by Alice Firgau

Folk Song from Thailand

วัน เพ็ญ_ เดือน สิบ สอง_ น้ำ ก็ นอง เต็ม_ตลิ่ง เราทั้ง__
wan pen__ deup sip song__ nam gau nong tem ta-ling rao tang
The ri - ver is ris - ing, the moon, it is full. Ev - 'ry -

หลาย_ ชาย หญิง สนุก กัน จริง วัน ลอย กระ ทง
lai _____ chai ying sa-nook gan - jing wan loi - gra-tong
one _____ feels so hap-py and glad on Loi - gra-tong.

ลอย ลอย กระ ทง ลอย ลอย กระ ทง ลอย กระ
loi loi - gra-tong loi loi - gra-tong loi - gra -
Loi, Loi - gra-tong, Loi, Loi - gra-tong, Loi - gra -

ทง กัน แล้ว ขอ_ เชิญ น้อง แก้วออก มา รำวง รำ วง รำ
tong gan lah-ow koh__ churn nong kay-oh ock ma lum wong lum
tong. Come, float your _ boat, then join the dance with me. We

วง วัน ลอย กระ ทง รำ วง วัน ลอย กระ ทง บุญ จะ
wong wan loi - gra-tong lum wong wan loi - gra-tong boon ja
dance on Loi - gra-tong, we dance on Loi - gra-tong, And we're

ส่ง ให้ เรา สุก ใจ บุญ จะ ส่ง ให้ เรา สุก ใจ
song hey rao sook jai boon ja song hey rao sook jai
hap - py as can be, and we're hap - py as can be.

Chanukah Lullaby

People of the Jewish faith celebrate Chanukah [HAHN-noo-kah], the Festival of Lights. During Chanukah, children of all ages play the *dreydl* [DREY-dl] game. The *dreydl* is a four-sided top with a Hebrew letter on each side. When the *dreydl* stops spinning, players exchange pennies and food according to which side of the *dreydl* faces upward.

Sing the traditional Chanukah song "*S'vivon*" [SEH-vee-vohn].

CD 21–15

S'vivon
(Dreydl)

Hebrew Words by L. Kipnis
English Words by Sue Ellen LaBelle and David Eddleman

Folk Song from Israel

S' - vi - von, sov sov sov, Cha - nu - kah _____ hu - chag tov.
S' - vi - von, turn and turn, Play the game, _ it's _ fun to learn.

Cha - nu - kah hu-chag tov, S' - vi - von _ sov sov sov. Chag sim - chah _
Cel - e - brate, take a turn, spin the top as can-dles burn. Cha - nu - kah, the

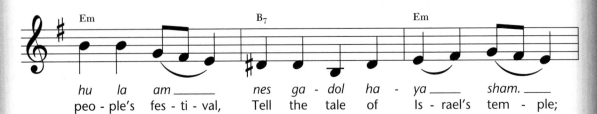

hu la am _____ nes ga - dol ha - ya _____ sham. ____
peo - ple's fes - ti - val, Tell the tale of Is - rael's tem - ple;

D.C. al Fine

Nes ga - dol ha - ya sham, _____ chag sim - chah _ hu la am.
Cel - e - brate the light and prayer, _ And how a won - der hap-pened there.

Chanukah Ensemble

Play percussion instruments as an accompaniment to *"S'vivon."* When the tambourine player plays a half note, you will shake, or rattle, the tambourine. Experiment by adding an *accelerando* to the music, or by playing the song at different tempos. **Describe** how changes to the tempo affect the character of the song.

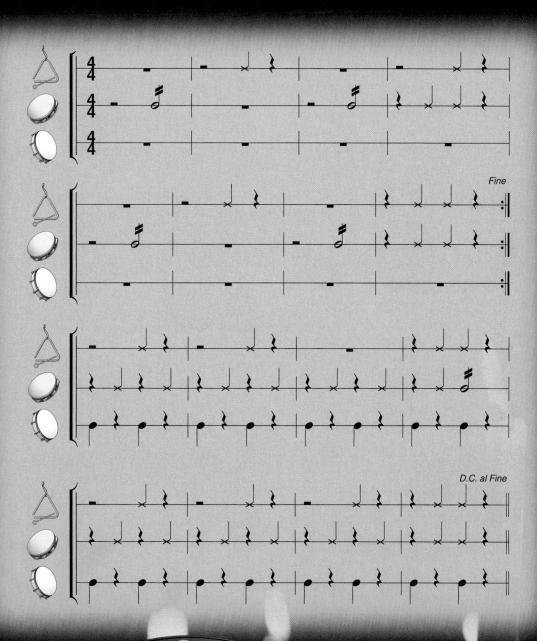

Fine

D.C. al Fine

Tune In

Chanukah is a Hebrew word that means "dedication."

Winter Celebrations

In many parts of the world people celebrate the change of seasons. Winter is a time of many celebrations.

Arts Connection

▲ *The Old Oaken Bucket in Winter* by Grandma Moses.
Grandma Moses (1860–1961) was over 70 years old when she began painting. Although she never had an art lesson, her work is praised by critics. She often painted scenes of simple rural life.

Wintertime Singing

Sing "Winter Song" in unison. After you know the melody, learn the harmony part and the countermelody part.

Read and clap the rhythm of measures 1 and 2. How many times does this rhythmic phrase appear?

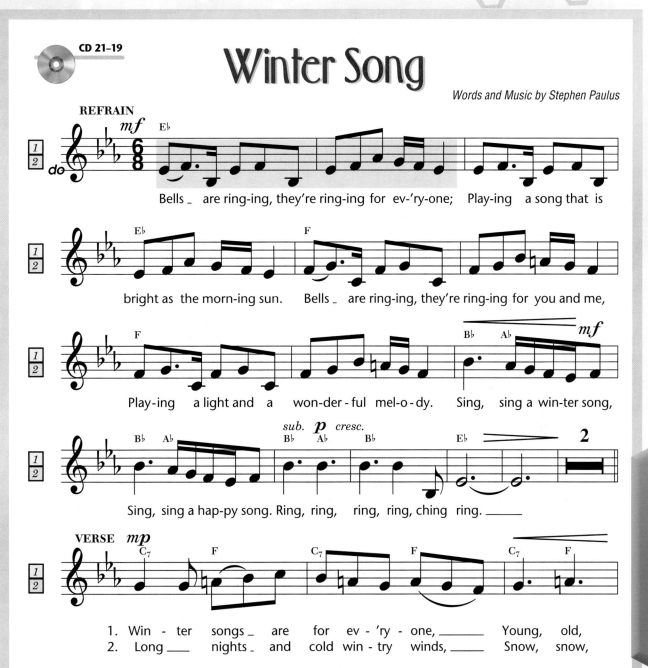

CD 21–19

Winter Song

Words and Music by Stephen Paulus

REFRAIN

Bells _ are ring-ing, they're ring-ing for ev-'ry-one; Play-ing a song that is

bright as the morn-ing sun. Bells _ are ring-ing, they're ring-ing for you and me,

Play-ing a light and a won-der-ful mel-o-dy. Sing, sing a win-ter song,

Sing, sing a hap-py song. Ring, ring, ring, ring, ching ring. _____

VERSE

1. Win - ter songs _ are for ev - 'ry - one, _____ Young, old,
2. Long ___ nights _ and cold win - try winds, _____ Snow, snow,

Troika Tune

Listen to this musical depiction of a *troika*, a Russian sleigh drawn by a team of three horses. How does the music convey the motion of the sleigh gliding across the snow-covered countryside?

CD 21–21
Troika

from *Lieutenant Kijé*
by Sergei Prokofiev

Prokofiev composed this music in 1933 for a film about the daring adventures of a lieutenant in the Czar's army.

M·U·S·I·C M·A·K·E·R·S

Sergei Prokofiev

Composer **Sergei Prokofiev** (1891–1953) grew up in Ukraine on his family's farm. His mother, a talented piano player, sparked her son's interest in music with visits to the opera in Moscow. At the age of 11, Prokofiev received private lessons in music theory and composition. At the age of 13, he began his formal training in music at the St. Petersburg Conservatory, the leading music school in Russia.

Prokofiev composed for ballet (*Romeo and Juliet*), opera (*The Love of Three Oranges*), and the orchestra (*Lieutenant Kijé*).

Arts Connection

▲ *Sergei Prokofiev* by Pyotr Konchalosky, 1934

Christmas Celebrations

Caroling is a traditional activity at Christmas. Singers sometimes walk from house to house singing Christmas carols. They may also go from room to room at a hospital or nursing home.

Sing the song "Caroling, Caroling."

CD 21–22

Caroling, Caroling

Lyrics by Wihla Hutson   *Music by Alfred Burt*

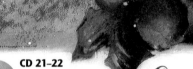

1. Car-o-ling, car-o-ling, now we go; Christ-mas bells are ring - ing!
2. Car-o-ling, car-o-ling, thru the town; Christ-mas bells are ring - ing!

Car-o-ling, car-o-ling, thru the snow; Christ-mas bells are ring - ing!
Car-o-ling, car-o-ling, up and down; Christ-mas bells are ring - ing!

Joy-ous voic-es sweet and clear, Sing the sad of heart to cheer.
Mark ye well the song we sing, Glad-some tid-ings now we bring.

Ding, dong, ding, dong, Christ-mas bells are ring - ing!
Ding, dong, ding, dong, Christ-mas bells are ring - ing!

Glorious Times

The music for "*Gloria, Gloria*" was composed by Franz Joseph Haydn. The lyrics are in Latin.

Sing the entire melody of "*Gloria, Gloria*." Then divide into groups and **perform** it as a round.

In the British Isles, carolers sang carols and received a drink of hot punch from the wassail bowl. *Wassail* means "be healthy."

Tune In

CD 21–24

Gloria, Gloria

Music by Franz Joseph Haydn

1. Glo - ri - a, Glo - ri - a in ex - cel - sis, Glo - ri - a.

2. Glo - ri - a, Glo - ri - a in ex - cel - sis, Glo - ri - a.

3. Glo - ri - a, Glo - ri - a in ex - cel - sis, Glo - ri - a.

1. Et in ter - ra pax ho - min - i-bus.

2. Et in ter - ra pax ho - min - i-bus.

3. Et in ter - ra pax ho - min - i-bus.

Celebrate the Day

A Kingly Carol

Who are the three characters in this Christmas ballad?

Sing the traditional carol "Good King Wenceslas."

CD 21–27
MIDI 34

Good King Wenceslas

Traditional

1. Good King Wen - ces - las looked out   On the Feast of   Ste - phen,
2. "Hith - er, page, and stand by me,   If thou know'st it,   tell - ing,

When the snow lay round a - bout,   Deep and crisp and   e - ven;
Yon - der pea - sant, who is he?   Where and what his   dwell - ing?"

Bright - ly shone the moon that night, Though the frost was   cru - el,
"Sire, he lives a good league hence, Un - der-neath the   moun - tain;

When a poor man came in sight, Gath-'ring win - ter   fu -   el.
Right a -gainst the for - est fence, By Saint Ag - nes' foun -   tain."

3. "Bring me flesh and bring me wine, Bring me pinelogs hither,
Thou and I will see him dine, When we bear them thither."
Page and monarch forth they went, Forth they went together;
Through the rude wind's wild lament, And the bitter weather.

4. "Sire, the night is darker now, And the wind blows stronger;
Fails my heart, I know not how, I can go no longer."
"Mark my footsteps, good my page! Tread thou in them boldly;
Thou shalt find the winter's rage Freeze thy blood less coldly."

5. In his master's steps he trod, Where the snow lay dinted;
Heat was in the very sod Which the saint had printed.
Therefore, Christian folk, be sure, Wealth or rank possessing;
Ye who now will bless the poor, Shall yourselves find blessing.

The Good King Continues

to this contemporary version of the same carol.

CD 21–29
Good King Wenceslas

Traditional Carol
as performed by Mannheim Steamroller

This arrangement features electronic timbres and
contemporary rhythms.

Kwanzaa Joy

Kwanzaa is a unique African American celebration that focuses on the traditional values of family, community responsibility, commerce, and self-improvement. The celebration begins on December 26 and continues through January 1. The *kinara* holds seven candles. The candles symbolize the principles of *Kwanzaa*. **Sing** "The Joy of Kwanzaa" with expression that matches its lyrics.

CD 22–1

The Joy of Kwanzaa

Words and Music by Reggie Royal

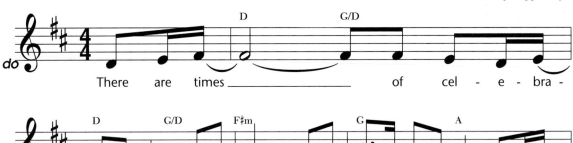

There are times _____ of cel - e - bra -

- tion _ in our lives, here or far a - way, _ That our love _

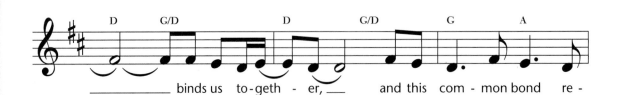

_____ binds us to-geth - er, _ and this com - mon bond re -

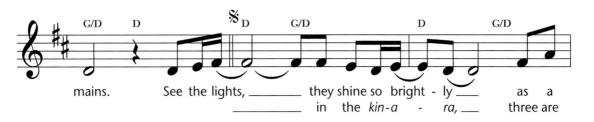

mains. See the lights, _____ they shine so bright - ly ___ as a
_____ in the *kin-a* - *ra,* ___ three are

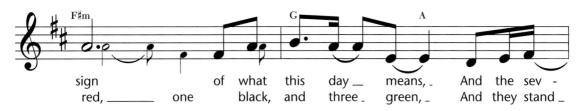

sign of what this day ___ means, _ And the sev -
red, _____ one black, and three _ green, _ And they stand _

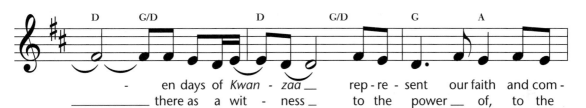

- en days of *Kwan* - *zaa* ___ rep - re - sent our faith and com -
_____ there as a wit - ness _ to the power ___ of, to the

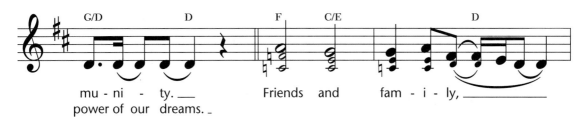

mu - ni - ty. ___ Friends and fam - i - ly, _____
power of our dreams. _

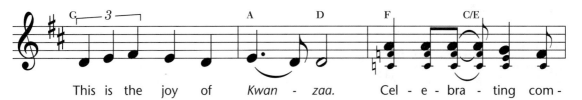

This is the joy of *Kwan* - *zaa.* Cel - e - bra - ting com -

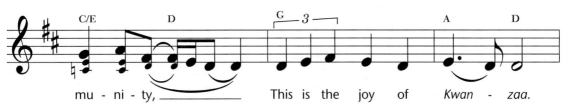

mu - ni - ty, _____ This is the joy of *Kwan* - *zaa.*

2nd time to Coda ⊕

D.S.

Can - dles burn _

Coda

And the road of life be-fore __ us is a

road with man - y turns, But if we will walk to -

geth - er, ___ there is so much we __ can learn, we can

learn. Un - i - ty, ___ de - ter - mi - na - tion, _ work-ing

with ___ re-spon-si - bil - i - ty, _ come to-geth - er for a pur-

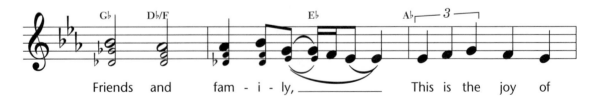

- pose, _ and cre - ate through faith what we want to __ be. __

Friends and fam - i - ly, ___ This is the joy of

Take It to the Net Visit *www.sfsuccessnet.com* to learn more about holiday music.

Kwan - zaa. Cel - e - bra - ting com - mu - ni - ty, _____

This is the joy of Kwan - zaa, This is the joy of

Kwan - zaa. _____

Martin Luther King Day

Martin Luther King Jr. was a man with a dream. He dreamed that all people could live together harmoniously. King was an important leader of the Civil Rights movement in the 1960s. His birthday, January 15, became a national holiday after his tragic death. "Abraham, Martin, and John" is about four political rights martyrs: Abraham Lincoln, Martin Luther King Jr., John F. Kennedy, and Robert F. Kennedy.

Sing "Abraham, Martin, and John." Start with the melody, then add the harmony parts.

Martin Luther King Jr. ▶

CD 22–3
MIDI 35

Abraham, Martin, and John

Words and Music by Dick Holler
Arranged by Joan R. Hillsman

Has an-y-bod-y here seen my old friend
1. A - bra - ham?
2. Mar - tin?
3. John? ___
4. Bob - by?

Can you tell me where he's gone? _____

John F. Kennedy and
Robert F. Kennedy ▶

1.-3. He freed a lot-ta peo-ple, but it seems the good die
4. I thought I saw him walk-in' up __ o - ver the

young, __ But I just looked a - round and he's
hill ___ with ___ A - bra - ham, Mar - tin, and

1.– 3.
1., 2. gone. _____ Has
3. gone. _____ (To Refrain) John. _____

4.
Fine

REFRAIN

Did-n't you love _ the things they _ stood for? Did-n't they try __ to

find some good for you and me? And we'll be free,

Some - day soon, it's gon-na be __ one day. Has

D.S. al Fine

African American slaves frequently sang spirituals such as "Free at Last." Like Martin Luther King Jr., they looked forward to a day when they would have true feedom.

Sing "Free at Last." Take turns singing the solo sections of the song.

CD 22–5

Free at Last

African American Spiritual
Arranged by Joan R. Hillsman

REFRAIN

Free at last, ___ free at last, ___
Thank God Al-might-y I'm free at last. ___
Free at last, ___ free at last, ___
Thank God Al-might-y I'm free at last. ___

VERSE

Solo

Eb

Way down yon-der in the grave-yard walk,
On a my knees __when the light pass'd by,
Some a these morn - ings, __ bright and fair,

Chorus

Thank God Al-might-y I'm

Bb7   Eb   *Solo*

Me and my Je-sus gon-na meet and talk, __
Thought _ my soul _would _ rise and fly, __
Gon-na meet __ King Je - sus __ in the air, __

free at last. __

Eb   Bb7   Eb   *D.C. al Fine*

Thank God Al - might - y I'm free at last. __

Chorus

Thank God Al - might - y I'm free at last. __

◀ Martin Luther King, Jr. Memorial in Atlanta, Georgia

Tune In

Martin Luther King's "I Have a Dream" speech ends with a reference to this spiritual—"Free at last! Free at last! Thank God Almighty, we are free at last!"

Freedom's Cry

Sing the melody of "I Wish I Knew How It Would Feel to Be Free," by the jazz pianist and educator Billy Taylor.

Listen to this jazz arrangement of the song, performed by the composer.

CD 22–7

I Wish I Knew How It Would Feel to Be Free

by Billy Taylor
as performed by the Billy Taylor Trio

The other members of the trio are Chip Jackson on bass and Steve Johns on drums.

CD 22–8

I Wish I Knew How It Would Feel To Be Free

Music by Billy Taylor
Words by Billy Taylor and Dick Dallas
Arranged by Buryl Red

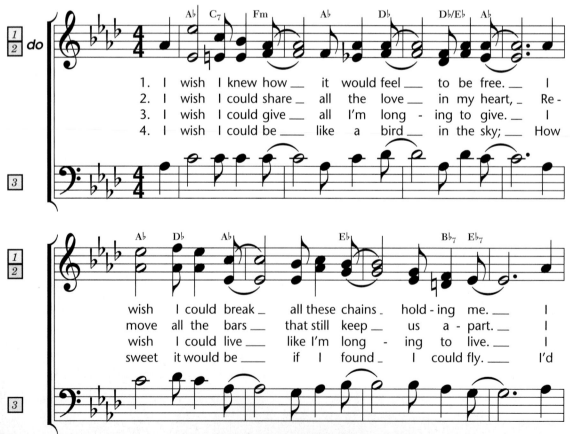

1. I wish I knew how ___ it would feel ___ to be free. ___ I
2. I wish I could share ___ all the love ___ in my heart, ___ Re-
3. I wish I could give ___ all I'm long - ing to give. ___ I
4. I wish I could be ___ like a bird ___ in the sky; ___ How

wish I could break ___ all these chains ___ hold - ing me. ___ I
move all the bars ___ that still keep ___ us a - part. ___ I
wish I could live ___ like I'm long - ing to live. ___ I
sweet it would be ___ if I found ___ I could fly. ___ I'd

wish I could say ___ all the things ___ I should say, ___ Say 'em loud, ___
wish you could know ___ what it means ___ to be me; ___ Then you'd see ___
wish I could do ___ all the things ___ I can do; ___ Though I'm 'way ___
soar to the sun ___ and look down ___ at the sea; ___ Then I'd sing, ___

___ say 'em clear, ___ for the whole ___ world to hear. ___
___ and a - gree, ___ ev-'ry man ___ should be free. ___
___ o - ver - due, ___ I'd be start - ing a - new. ___
___ 'cause I'd know ___ how it feels ___ to be free. ___

Billy Taylor (born 1921) has been playing the piano since he was seven years old. He began his professional jazz piano career at the age of 13 when he played in a jazz club for exactly one dollar. After graduating from Virginia State College, Taylor went to New York City. Billy Taylor has headlined at major jazz clubs in New York City, he has produced more than 32 CDs, and he has received 16 honorary degrees from universities throughout the United States.

Presently Taylor focuses on jazz education and on recording with his trio, the Billy Taylor Trio. He also serves on the National Council of the Arts.

Valentines for friends

Valentine's Day, observed on February 14, is a day to tell your family that you love them. It is also a great day to tell your friends that you appreciate their friendship.

You can give a Valentine greeting by speaking your feelings, giving a hug, or sending a Valentine's card. You can also sing your Valentine greeting. The Spanish song "*Eres tú*" is a song about love. It has a good message for this special day.

Tune In

In Denmark, people send pressed white flowers as Valentines to their friends. The flowers are *snowdrops*.

Sing *"Eres tú"* and imagine you are expressing your feelings to your Valentine.

CD 22–10

Eres tú
(Touch the Wind)

English Words by Mike Hawker *Words and Music by Juan Carlos Calderón*

1. Co-mo u-na pro - me - sa, ___ e - res tú, ___ e - res tú.
1. I woke up this morn - ing, ___ and my mind ___ fell a - way,

Co - mo u-na ma - ña - na, ___ de ve - ra - no.
Look-ing back sad - ly ___ from to - mor - row.

Co - mo u-na son - ri - sa, ___ e - res tú, ___ e - res tú, ___ A - sí, ___
As I heard an ech-o ___ from the past ___ soft-ly say ___ Come back, _

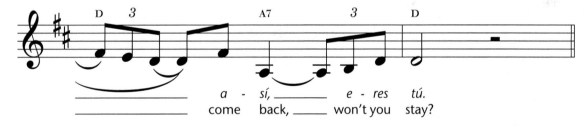

___ a - sí, ___ e - res tú.
come back, ___ won't you stay?

VERSE

D   *3*   A   G   D

2. To - da mi es-pe-ran - za, ___ e - res tú _____ e - res tú.
3. Co - mo mi po - e - ma, ___ e - res tú, _____ e - res tú.
2. I Want-ed to reach you, __ let you know ___ I still care,
3. And on - ly for - ev - er _____ can I say _____ I love you.

D   *3*   A   *3*   G   A

Co - mo llu - via fres - ca _____ en mis ma - nos.
Co - mo u - na gui - ta - rra _____ en la no - che.
I'm lost in the si - lence ___ of my sor - row.
And on - ly for - ev - er _____ have I lost you.

D   *3*   A   G   F#m   G

Co - mo fuer - te bri - sa, __ e - res tú, ___ e - res tú, _____ a - sí, ___
Co - mo mi ho - ri - zon - te, __ e - res tú, ___ e - res tú, _____ a - sí, ___
And I put a prom - ise __ in the wind, _ on the air, _____ to fly ___
But on - ly a dream - er ___ could wake up, ___ as I do, _____ and hope _

D   *3*   A7   *3*   D   A

_____ a - sí, _____ e - res tú.
_____ a - sí, _____ e - res tú.
_____ a - way _____ to you there.
_____ it's still _____ yes - ter - day.

REFRAIN

D   F#m   Bm   G   E/G#   D/A   A

E - res tú, co - mo el a - gua de mi fuen - te,
Touch the wind, catch my love as it goes sail - ing,

A   A/C#   D   G   D   A7   D

E - res tú, __ el fue - go de _____ mi ho - gar.
Touch the wind, _ and I'll be close _____ to you.

474

A World of Love

Although we have different backgrounds and traditions, we all know what love is—no matter which language we speak. Practice saying "I love you" in French, Spanish, Russian, and Hebrew. Then **sing** the song "Love in Any Language."

CD 22–14

Love in Any Language

Words and Music by Jon Mohr and John Mays

Je t'aime.   Te a - mo.   Ya tri-bya lyu-blyu.
(French)   (Spanish)   (Russian)

A - ni o - he - vet ot - ka.   I   love you. __   The
(Hebrew)

sounds are all   as dif - f'rent   as the lands from which they came. __   And

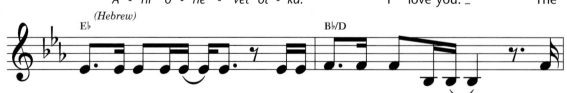

though our words are all __   u-nique, __ our hearts are still the same. _____

476

Signing with Love

Learn to sign these words as you sing "Love in Any Language."

▲ Je t'aime

▲ Te amo

▲ I love you

REFRAIN

Love in an - y lan - guage, _ straight from the heart, _

Pulls us all ___ to - geth - er, _____ nev - er a - part. _ And

once we learn _ to speak _ it, _____ all the world _ will hear, _

Love in an - y lan - guage _ flu - ent - ly spo - ken ___

here. We teach the young _ our dif-f'renc-es, yet look how we're the same. _ We

Birthdays and Anniversaries

Birthdays and anniversaries are reasons to celebrate. Mexicans and Mexican Americans sing this song about "morning" as a birthday greeting.

Sing the song in two-part harmony. The harmony part is a third above the melody.

Las mañanitas

English Words by Lupe Allegria

Folk Song from Mexico

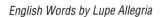

Es - tas   son   las ma - ña - ni - tas   Que can -
Hear   us   sing   las ma - ña - ni - tas   as the

ta - ba el Rey Da - vid,   A las   mu - cha - chas bo -
morn - ing light ap - pears,   And the gen - tle bird will

ni - tas Se las can - ta - mos   a - quí.   Des -
join   in the hap - py   mu - sic   he   hears.   Oh,

pier - ta, mi bien, des - pier - ta,   Mi - ra   que ya a - ma - ne -
wake   up and see the sun - shine. Oh,   wake   up and meet the

ció;   Ya los   pa - ja - ri - llos   can - tan, La lu - na
day.   Hear, the morn - ing bird is   sing - ing, the sil - ver

ya   se   me - tió.
moon has gone   a - way.

Carnaval Celebration

Many cultures celebrate *Carnaval* before Lent. In northwest Argentina, the people of the mountainous region of *Quebrada de Humahuaca* celebrate with singing, playing, and dancing. **Sing** "*El carnavalito humahuaqueño*" in the lively spirit of *Carnaval*.

CD 22–21 El carnavalito humahuaqueño
(The Little Humahuacan Carnival)

English Words by Donald Kalbach

Folk Song from Argentina

1. Lle - gan-do es-tá el _ car-na - val, que-bra-de - ño mi _ cho - li - ta.
2. La la la la__ la la la, la la la la la__ la la la.
1. The car - ni - val _ has be-gun, so be hap-py, my _ dear-est one.
2. La la la la__ la la la, la la la la la__ la la la.

Lle - gan-do es-tá el _ car-na - val, que-bra-de - ño mi _ cho - li - ta.
La la la la__ la la la, la la la la la__ la la la.
The car - ni - val _ has be-gun, so be hap-py, my _ dear-est one.
La la la la__ la la la, la la la la la__ la la la.

Fies - ta de la que - bra - da hu - ma-hua - que - ña pa - ra can - tar.
Fes - ti - val from *que - bra - da,* Come to the par - ty and sing and play.

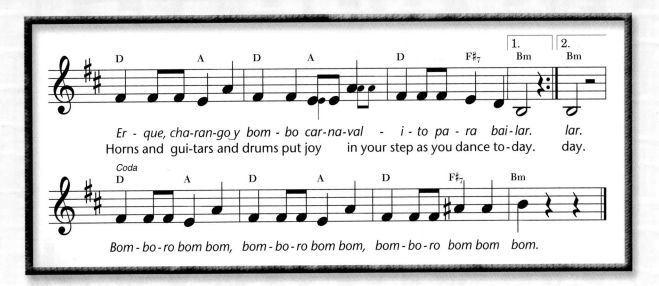

Er - que, cha-ran-go y bom - bo car-na-val - i - to pa - ra bai - lar. lar.
Horns and gui-tars and drums put joy in your step as you dance to-day. day.

Bom - bo - ro bom bom, bom - bo - ro bom bom, bom - bo - ro bom bom bom.

Festive Harmonies

Play this arrangement of *"El carnavalito humahuaqueño"* for mallet instruments. Are the harmonies in this arrangement the same or different than the song recording?

Arranged by Konnie Saliba

Soprano Xylophone

Alto Xylophone (2 players)

Bass Xylophone/Contrabass Xylophone

Coda

patriotism sings

We celebrate patriotism with songs about our country. "America" is a patriotic melody we share with Great Britain. The British sing "God Save the Queen." Which country used the melody first? Why?

Sing "America." What style will you use to express the meaning of the words?

CD 23–1

America

Words by Samuel Francis Smith

Traditional Melody

1. My coun-try! 'tis of thee, Sweet land of lib-er-ty,
2. My na-tive coun-try, thee, Land of the no-ble free,

Of thee I sing; Land where my fa-thers died, Land of the
Thy name I love; I love thy rocks and rills, Thy woods and

Pil-grims' pride, From ev-'ry __ moun-tain-side Let __ free-dom ring!
tem-pled hills; My heart __ with __ rap-ture thrills Like __ that a-bove.

3. Let music swell the breeze,
And ring from all the trees
Sweet freedom's song;
Let mortal tongues awake,
Let all that breathe partake,
Let rocks their silence break,
The sound prolong.

4. Our fathers' God, to Thee,
Author of liberty,
To Thee we sing;
Long may our land be bright
With Freedom's holy light,
Protect us by Thy might,
Great God, our King!

Beautiful America

The beauty of the land that became America is something to celebrate. Katharine Lee Bates wrote this poem that expresses her feelings about our beautiful country. The poem was later set to a hymn tune composed by Samuel A. Ward.

Sing "America, the Beautiful."

Then **listen** to a gospel version of the song.

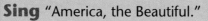

CD 23–3
America, the Beautiful

by S.A. Ward and Katharine Lee Bates

CD 23–4
MIDI 36

America, the Beautiful

Words by Katharine Lee Bates   *Music by S. A. Ward*

1. O beau-ti-ful for spa-cious skies, For am-ber waves of grain, For
2. O beau-ti-ful for pil-grim feet, Whose stern im-pas-sioned stress A
3. O beau-ti-ful for pa-triot dream That sees be-yond the years Thine

pur-ple moun-tain maj-es-ties A-bove the fruit-ed plain! A-
thor-ough-fare for free-dom beat A-cross the wil-der-ness! A-
al-a-bas-ter cit-ies gleam, Un-dimmed by hu-man tears! A-

mer-i-ca! A-mer-i-ca! God shed His grace on thee And
mer-i-ca! A-mer-i-ca! God mend thine ev-'ry flaw, Con-
mer-i-ca! A-mer-i-ca! God shed His grace on thee And

crown thy good with broth-er-hood From sea to shin-ing sea!
firm thy soul in self-con-trol, Thy li-ber-ty in law!
crown thy good with broth-er-hood From sea to shin-ing sea!

young country was struggling to retain its freedom.
We should all reflect on the freedom and
opportunities we now enjoy in the United States.

Sing our National Anthem.

CD 23–6

The Star-Spangled Banner

Words by Francis Scott Key

Music by John Stafford Smith

1. Oh, __ say! can you see, by the dawn's ear - ly light, What so
2. On the shore, dim - ly seen through the mists of the deep, Where the
3. Oh, __ thus be it ever when __ free men shall stand Be -

proud - ly we hailed at the twi - light's last gleam - ing, Whose broad
foe's haugh - ty host in dread si - lence re - pos - es, What is
tween their loved homes and the war's des - o - la - tion! Blest with

stripes and bright stars, through the per - il - ous fight, O'er the
that which the breeze, o'er the tow - er - ing steep, As it
vic - t'ry and peace, may the heav'n - res - cued land Praise the

ram - parts we watched were so gal - lant - ly stream - ing? And the
fit - ful - ly blows, half con - ceals, half dis - clos - es? Now it
Pow'r that hath made and pre - served us a na - tion! Then __

486

A Patriotic Celebration

The selection below, by the American composer and pianist
Louis Moreau Gottschalk, is a musical celebration of America.

Listen for three familiar melodies. Can you name them?

CD 23–8
L'union

by Louis Moreau Gottschalk

Gottschalk (1829–1869) spent most of his childhood in
New Orleans. His music reflects Creole, French, and Latin
American styles.

Music Reading Practice

CD 1–8
MIDI 38

Reading Sequence 1, page 10

Rhythm: Review ♩, ♫♩, ♩, and Ties

As you conduct in meter in 4, use rhythm syllables to **read** and **perform** this counter-rhythm for "Red River Valley." Note how the ties change the rhythm.

CD 1–17
MIDI 39

Reading Sequence 2, page 12

Rhythm: Review ♫♫, ♫♫, ♩. ♩, and Upbeats

Read and **perform** this counter-rhythm for "*Bắt kim thang,*" using rhythm syllables.

Melody: Reading Melodic Patterns

Using pitch syllables, **read** and **sing** this countermelody for
"Bury Me Not on the Lone Prairie."

Melody: Reading Melodic Contour

Read and **sing** this countermelody for "Gonna Build a
Mountain," using pitch syllables.

Reading Sequence 5, page 42

CD 3–3
MIDI 42

Rhythm: Reading Rhythms in ¾

Find the dotted-rhythm patterns below. As you conduct a three-beat pattern, use rhythm syllables to **read** the rhythms. Then **perform** them as an accompaniment for "Farewell to Tarwathie."

Reading Sequence 6, page 44

CD 3–9
MIDI 43

Rhythm: Reading Rhythms in ¾

Using rhythm syllables, **read** and **perform** these rhythms for "Barb'ry Allen."

Melody: Reading a Major Scale

Using pitch syllables and hand signs, **read** and **sing** this countermelody for "*Adiós, amigos.*"

Melody: Reading a Minor Scale

As you tap a steady beat, use pitch syllables to silently **read** and **sing** this countermelody for "*La mariposa.*" This will help develop your inner hearing.

Reading Sequence 9, page 80

CD 5–10
MIDI 46

Rhythm: Reading Augmentation and Diminution

Using rhythm syllables, **read** and **perform** this three-part rhythm accompaniment for *"Do, Re, Mi, Fa."*

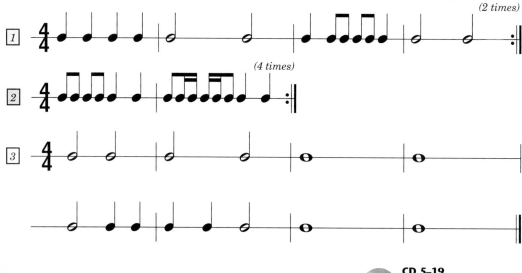

 Reading Sequence 10, page 82

CD 5–19
MIDI 47

Rhythm: Reading Augmentation and Diminution

As you lightly tap the beat, use rhythm syllables to **read** and **perform** this two-part rhythm accompaniment for *"Hava nashira."*

CD 6–6

MIDI 48

Reading Sequence 11, page 94

Melody: Reading in Modes

Using pitch syllables and hand signs, **read** and **sing** this minor countermelody for "Scarborough Fair," which is in dorian mode.

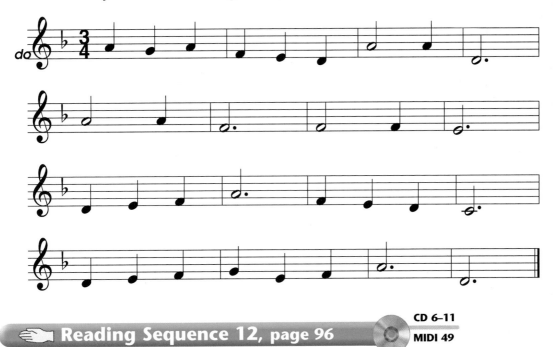

MIDI 49

Reading Sequence 12, page 96

Melody: Reading in Mixolydian Mode

Locate the measures that are identical in each phrase. How are the last two measures of each phrase alike, or different? Then, use pitch syllables to **read** and **sing** this countermelody for "Harrison Town."

Music Reading Practice

Reading Sequence 13, page 118

Rhythm: Reading Rhythms in $\frac{2}{2}$

As you conduct in meter in 2, use rhythm syllables to **read** and **perform** this counter-rhythm for "Swanee."

Reading Sequence 14, page 120

Rhythm: Reading Rhythms in $\frac{3}{8}$

Using rhythm syllables, **read** and **perform** this two-part rhythm accompaniment for "One Morning in May."

Melody: Reading in Harmonic Minor

Read and **sing** this countermelody for *"Lo yisa,"* using hand signs and pitch syllables.

Melody: Reading Melodic Sequences

Identify the melodic sequence in this countermelody for *"Alleluia."* Then, **read** and **sing** it using pitch syllables.

Music Reading Practice

👆 **Reading Sequence 17, page 156**

CD 8–30
MIDI 54

Rhythm: Reading ♪♩ ♪ Syncopation

Using rhythm syllables, **read** and **perform** this counter-rhythm for "Let Us Sing Together." As you do so, tap a steady beat with your foot.

👆 **Reading Sequence 18, page 158**

CD 9–3
MIDI 55

Rhythm: Reading ♪♩♪ Syncopation

Tap a steady beat with your foot. Using rhythm syllables, **read** and **perform** this three-part rhythm accompaniment for "Lost My Gold Ring."

Melody: Reading Intervals (Seconds and Thirds)

Using hand signs and pitch syllables, **read** and **sing** this countermelody for *"O lê lê O Bahía."*

Melody: Reading Intervals (Major)

Locate and sing the intervals of a third, a fourth, a fifth, and an octave in this exercise. Then, using pitch syllables, **read** and **sing** it as a countermelody for "Like a Bird."

Music Reading Practice

Reading Sequence 21, page 194

Rhythm: Reading Syncopation

Using rhythm syllables, **read** and **perform** this syncopated counter-rhythm for "Paths of Victory." Conduct in meter in 4 as you say the syllables.

Reading Sequence 22, page 196

CD 10–37
MIDI 59

Rhythm: Reading Mixed Meter

Using rhythm syllables, **read** and **perform** this counter-rhythm for "New Hungarian Folk Song." Then, conduct it, paying close attention to the meter changes.

Melody: Reading Intervals (Fourths and Fifths)

Using hand signs and pitch syllables, **read** and **sing** this melody for "Blue Mountain Lake." **Identify** and **sing** the intervals of fourths and fifths.

Melody: Reading Intervals (Harmonic Minor)

Using pitch syllables and hand signs, **read** and **sing** this countermelody for "*Kyrie.*"

Playing the Recorder

Recorders come in different sizes. As seen in this picture, the soprano recorder is smaller than the alto recorder. Both instruments use the same set of fingerings but produce different pitches. The fingerings below are for soprano recorder.

Alto recorder

Soprano recorder

Getting Ready

Look at the diagram for the note G. Using your left hand, cover the holes that are darkened. Press hard enough so that the holes make a light mark on each finger and thumb. Cover the tip of the mouthpiece with your lips. Blow gently as you whisper *daah*. **Play** a steady beat on the note G. After you can play G, try practicing A, B, high C, and high D. The diagrams will help with finger placement.

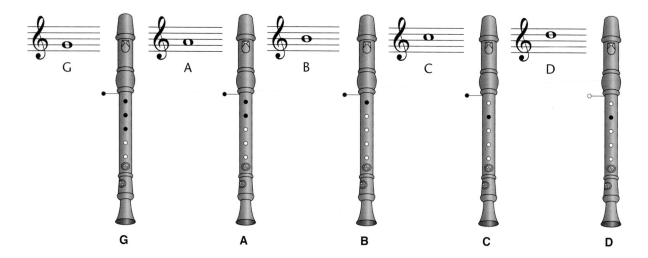

Beginning with "B-A-G" Plus Two

Now that you can play B, A, G, high C, and high D, **play** this simplified melody of "Bridges," page 86. Does the recorder part move mostly by steps, leaps, or repeats?

Building Right-Hand Strength

Here are two pairs of new notes: D and E; F and C. As you practice these note pairs, cover the holes securely with your fingers flat, not arched, and whisper *daah*. When playing notes in the low register of the recorder, remember to use very little air.

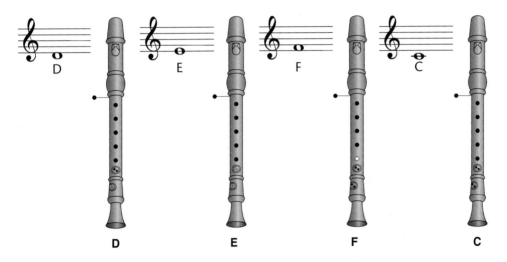

After learning D and E, **play** the melody of "Peace Like a River," page 190. Be sure to whisper *daah* gently in the style of the music. The two phrases of this song are written below so you can begin to practice.

Play this part for the recorder throughout the song "*Adiós, amigos,*" page 57. It uses F and C. How is it the same as the melody on the recording?

Learning Notes in Pairs

Try learning these new notes paired with some notes you already know: F♯ with G, G♯ with A, and B♭ with B. This half-step rule will help you remember how to finger F♯ and G♯.

Think of the fingering for the note that is a half step higher than the note with the accidental.

Skip a hole on your recorder and then cover the next two holes.

If you are attempting to play G♯, think of the fingering for A. Leave the next hole uncovered and then cover the following two holes. Check the diagram below to see if you have fingered G♯ correctly. Use the same rule to learn to play F♯ and B♭. What notes will you think about first?

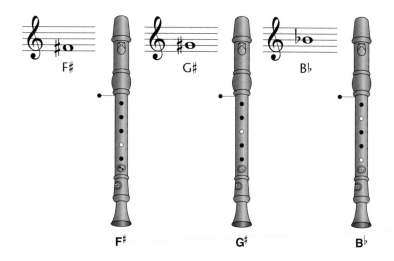

New Recorder Challenges

After learning F♯, **play** this ostinato from "Hey, Ho! Nobody Home," page 28. Is it easier to play from E up to F♯ or from G down to F♯?

F♯

When you can play G♯ and B♭, **play** the verse of "You Are My Sunshine," page 246. Before playing with the recording, practice each phrase slowly. Remember to **sing** the refrain.

The Virtuoso Recorder

Michala Petri is one of the world's best recorder performers. She is called a virtuoso because her technical and artistic playing are at a very high level. **Listen** to her skillful playing on these contemporary pieces.

CD 23–9, 10

Nele's Dances, No. 17 and No. 18

by Thomas Koppel
as performed by Michala Petri

Koppel, a Danish composer, wrote *Nele's Dances* specifically for Michala Petri and her virtuoso recorder playing.

Recorder Fingerings

This fingering chart will help you learn alto recorder fingerings by relating them to the soprano recorder.

Soprano Recorder

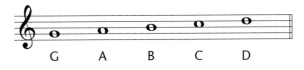

G   A   B   C   D

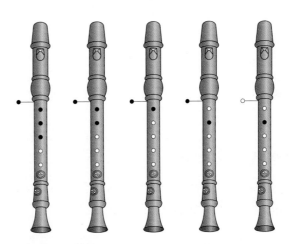

Alto Recorder

C   D   E   F   G

Mallet Instruments

Playing Mallets

When using mallets to play barred instruments, follow these simple suggestions.

Holding the Mallets

Fold your fingers and thumbs around the mallet handle—the thumb should lie alongside the handle, but the pointer finger should not sit on top of the mallet. The backs of your hands should face the ceiling. Grip the handles on the hand grips, but not at the very end. (Smaller hands may need to grip further up toward the mallet head.) Elbows should hang easily at your sides. Avoid elbows that stick out to the side or hug the body.

Striking the Bars

Strike each bar at its center, not at either end. Let your mallet strike quickly and then bounce away. If you let the mallet stay on the bar, the sound is stopped.

Matching Mallets to Instruments

It is important to choose the appropriate mallet for each instrument to make the best sound.

For special effects, use hard wood mallets or mallet handles.

Bass instruments need large felt or yarn heads. Choose softer mallets for metallophones, and harder mallets for xylophones.

Alto/soprano xylophones need medium-sized felt or yarn heads with a hard core. Alto/soprano metallophones need the same, but with a softer core. ▼

Glockenspiels need small wood, hard rubber, or composition heads. ▼

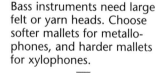

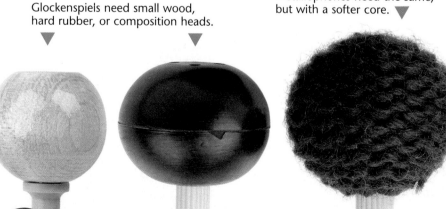

Avoid anything that would damage the surface of the bars.

Sit on the floor. ▶

Sit in a chair to play bass instruments. ▶

◀ Stand.

Sit in a chair. ▶

Playing the Guitar

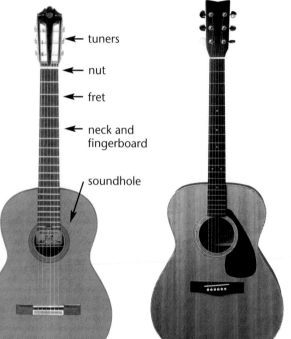

Why Play the Guitar?

The guitar is a very popular and versatile instrument. Once you learn some basics, you can create your own "musical voice" in the special way you play the guitar. You can quickly learn some of these basics by following the suggestions included in these pages.

Types of Guitars

There are three types of guitars—nylon-string classical, steel-string acoustic, and electric. Look at these photographs and learn the names of their parts:

← tuners

← nut

← fret

← neck and fingerboard

soundhole

pick-ups

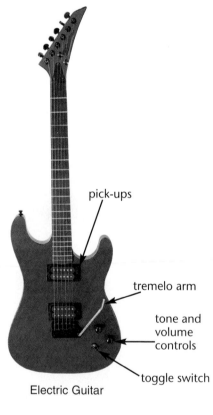

tremelo arm

tone and volume controls

toggle switch

Nylon-String Classical Guitar   Steel-String Acoustic Guitar   Electric Guitar

Tuning the Guitar

- Guitar strings are numbered 1, 2, 3, 4, 5, 6, with the sixth string being the lowest in pitch.

- You can tune the guitar using the keys of the piano. The illustration below shows what keys to use for tuning each guitar string.

- You can also tune your guitar by using an electronic tuner, which allows you to "see" when each string is in tune.

middle C

E   A   D   G   B   E
6   5   4   3   2   1

- You can also tune the guitar by using a method called relative tuning. Follow these steps:

1. Tune the sixth, or lowest-pitched, string to E on the piano or pitch pipe.

2. Press the sixth string on fret 5 and pluck it with your right thumb, producing the note A, which you use to tune the next, or fifth, string.

3. Reach your right hand over to the tuning keys, and turn the fifth-string key until the two sounds match. Now the fifth string is in tune.

4. Press the fifth string on fret 5, and use the pitch to tune the fourth string, repeating the tuning process as before.

5. Press the fourth string on fret 5, and use the pitch to tune the third string.

6. Press the third string on fret 4, and use the pitch to tune the second string.

7. Press the second string on fret 5, and use the pitch to tune the first string. Now you are in tune!

The Best Playing Positions

There are three ways to hold your guitar comfortably and correctly. Notice the different ways that are pictured here:

- Always raise the guitar neck slightly, because this allows the left hand to play chords without extra tension and effort.

- Always keep the front of the guitar completely vertical, because this also helps the left hand to play chords easily.

- You can also play standing up with the help of a guitar strap, but make sure to keep the neck slanted slightly upwards, and hold the guitar high enough so that it is not difficult to see what you are doing.

Guitar

507

Playing Basics

Here is some basic information on how to play the guitar:

- The left-hand fingers press the strings on the frets to produce chords, which are used to accompany songs.

- The right-hand thumb brushes the strings to make the sounds.

- You may also use a "pick," a small triangular-shaped piece of soft plastic, to play the strings with your right hand.

- Notice how the left-hand fingers are numbered; you will use these numbers when you begin reading the guitar chords.

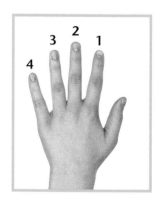

Playing Guitar Chords

- All chords have note names—these are indicated in many song scores in this book. The position of the chord names tells you what chords you will use, and when you will be changing chords in the song. They look like this:

Guitar Chords Used in This Book

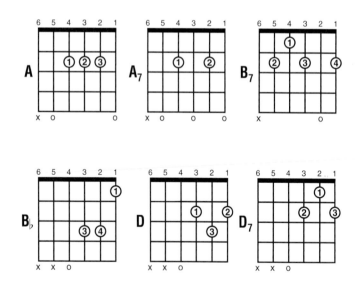

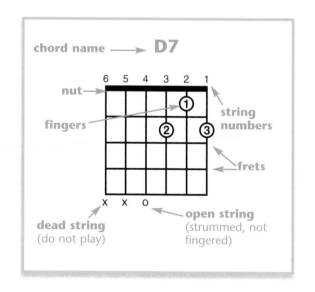

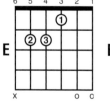

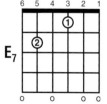

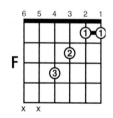

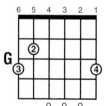

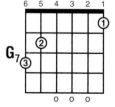

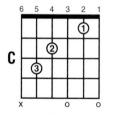

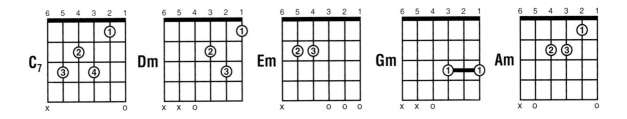

Using a Capo

- A capo is a clamp-like device that allows guitarists to use easy, first-position guitar chords to play songs in virtually any key (changing the key of a song is called transposing).

How You Can Tell You're Improving

You are improving if you answer "yes" to more and more of these questions:

- Can you make chord changes without looking?
- Can you play at an even tempo?
- Can you sing along while you play?
- Do your fingertips hurt less when you play?
- Can you play for longer periods of time?
- Can you play some songs from memory?

Guitar

Playing the Keyboard

Sitting Position

Sit slightly forward on the bench with your feet resting on the floor at all times. Your knees should be just under the front edge of the keyboard. Sit comfortably.

Hand Position

Your hand position is the shape of your hand as it hangs naturally at your side. When you bring your hand up to the keyboard, your fingers should be slightly curved at the middle joint and the wrist should be parallel to the keyboard. Your elbows should be flexible as they hang near your side. Do not "hug" your elbows too close to your sides.

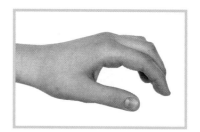

Finger Numbers

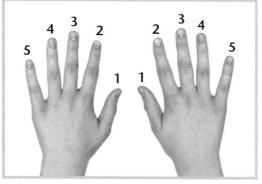

Fingering for Steps and Skips

You have learned that melodies move by steps, by leaps (skips), and by repeats. How a melody moves determines the fingering to be used to play that melody on the keyboard. The examples, on page 511, show the relationship between right/left movement on the keyboard and up/down movement on the staff.

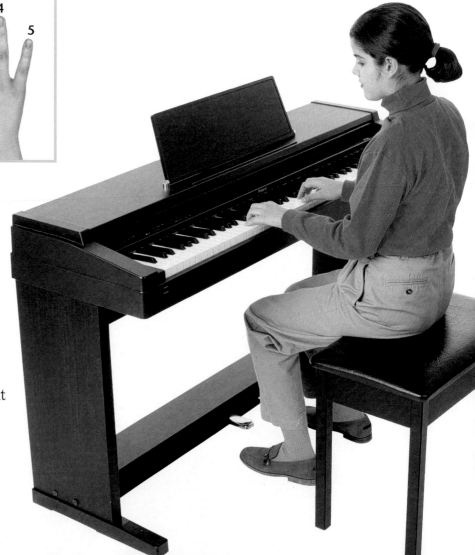

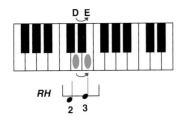

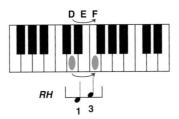

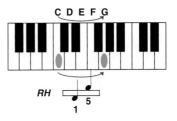

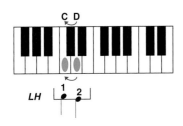

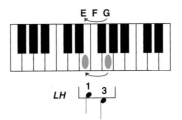

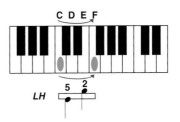

Three-Line Reading

Play the following examples. Determine a logical fingering before you begin each one.

RH   Begin on E:

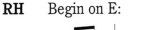
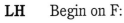

LH   Begin on F:

Playing from Treble and Bass Clefs

When singing music, you have learned to follow the upward/downward direction of a melody and to determine if it moves by step, by leap, or if it stays on a repeated tone. When playing music, you must read music in the same way as well as determine where to play the notes on the keyboard. Each note in printed music indicates one place, and only one place, where it can be played. **Play** the following examples in the treble and bass clefs.

Sound Bank

◀ **Accordion** A keyboard instrument with bellows that expand and compress to produce sound. The concertina is a relative of the accordion and has buttons. The accordion and concertina are popular in European and Cajun music. CD 23–11

◀ *Bandura* A traditional string instrument of Ukraine that sounds similar to a harpsichord. Each string produces only one pitch. There are no frets as with a guitar. A bandurist usually plucks notes with the fingers or a pick. The left hand plays bass notes. *Banduras* range in size from treble to bass and have 30 to 60 strings. CD 23–12

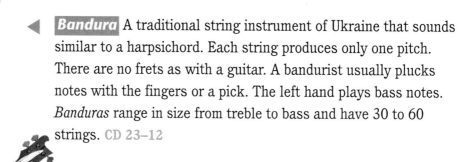

◀ **Bass Guitar** An electric guitar with four bass strings played by plucking. The bass guitar plays bass lines and is important in rock, pop, and jazz. CD 23–13

◀ **Bassoon** A large, tube-shaped woodwind instrument with a double reed. Lower notes on the bassoon can be gruff or comical. Higher notes are softer, sweeter, and more gentle-sounding. CD 23–14

◀ *Bodhrán* [boh-RAHN] An Irish wood-frame drum played with a double-ended small stick. CD 23–15

Instrument Key: strings   percussion   woodwind   brass   keyboard

Cello [CHEH-loh] A large, wooden string instrument played with a bow or by plucking the strings. The player sits with the cello between the knees. The cello has a low, rich-sounding, warm tone. CD 23–16

Clarinet A wind instrument shaped like a long cylinder with a flare at the end. It is usually made of wood and has a reed in the mouthpiece. Low notes on the clarinet are soft and mellow. The highest notes are clear and resonant. CD 23–17

Conga [KOHN-gah] An Afro-Cuban drum with a long, barrel-shaped body. Conga drums come in several sizes: the smaller *quinto,* the standard *conga,* and the larger *tumba.* A *tumbador* is a conga player. The conga is struck with the fingers and the palms of the hands. CD 23–18

Didgeridoo [dih-jehr-ee-DOO] A long, hollow tube made from a Eucalyptus tree, played with the breath and vibrating lips like the tuba. The *didgeridoo* is a traditional instrument of the Aborigines in Australia. Players use circular breathing to create drone tones. CD 23–19

Djembe [JEHM-beh] An African, medium-sized drum made from an animal hide stretched across a wooden frame. CD 23–20

◀ **Donno** [doh-noh] An hourglass-shaped talking drum played with an L-shaped stick. The *donno* is also known as a *dundun.* CD 23–21

◀ **Dombak** [DOM-bak] A Middle Eastern, goblet-shaped drum that produces a deep bass ("dom") and a high, sharp tone ("bak"). The *dombak* is also known as a *dombek, tombak,* and *darabukka.* It is sometimes spelled *doumbek.* CD 23–22

◀ **Drums** (Trap Set) A drum set (or "kit") consisting of bass and snare drums, tom toms, hi-hat, and cymbals. The drum set is important in all forms of rock, pop, and jazz. CD 23–23

◀ **Erhu** [EHR-hoo] A two-string Chinese instrument. It is played by a bow with the hand inserted between the two strings. The *erhu* sounds something like a violin and is an important instrument in modern Chinese orchestras. CD 23–24

◀ **Flute** A small metal instrument shaped like a pipe. The player holds the flute sideways and blows across an open mouthpiece. The flute's sound is pure and clear. CD 23–25

Instrument Key: strings   percussion   woodwind   brass   keyboard

French Horn A medium-sized instrument made of coiled brass tubing with a large bell at one end. The player holds the horn on his or her lap and keeps one hand inside the bell. The horn has a mellow, warm tone. CD 23–26

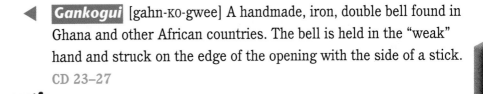

Gankogui [gahn-KO-gwee] A handmade, iron, double bell found in Ghana and other African countries. The bell is held in the "weak" hand and struck on the edge of the opening with the side of a stick. CD 23–27

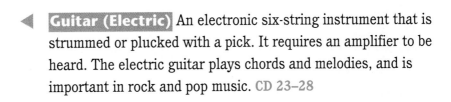

Guitar (Electric) An electronic six-string instrument that is strummed or plucked with a pick. It requires an amplifier to be heard. The electric guitar plays chords and melodies, and is important in rock and pop music. CD 23–28

Kendang [KEN-dang] An Indonesian, barrel-shaped, double-headed drum. The *kendang,* sometimes spelled *kendhang,* is similar to the *mridangam* of southern India and plays a leading role in the gamelan orchestra. CD 23–29

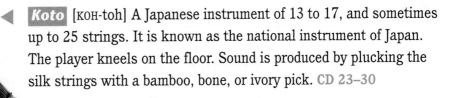

Koto [KOH-toh] A Japanese instrument of 13 to 17, and sometimes up to 25 strings. It is known as the national instrument of Japan. The player kneels on the floor. Sound is produced by plucking the silk strings with a bamboo, bone, or ivory pick. CD 23–30

 ◄ **Kpanlogo** [pahn-LOH-go] A barrel-shaped drum, carved from a single tree, found among the Ga people of Ghana, West Africa. The antelope-hide drum head is held tight by wooden stakes driven into the sides of the drum. CD 23–31

 ◄ **Mbira** [mm-BEE-rah] An African finger xylophone of 5 to 30 or more thin metal, wood, or cane tongues attached to a sounding board. The tongues are plucked with the thumbs and fingers to produce a sound similar to that of a xylophone. CD 23–32

 ◄ **Mridangam** [MREE-dan-gam] A double-headed, barrel-shaped drum that is made of wood with animal hide drawn across the top. The *mridangam* is the classic drum of southern India and is primarily used for accompanying the *vena,* flute, violin, or voice. CD 23–33

 ◄ **Odaiko** [oh-DIE-ko] A large drum from Japan that is struck with large cylindrical sticks. One of several Japanese drums played in the tradition of *taiko*. CD 23–34

◄ **Recorder** A simple wind instrument made of wood or plastic with a "whistle" mouthpiece. Recorders come in many sizes and have a gentle, hollow sound. CD 23–35

Instrument Key: strings   percussion   woodwind   brass   keyboard

Saxophone The saxophone is a member of the woodwind family and is made of metal. Sound is made by blowing air into a mouthpiece with a reed and pressing keys to play different pitches. CD 23–36

Shekere [SHEH-keh-reh] A large, calabash-gourd rattle with outside netting and shells. This West African rattle is either hit against the thigh or the hand. CD 23–37

Snare Drum A small, cylinder-shaped drum with two heads. Snares are stretched across the bottom head to create a vibrating sound. A snare drum is played with drumsticks and plays non-pitched rhythm patterns. CD 23–38

Steel Drums Steel drums are fashioned from oil drums and the top surfaces are shaped into facets that sound musical pitches when struck by mallets. Steel drums have a unique sound and are popular in the islands of the Caribbean. CD 23–39

String Bass This is the largest of the string instruments. It is often played standing. The bass strings produce low bass tones and are either bowed or plucked. It is played in orchestral, jazz, and pop music. CD 23–40

◀ **Synthesizer** An electronic keyboard instrument found in many styles of rock and pop music. Synthesizers create sounds through electronic synthesis and can produce many instrument sounds. CD 23–41

◀ *Tabla* [TAH-blah] Drums used in the classical music of northern India, similar to the timpani. *Tablas* produce pitched and nonpitched sounds by being played on different parts of the drumhead. CD 23–42

◀ *Tamboura* [TAM-boo-rah] A four-string drone instrument popular in India. The *tamboura* strings are tuned to the intervals of an octave and a fifth, and are played in a continuous drone style. CD 23–43

◀ **Timpani** Large, pot-shaped drums, also called kettledrums. The timpani can be tuned to specific pitches. Several timpani are used to play melody patterns. CD 23–44

◀ **Trombone** A large brass instrument with a bell at one end of the tubing. Pitch is changed by moving a long slide on the side of the instrument. The trombone is found in bands, orchestras, and jazz ensembles. CD 23–45

Instrument Key: strings percussion woodwind brass keyboard

Trumpet A small brass instrument with a bell (a flared opening) at one end of its coiled tubing. The player presses valves to change pitch. The sound of the trumpet is bold and bright. CD 23–46

Tuba The largest brass instrument, with a large bell that points upward. The player changes the pitch by pressing valves. The tuba's sound is very low, deep, and sturdy. CD 23–47

Violin The smallest string instrument in a Western orchestra. It is held under the player's chin and is bowed or plucked. The violin's tone can be brilliant, warm, harsh, or mellow. CD 23–48

Xylophone A keyboard of wooden bars played with mallets. The xylophone has a bright, brittle sound. CD 23–49

a cappella Vocal music performed without instrumental accompaniment. p. 207

accelerando A gradual increase in tempo. p. 152

accent (>) A single tone or chord that is performed louder than those around it. p. 194

accompaniment The musical background, such as chords and rhythms, that supports the melody. p. 142

acoustics The science of the production, control, and transmission of sound. p. 330

aerophone An instrument that produces sound by a vibrating air column. The aerophone family includes woodwinds, brass, organs, and the human voice. p. 362

augmentation Rhythm that is notated to be twice as slow. p. 80

backbeat The strong offbeat in a measure, such as the snare drum playing on beats 2 and 4 in rock rhythms. p. 84

ballad A folk song that tells a story, often with many verses. In pop music, a slow, lyric song that is often about love. p. 44

band A balanced group of instruments, consisting of woodwinds, brass, and percussion. p. 136

beat A repeating pulse that can be felt in most music. p. 12

blues A style of music that has emotional lyrics; slow, offbeat rhythms; and improvised singing and playing. p. 240

boogie-woogie A special blues progression that uses blues chords and swing rhythm. Boogie-woogie is sometimes called "eight-to-the-bar." p. 93

call and response A style of performance in which a leader plays or sings a call, and a group responds. p. 230

canon A form in which each part performs the melody, entering at different times on the same or different pitches. p. 124

cantata A large dramatic work, sometimes of a religious nature, for choir and instruments. Many cantatas contain solo and chorus sections, with continuous narration (recitative). p. 338

choir Commonly used to mean a group of singers performing together. Also a group of instruments, as in a brass *choir*. p. 210

chord Three or more different tones played or sung simultaneously. p. 92

chord progression The order of chords in a segment of a piece of music. p. 92

chordophone An instrument that produces sound by vibrating strings. The chordophone family includes the orchestral strings, guitar, and piano. p. 363

chromatic scale A scale consisting of 12 consecutive half steps. p. 168

compound meter A meter in which the beat is divided into three equal parts. The dotted quarter note gets the beat. p. 120

countermelody A melody that runs counter to, or against, the main melody. p. 104

crescendo (━━━) Gradually getting louder. p. 76

cut time ($\frac{2}{2}$ or ¢) A meter of two beats per measure. The half note gets the beat. This is also called $\frac{2}{2}$ meter. p. 119

decrescendo (━━━) Gradually getting softer. p. 76

diminution Rhythm that is notated to be twice as fast. p. 80

disco Dance music of the 1970s that marked the beginnings of today's dance genre. Named after "discothèques" (dance clubs), disco was dominated by its straight steady beat played by the bass drum. p. 368

DJ A "disc jockey" who plays (spins) records for dance parties. Today's DJs produce, write, and "mix" music in the styles of dance, techno, and hip-hop music. p. 368

downbeat The strong beat in music. Usually, the first accented beat of the measure. p. 12

duet A piece written to be played or sung by two performers. p. 172

duple meter A meter of two beats per measure. p. 119

dynamics The degrees of loudness and softness of sound. p. 38

electrophone An instrument that produces sound either electronically or digitally with no acoustic generation. The electrophone family includes electronic keyboards, synthesizers, and samplers. p. 366

form The structure of a composition; the way its musical materials are organized. p. 46

fugue A musical form in which the main melody is stated in one voice and then is imitated by two or more voices, each entering successively. p. 128

gamelan An Indonesian ensemble consisting primarily of gongs, gong-chimes, metallophones, and drums. p. 384

gospel An African American style of music that combines jazz rhythms and blues singing with religious music. It may be accompanied by hand clapping, swaying, foot stomping, and other movements. p. 232

ground bass A bass line that continually repeats throughout a composition. p. 202

harmony Two or more different tones sounding at the same time. Harmony is most often structured around stylistic and historical rules and principles. p. 26

highlife A musical style that combines elements of traditional West African styles and jazz. Some common instruments are saxophones, brass, electric guitars, and percussion. p. 294

homophonic A musical texture consisting of a melody supported by harmony. p. 173

idiophone An instrument that produces sound by vibration of the body of the instrument. The idiophone family includes cymbals, bells, and woodblocks. p. 363

improvise To make up music as it is performed. p. 55

interval The distance between two notes. p. 130

jazz A style that grew out of the music of African Americans, then took many different substyles, such as big band, boogie, cool jazz, swing, bebop, Chicago, and New Orleans. It features solo improvisations over a set harmonic progression. p. 250

key The scale on which a piece of music is based, named for its tonic, or "home" tone. p. 56

key signature The musical symbol set, comprised of sharps or flats placed on the staff, that defines the key of a piece of music. p. 56

legato Notes that are connected to each other and played or sung smoothly. p. 38

major scale An arrangement of eight tones in a scale according to the following steps: whole, whole, half, whole, whole, whole, half. p. 56

melodic contour The shape of a musical phrase. p. 20

melodic sequence The repetition of a melodic pattern usually at different stepwise pitch levels. p. 132

membranophone An instrument that produces sound by vibration of a stretched membrane or skin. The membranophone family includes most drums. p. 362

meter The organization of beats into groups, most often in sets of two or three. p. 118

minor scale Any of several arrangements of eight tones in a scale in which the scale begins and ends on *la* (the tonic), one and one-half steps down from the home tone (*do*). For example, in natural minor: whole, half, whole, whole, half, whole, whole. p. 58

mixed meter The use of more than one time signature in a piece of music. p. 196

mode A musical scale with a specific set of half-steps and whole-steps that give it a unique sound. p. 94

monophonic A musical texture consisting of a single melodic part. p. 207

motive A short musical idea or pattern that repeats throughout a composition. p. 98

musical expression The qualities of music that determine emotional content. Some of these qualities are loud, soft, slow, and fast. p. 6

new wave A popular style of rock in the 1980s that was heavily influenced by electronic music, drum machines, and synthesizers. p. 368

orchestra A performing group of various instruments. The term can be applied to many different ensembles, such as the Western symphony orchestra or the Chinese string orchestra. p. 102

ostinato A musical idea that is continually repeated. Ostinatos can be melodic, rhythmic, or harmonic. p. 29

pentatonic A scale consisting of five tones. A common pentatonic scale corresponds to tones 1, 2, 3, 5, and 6 of the major scale. p. 56

phrase A musical unit comparable to a sentence, each phrase expresses a thought ending with a sense of pause or closure. p. 22

pitch The identification of a tone with respect to highness or lowness. p. 354

polyphonic A musical texture in which two or more melodic parts occur at the same time. This creates layers of harmony. p. 207

power chords Chords containing only a root and fifth (no third), often used by rock guitarists. p. 64

question-and-answer drumming An African style of playing rhythms. A leader plays a phrase (the question), which is answered by other phrases from the group (the answer). p. 279

recitative A sung narration with *rubato* tempo and minimal accompaniment used to carry the story forward. p. 74

reggae A Caribbean style of rock music popularized by Bob Marley. Offbeat rhythms are prominent in this style. p. 140

ritardando (*rit.*) A gradual decrease in tempo. p. 152

root position A chord in which the pitch called the root is the lowest note of the chord. For example, C is the root of a C chord. p. 144

round A composition in which two or more parts enter in succession with the same melody. p. 122

rubato A change of tempo in which the music pushes ahead and/or pulls back slightly to allow greater expression. p. 191

salsa A Latin style of music with syncopated bass lines, energetic percussion rhythms, and vibrant horn parts and vocal harmonies. Popularized by Tito Puente in the 1940s, *salsa* is still popular today. p. 265

scale (mode) An arrangement of pitches from lower to higher, according to a specific pattern of intervals. p. 56

scat singing A special style of jazz singing that uses nonsense syllables to sing instrument-like melodic lines. p. 64

score Written music or notation of a composition, with each of the vocal or instrumental parts appearing in vertical alignment. p. 211

sequence See *melodic sequence.*

sforzando (*sƒz*) A sudden accent on a note or chord. p. 78

sight-reading The ability to read music accurately the first time. p. 126

simple meter A meter in which the beat is divided into two equal parts. Usually, the quarter note gets the beat. p. 119

staccato (♩) Notes that are performed short and separated from each other. p. 38

style A description given to music that has a special character or sound derived from the way it uses musical elements—melody, rhythm, timbre, harmony, texture, and form. p. 60

subject The main theme, or melody, in a fugue. The subject is contrasted by the episode. p. 128

symphony A large, usually lengthy, piece of art music for a full Western orchestra. The term is also sometimes used to mean "symphony orchestra." p. 98

syncopation A term used to describe accented rhythms that are off the beat. p. 156

techno and dance music A contemporary style of music created with electronic keyboards, synthesizers, and samplers. The music has a strong dance beat, bass line, and melodic patterns. p. 368

tempo The speed of the beat. p. 114

texture The layering of sounds to create a thick or thin quality in music. p. 26

theme An important melody that occurs several times in a piece of music. p. 160

theme and variations A composition, each section of which is an alteration of the initial theme. p. 160

tie (♩‿♩) A symbol that joins two notes of the same pitch to make the sound longer. p. 10

timbre The tone color, or unique sound, of an instrument or voice. p. 24

time line An African rhythm in which a pattern repeats and becomes the main beat that holds the music together. p. 280

time signature ($\frac{4}{4}$) The musical symbol that indicates how many beats are in a measure (top number) and which note gets the beat (bottom number). p. 42

tone row An early twentieth-century composition technique in which the pitches of the chromatic scale are ordered in a non-tonal way. p. 168

tonic The home tone of a scale. In a major scale, the tonic is *do*. p. 56

triple meter A meter of three beats per measure. p. 120

unison The same pitch sounded by more than one source. p. 207

variation A significant change in a musical theme. p. 160

Classified Index

Listening selections appear in *italics*.

Holidays

Celebrations

El carnavalito humahuaqueño (The Little Humahuacan Carnival) 482
I Am But a Small Voice 446
Las mañanitas 481
Loigratong 451
Round Dance 445

Chanukah

S'vivon (Dreydl) 452

Christmas

Angels on the Midnight Clear 423
Caroling, Caroling 458
Cowboys' Christmas Ball 239
Cowboys' Christmas Ball 238
Ding Dong! Merrily on High 427
Gloria, Gloria 459
Good King Wenceslas 460
Good King Wenceslas 461
O Christmas Tree 24

Fall Harvest

Alumot (Sheaves of Grain) 306

Halloween

Purple People Eater, The 448

Kwanzaa

Joy of Kwanzaa, The 462

Martin Luther King Day

Abraham, Martin, and John 466
Free at Last 468
I Wish I Knew How It Would Feel to Be Free 470
I Wish I Knew How It Would Feel to Be Free 470

Patriotic

America 484
America, the Beautiful 485
America, the Beautiful (Gospel) 485
L'union 487
Star-Spangled Banner, The 486

United Nations Day

United Nations on the March, The 443

Valentine's Day

Eres tú (Touch the Wind) 473
Love in Any Language 476

Winter

Lieutenant Kijé, "Troika" 457
Winter Song 455

Listening Selections

Allison, Petty, and Holly: *That'll Be the Day* 256 CD 13–15
Anthony and Rooney: *You Sang to Me* 335 CD 17–4
Appell and Mann: *Let's Twist Again* 257 CD 13–16
Arban: *Variations on "The Carnival of Venice"* 161 CD 9–12
Arnold: *Four Scottish Dances*, "Allegretto" *Op. 59* 43 CD 3–6
Bach: *Jesu, Joy of Man's Desiring* 87 CD 5–30

Bach: *"Little" Organ Fugue in G Minor* (brass) 129 CD 7–22
Bach: *"Little" Organ Fugue in G Minor* (organ) 129 CD 7–21
Bach: *Orchestral Suite No. 2*, "Minuet" 192 CD 10–28
Beethoven: *Symphony No. 5 in C Minor*, Movement 1 98 CD 6–14
Berg: *Lyric Suite*, "Allegretto Gioviale" 169 CD 9–26
Berman, Berman, and Cremers: *This Is Your Night* 368 CD 18–21
Berman, Berman, and Cremers: *This Is Your Night* (Dance Mix) 369 CD 18–22
Bernstein: *Mass*, "Responsory: Alleluia" 217 CD 11–25
Bernstein: *Overture to "Candide"* 218, 219 CD 11–26, 27
Bizet: *L'arlésienne*, "Farandole" No. 2 68 CD 4–28
Borde: *Gidden riddum* 299 CD 15–9
Broonzy and Segar: *Key to the Highway* 243 CD 12–21
Cage: *Concert for Piano and Orchestra* 209 CD 11–17
Clarke: *Prince of Denmark's March* 55 CD 3–30
Copland: *El Salón México* 199 CD 10–40
Davis and Mitchell: *You Are My Sunshine* 247 CD 13–6
de Vita: *Lluvia* 332 CD 17–1, 2
de Vita: *Si tú no estás* 267 CD 14–2
Dikshitar: *Maha ganapathim* 305 CD 15–23
Driftwood: *Battle of New Orleans, The* 105 CD 6–23
Dylan: *Mr. Tambourine Man* 148 CD 8–20
Ellington: *It Don't Mean a Thing If It Ain't Got That Swing* 386 CD 19–21
Estefan, Cass and Ostwald: *Oye mi canto* 114 CD 6–34
Estefano: *Mi tierra* 365 CD 18–18
Garland: *In the Mood* 110 CD 6–28
Gershwin: *Summertime* 252 CD 13–12
Gershwin, Webster, Fain, Cobb: *Medley: Strike Up the Band, Mardi Gras March, Listen to that Dixie Band* 25 CD 2–18
Glass and Byrne: *Open the Kingdom* 31 CD 2–24
Gottschalk: *L'union* 487 CD 23–8
Gould: *Fanfare for Freedom* 139 CD 8–4
Grieg: *Lyric Suite*, "Wedding Day at Troldhaugen" *Op. 65 No.6* 9 CD 1–5
Hancock: *Watermelon Man* 270 CD 14–5
Hardiman: *Lord of the Dance Medley* 326 CD 16–14
Hardin Armstrong: *Hotter Than That* 65 CD 4–25
Hart: *Evening Samba* 297 CD 15–8
Hart: *Hunt, The* 363 CD 18–12
Hart: *Lost River* 283 CD 14–15
Haydn: *Canon No. 110 in G* 133 CD 7–35
Holst: *Suite No. 2 in F, Movement 1*, "March" 139 CD 8–3
Horner: *Coming Home from the Sea* 345 CD 17–14, 15
Horner, Mellencamp, and Green: *Yours Forever* 344 CD 17–13
Ingalls: *Northfield* 25 CD 2–15
Ives: *Variations on "America"* 162 CD 9–13
Jing-Ran Zhu and Qui-Hong Her: *Colours of the World* 271 CD 14–7
John and Rice: *The Circle of Life* 316 CD 16–6
Joplin: *Bethena Waltz* 157 CD 8–33
Joplin: *Elite Syncopations* 159 CD 9–9
Koppel: *Nele's Dances, No. 17* 503 CD 23–9
Koppel: *Nele's Dances, No. 18* 503 CD 23–10
Lebo M.: *Welcome to Our World* 272 CD 14–9

Other Integrated Recordings

Poems and Stories

Recorded Interviews

Design and Electronic Production: Kirchoff/Wohlberg, Inc.
Listening Maps and Music Reading Practice: MediaLynx Design Group
Photo Research: Feldman & Associates, Inc. and Kirchoff/Wohlberg, Inc. Every effort has been made to obtain permission for all photographs found in this book and to make full acknowledgment for their use. Omissions brought to our attention will be corrected in subsequent editions.

Illustration Credits

Photograph Credits

Index of Songs

Song Index

531